In the second half of the nineteenth cen
twentieth, Japan underwent two major shifts in political control. In the
1910s, the power of the oligarchy was eclipsed by that of a larger group of
professional politicians. In the 1930s, the locus of power shifted again,
this time to a set of independent military leaders.

In *The Politics of Oligarchy*, J. Mark Ramseyer and Frances M. Rosenbluth examine a key question of modern Japanese politics: Why were the
Meiji oligarchs unable to design institutions capable of protecting their
power? Using an analytical framework for oligarchic governments not
specific to Japan, the authors ask why the oligarchs chose the political
institutions they did, and what consequences those choices engendered
for Japan's political competition, economic development, and diplomatic
relations. Ramseyer and Rosenbluth argue that understanding these shifts
in power may clarify the general dynamics of oligarchic government, as
well as theoretical aspects of the relationship between institutional structure and regime change.

After reviewing scores of original documents and secondary literature,
Ramseyer and Rosenbluth conclude that the oligarchs were much like the
rest of the human race – prone to self-interest and contentiousness. By
failing to cooperate, the oligarchs were unable to protect and enlarge
their political rents. Indeed, as they sought political support outside the
oligarchy, paradoxically they weakened themselves by enlarging the segment of the population that was sufficiently organized to lobby for political power. Untimately, it was the oligarchs' very inability to agree among
themselves on how to rule that prompted them to release the military
from civilian control – a decision that was to have disastrous consequences both for Japan and for the rest of the world.

THE POLITICS OF OLIGARCHY

POLITICAL ECONOMY OF INSTITUTIONS AND DECISIONS

Editors

James E. Alt, Harvard University
Douglass C. North, Washington University in St. Louis

THE POLITICS OF OLIGARCHY

Institutional choice in Imperial Japan

J. MARK RAMSEYER

The University of Chicago

FRANCES M. ROSENBLUTH

Yale University

CAMBRIDGE
UNIVERSITY PRESS

CAMBRIDGE UNIVERSITY PRESS
Cambridge, New York, Melbourne, Madrid, Cape Town, Singapore, São Paulo

Cambridge University Press
The Edinburgh Building, Cambridge CB2 8RU, UK

Published in the United States of America by Cambridge University Press, New York

www.cambridge.org
Information on this title: www.cambridge.org/9780521473972

First published 1995
First paperback edition 1998

A catalogue record for this publication is available from the British Library

ISBN 978-0-521-47397-2 hardback
ISBN 978-0-521-63649-0 paperback

Transferred to digital printing 2007

For James Rosenbluth and Norma Wyse

Contents

Contents

CHAPTER 3
CONCESSION OR FACADE:
THE MEIJI CONSTITUTION

CHAPTER 4
ELECTORAL RULES AND PARTY COMPETITION:
THE STRUGGLE FOR POLITICAL SURVIVAL

CHAPTER 5
THE BUREAUCRACY: WHO RULED WHOM?

CHAPTER 6
THE COURTS: WHO MONITORED WHOM?

Contents

CHAPTER 7
THE MILITARY: MASTER OF ITS OWN FATE

CHAPTER 8
FINANCIAL POLITICS

Contents

CHAPTER 9
RAILROAD POLITICS

CHAPTER 10
COTTON POLITICS

CHAPTER 11
CONCLUSION: INSTITUTIONS AND POLITICAL CONTROL

x

Contents

Tables and figure

TABLES

Tables and figure

FIGURE

xiii

Series editors' preface

The Cambridge series on the Political Economy of Institutions and Decisions is built around attempts to answer two central questions: How do institutions evolve in response to individual incentives, strategies, and choices, and how do institutions affect the performance of political and economic systems? The scope of the series is comparative and historical rather than international or specifically American, and the focus is positive rather than normative.

This book challenges conventional preconceptions and historical interpretations about institutional design in Meiji Japan. For some scholars, the oligarchs creating the Meiji Constitution were selfless state-builders, designing an independent bureaucracy and judiciary to maximize the economic growth of the country as a whole. Ramseyer and Rosenbluth carefully delineate the private interests of the Meiji oligarchs as well, and trace out the many ways in which competition among these oligarchs and their repeated failure to cooperate with each other led instead to the creation of institutions facilitating lobbying as a byproduct of factional conflict. Studying the actual institutions in great detail, the authors show how the electoral system created incentives for politicians to provide private goods rather than productive investment, and the ways in which bureaucrats did not act as independent principals. Their careful historical examination of the strategies of leaders embedded in a straightforward rational choice model of institutional development, and the principal results that followed, are reinforced by an examination of the development of three economic sectors – banks, railroads, and textiles. The result is an impressive political-economic analysis of state-building in Japan that transcends the boundaries of that individual case to serve as a general foundation for scholarly investigation into the origins and economic effects of political institutions.

Acknowledgments

Throughout the text of this book, we have written Japanese names in customary Japanese fashion: family name first, given name last. In making bibliographical references, however, we have referred to Japanese and non-Japanese authors in a consistent manner: family names last.

In the course of writing and rewriting the manuscript, we received helpful suggestions from many thoughtful friends. They include Richard Anderson, Kathy Bawn, Richard Epstein, Steven Ericson, Eric Feldman, Miles Fletcher, David D. Friedman, Sheldon Garon, John Haley, Gail Honda, William Klein, Margaret McKean, Geoffrey Miller, Gregory Noble, Eric Rasmusen, Arthur Rosett, Richard Ross, Richard Smethurst, Cass Sunstein, David Titus, David Weinstein, Stephen Yeazell, and participants in a workshop at Indiana University. Without their help, this would have been a vastly inferior book.

We gladly acknowledge the generous financial assistance of the John M. Olin Foundation, the Lynde and Harry Bradley Foundation, the National Science Foundation (NSF grant nos. SES 9113795 and SES 9113738), the Sarah Scaife Foundation, the UCLA Academic Senate, the UCLA Career Development Award program, the UCLA Center for Japanese Studies, the University of Chicago Committee on Japanese Studies, and the Yale Center for International Studies.

During the peripatetic years over which we wrote this book, we were affiliated with many universities. In each place, the administrators, faculty, and library staff were far more gracious and helpful than we could fairly expect: the Harvard Law School, the UCLA School of Law and Political Science Department, the UC San Diego School of International Relations & Pacific Studies, the University of Chicago Law School, the University of Tokyo Law Faculty, and the Yale University Political Science Department.

Portions of this book appear as J. Mark Ramseyer, "Credibly Committing to Efficiency Wages: Cotton Spinning Cartels in Imperial Japan,"

Acknowledgments

The University of Chicago Law School Roundtable, 1993: 153 (1993), © The University of Chicago; J. Mark Ramseyer, "Hogohō no keizai to seiji: 1911-nen Nihon no kōjōhō," in *Soto kara mita Nihon hō* (Shirō Ishii & Norio Higuchi, eds.: University of Tokyo Press, 1995); and J. Mark Ramseyer, "The Puzzling (In)dependence of Courts: A Comparative Approach," *Journal of Legal Studies*, 23: 721 (1994), © The University of Chicago Press.

We dedicate this book to Jim Rosenbluth and Norma Wyse. They keep us honest.

1

Introduction

1. BACKGROUND

During the last three decades of the nineteenth century and the first four of the twentieth,[1] basic political control in Japan shifted twice. In the 1910s it shifted from a handful of oligarchs[2] to a larger group of professional politicians. In the 1930s it shifted again, this time to a set of independent military leaders.

In this book we explore those shifts. We ask why the oligarchs failed to design institutions that protected their power, why the elected politicians did no better, and what political and economic consequences the various institutions had. More generally, we ask whether the shifts may explain some of the dynamics of oligarchic government and clarify some of the theoretical aspects of the relationship between institutional structure and regime change.

1.1. The puzzle

In explaining political control in Imperial Japan, most scholars implicitly posit three hypotheses. In their concern for authenticity and precision, they seldom state them as baldly as we do here. We admit that we strip their accounts of much of the richness and nuance that they give them. Although we do this reluctantly, we do it intentionally — for what we lose in subtlety we capture in clarity. Richness and sophistication can confuse as well as contextualize, and we simplify the discussion here because we think the simplicity clarifies the essential logic at stake.

First, most scholars argue that the oligarchs who controlled the government in the late nineteenth century largely (not exclusively) tried to promote the national interest. In part, they acted to protect Japan from the West. In part, they tried to implement their own convictions about what served Japan best. Toward both ends, they restricted their own powers

1

through a constitution, and adopted policies they hoped would promote economic growth and military might. Rather than promote their selfish personal welfare, they fought for the common weal. Rather than act as a junta, they served as statesmen.

In the *Cambridge History*,[3] historian Akira Iriye captures the gist of this approach. The oligarchs, he writes, were ultimately "intent on providing national leadership for economic development so that the country as a whole would 'increase production and create industry'" (1989: 729). In his study of the Meiji Constitutional structure, historian George Akita (1967: 172–73) made the point more elaborately:

The aim of the Meiji oligarchs was to create a strong, modern Japan capable of taking its place in the family of advanced, respected, civilized nations. They believed that constitutionalism was inextricably tied to success in this endeavor.

"What is particularly impressive about the statecraft of the Japanese leaders," William Beasley (1989: 697) concluded (again in the *Cambridge History*), "is the clarity with which they understood the historical process through which they were leading the nation."

Second, most scholars argue that Japanese bureaucrats and judges acted autonomously. Granted, few observers claim oligarchs and politicians never influenced bureaucratic behavior. Many do suggest, however, that such influence was the exception not the norm.

For example, political scientist Bernard Silberman – the leading authority on pre-war Japanese bureaucrats – writes that "the civil bureaucracy had emerged by 1900 as the primary instrument of decision making and the primary structure of political leadership selection."[4] Chalmers Johnson echoes the point in his study of the modern Japanese bureaucracy: The pre-war bureaucrats were "at the center of government" and steadily "arrogated more and more power to themselves" (1982: 37). By the early twentieth century, "they had effectively preempted most of the centers of power from which they might be challenged" (id., 38). And in his magisterial account of Japanese legal history, John Haley (1991: 80) argues that the imperial "judiciary could claim full autonomy from all outside interference."

The *Cambridge History* again restates these themes. To Iriye (1989: 729), the Meiji government became "administratively and politically centralized, a system in which professional bureaucrats would play a pivotal role." To Beasley (1989: 668), the civil service system "helped protect the bureaucracy, both civil and military, from political meddling. What it did not do, as the twentieth century was to demonstrate, was to prevent the bureaucracy from meddling in politics."

Last, many scholars argue that these public-spirited oligarchs and bureaucrats instituted policies that effectively fostered economic growth. That some of the measures may have fostered growth seems unexceptional. Virtually all economists agree that enforceable property rights and independent central banks promote growth. Yet some of the other measures seem more dubious. Some schemes – like the state-owned model textile factories – were simple failures. Others – like the state-owned telegraphs and railroads – were projects that private firms probably could (and would) have undertaken as efficiently.

Perhaps more troubling, many scholars argue that even the early government's attempts overtly to manipulate investment and consumption patterns promoted growth. Peter Duus (1988: 18), for example, identifies in the *Cambridge History* as key aspects of the pre-war and post-war "sociopolitical environment of growth": "a tolerance of the government's flexible involvement in promoting economic growth; a disincentive to cling to pure market models of the economy; [and] a predilection for oligopolistic organization." E.S. Crawcour (1989: 616), writing in the *Cambridge History* as well, concludes: "Japan's success depended significantly and perhaps critically, on the ability of the Meiji government and its supporters to restrict consumption in the interests of industrial and military investment." Growth required government manipulation, in short, not market competition (id., 617):

Japanese governments have, in the areas that they considered most important, generally put more faith in manipulation than in free competition and the market mechanism. . . . [This] heritage of manipulation may have contributed as much to Japan's economic development as did the heritage of individual enterprise.

Of this composite story, we are skeptical. It is not that the three hypotheses plainly contradict the apparent facts of Japanese history. It is not even that the hypotheses are logically impossible. It is rather a question of plausibility. By the canons of modern social science, each of the three hypotheses taken separately is highly improbable. Taken together, that improbability cubes itself.

Consider each hypothesis in turn. Certainly, the Meiji (1868–1912) oligarchs might have acted as statesmen. Under their rule, Japan did transform itself into a major world power. Whatever selfish motives they occasionally entertained, they could have governed in the public interest. Altruism is an occasional (and fortunate) fact of life, even among military juntas.

Certainly, the Meiji oligarchs might have created an independent bureaucracy. Whatever control they wielded over others they employed, they could have kept their bureaucrats independent. Some principals do give their agents autonomy, even – again – in military governments.

Certainly, the Meiji oligarchs might have manipulated markets in ways that promoted efficient growth. Under their rule, the Japanese economy did grow fast. Whatever other mistakes they made in life, in economic policy they could have been prescient or lucky or both. Even ardently market-oriented social scientists admit governments can – hypothetically – intervene efficiently.

None of the statements is impossible. Rather, each is improbable, and the set of all three much more so. Altruism is not a major part of most oligarchic government programs. Independence is not something oligarchs commonly assign their hired agents. And prescience and luck are not attributes most governments show in manipulating markets.

Nor is there much evidence from modern Japan to support these hypotheses. Altruism is not something of which anyone has accused postwar Japanese government leaders, and some of the Meiji "statesmen" did reward themselves handsomely.[5] Independence is not something the postwar Japanese politicians have given their judges and bureaucrats.[6] And prescient economic management is not something for which many – if any – economists cite modern Japanese bureaucrats.[7]

We find all this a problem. Effectively, scholars have "explained" large swaths of Japanese history through a set of hypotheses that directly contradict basic working assumptions in modern social science. Effectively, scholars have posited Japan an "exceptional" case in three fundamental but very distinct ways.

1.2. This project

In this book we search for a less "exceptional" approach. We ask whether the fundamental contours of Japanese history might not follow from a pair of parsimonious assumptions more consistent with modern scholarship. Working within the "rational-choice" tradition, we posit that firms try to maximize profits and that government officials try to stay in office. Through these simple (many will say "simple-minded") postulates, we explore some of the basic contours of Imperial Japanese history.

In truth, we think we do more than explain the basic contours of that history – though we do think we accomplish that. First, because we use an analytical framework not specific to Japan, we think we clarify some of the strategic choices oligarchs everywhere face – an under-explored issue in political science. Second, because we ask different questions than most scholars ask, we think we find new facts. We can state this more bluntly: We think some of the "facts" of Japanese history as scholars have traditionally understood them are not facts at all. All too often, in Japanese history scholars have used implausible hypotheses to explain phenomena that never occurred.

Although our model is standard to economics and much of modern political science, we recognize that few of our Japanological colleagues will sympathize. Some will complain that it describes no society anywhere. Others will complain that it imputes a late twentieth-century calculus to people living in a different world in a different age. Indeed, honest readers of earlier drafts made both observations.

We are grateful to our readers, but these objections miss the point. First, we do not deny that humans are more complex than our model allows. We claim neither that all firms always maximize profits, or that all political actors worry only about their office. Instead, we make a more basic and mundane point: that most firms usually try to maximize profits and most political actors usually try to keep their office. The reason is simple: In most cases, firms that do not try to sell good products cheap eventually fail, and politicians who ignore their competitors eventually disappear. That much is true in the United States and is true in Japan. It is true now and was true a century ago.

Second, simple hypotheses clarify some of the more salient dynamics at work. It is not that richer theories of human behavior cannot help. Our parsimonious approach leaves a wide range of phenomena unexplained, and even within the rational-choice tradition, many scholars expand our postulates about human behavior to capture a fuller range of experience (for example, Przeworski, 1991; Coleman, 1990). It is rather that richer theories advance a different enterprise than we undertake here. We do not use such richer theories – but not because we think them invalid. Rather, we retain our more parsimonious assumptions because we think they clarify the larger strategic decisions that the actors made.

Before summarizing the argument that follows, we note three additional points. First, we focus on conflicts within the oligarchy. We find that these conflicts explain many of the more prominent puzzles of Japanese political history. It is precisely because most historians slight these conflicts, we suspect, that many seem so inclined both to characterize the men who wielded power as statesmen, and to take their self-serving rhetoric at face value.

Second, we suggest that international pressures may have mattered less than most scholars assert. Whether unelected oligarchs or elected politicians, government leaders must placate large swatches of their own populations or they will not retain power. Almost invariably, unless they can credibly threaten war, foreign governments have less influence. Imperial Japanese leaders generally answered to their domestic populations. As a result, we suggest that regime change in Imperial Japan may have been less the inadvertent result of any efforts to renegotiate treaties; it may have been more the foreseeable result of domestically oriented strategies – of the persistent attempts by several oligarchs to cater to those outside the circle of power.

Last, although we largely exclude intellectual and ideological phenomena from our analysis, our conclusions are consistent with the most prominent finding of recent intellectual historians: that as a symbol the imperial house was highly manipulable and effectively indeterminate. In her explorations of Meiji ideology, Carol Gluck (1985: 277) describes the Meiji intellectual world as "a plural ideological universe." Symbols, she suggests, were grossly manipulable and routinely manipulated. In this environment, even the emperor had a profoundly uncertain effect. Exactly because of his inherent indeterminacy, we have not focused on the ways government leaders used him symbolically – a task Gluck herself has pursued marvelously well. We focus instead on the institutional framework of government – on factors with perhaps a more determinate impact on history.

We begin by explaining why the late nineteenth-century oligarchs chose the constitution (and other aspects of the institutional structure) that they did (Chapters 2–4). We then trace two sets of implications that followed: how that institutional structure determined who formed and implemented policy over time (Chapters 5–7), and how that structure shaped the allocation of political rents over time (Chapters 8–10). In the remainder of this Chapter 1, we summarize our results.

2. THE ARGUMENT

2.1. The internal logic to oligarchies (Chapters 2–4)

The fragility of cooperation. At root, the leaders of Imperial Japan chose many aspects of the institutional structure that they did because they could not cooperate (Chapter 2). They were an oligarchy, not a dictatorship, and their numbers made all the difference. If they could have cooperated with each other, they could have protected and perhaps even enlarged their collective rents. Just as firms that cooperate can sometimes earn monopoly rents, so they – if they could but have cooperated – could potentially have earned large political rents. Through those rents, they could have increased the wealth, status, and other perquisites of power that they consumed.

In economic markets, rival sellers can rarely cooperate very long. Unfortunately for producers but fortunately for consumers, cartel members usually have an incentive to cheat (Stigler, 1964). Although they maximize their collective profits by raising prices, they maximize their individual profits by cheating – by underselling the cartel by a hair. If firm A cheats and all other cartel members cooperate, consumers will turn to A. The cartel as a whole will earn less, but A individually will earn more. Because every firm has an incentive to play A, every firm will cheat, and no firm will earn a monopoly rent.

So too in political markets. Although the Japanese oligarchs could have maximized their collective political rents by cooperating, they maximized their individual rents by cheating relentlessly. The paradox derives from the well-known game-theoretic problem of "empty cores." In splitting the political rents among themselves, oligarchs will seldom find a stable equilibrium (the "core" of their game being "empty"): Whatever agreement they negotiate, a majority of the members of the group will always have an incentive to fight it.[8] However they split the political rents, a majority of the oligarchy will be able to improve their individual positions by promoting a different split. Because of all this, the oligarchs found their fratricidal battles chronic. For reasons that follow, they also found them suicidal.[9]

First, in dividing the political rents among themselves, the oligarchs found that it paid to prove that they could threaten the oligarchy. To strengthen their bargaining position within the oligarchy, some members solicited support outside it. To improve the position from which they bargained for a division of the oligarchic spoils, they solicited support from the politically dispossessed. By doing so, they effectively showed that they could do well for themselves even if they quit playing the cooperative oligarch.

Second, the oligarchs played this self-destructive game relentlessly. When one oligarch wanted to increase his share of the oligarchic spoils, he organized one segment of the population. When another oligarch wanted to retaliate, he organized another. Once organized, however, these groups tended to endure (Olson, 1982). Gradually but steadily, the oligarchs enlarged the fraction of the population informed and organized enough to lobby for political power. Gradually but steadily, they caused power to devolve from oligarchy to democracy. In the process, by the time they died they had helped create two new groups: Citizens sophisticated, organized, and informed enough to capture power for themselves, and a cadre of party politicians who – by appealing to those citizens – could capture a large share of the political rents for themselves.

Third, asymmetries in demogogic talent prevented the oligarchs from designing institutions that would stop this suicidal game. When firms in a cartel have similar cost curves, they find it relatively easy to limit the quantity of goods they each produce. When they lack those similarities, they find it relatively hard. In late nineteenth-century Japan, the oligarchs faced just such heterogeneities in the cost of generating political support. Some oligarchs had crowd appeal, others did not. As with cartelized firms, these cost-asymmetries prevented the oligarchs from setting and enforcing the limits to their fratricidal competition. Although they collectively could have gained if they together could have limited their appeals to the dispossessed, several of them individually gained if they reneged. They did renege, and the relentless devolution of power ensued.

7

The politics of oligarchy

Alternatives. If this hypothesis seems peculiar, consider three alternatives (Chapter 3). First, perhaps the oligarchs created the electoral institutions they did to maximize their personal wealth. Because economic growth would have expanded the stock of wealth from which they could extract their shares, all else being equal they would have preferred a growing economy. Maybe they installed competitive electoral markets because democratic institutions promote growth. Although they also limited their own power to expropriate, maybe that was the point: By limiting their own power, they (a) increased their ability credibly to promise investors safe returns, (b) stimulated investment, and (c) expanded the stock of national wealth.

Perhaps, in other words, with a bigger economy to tax, the oligarchs maximized their cash returns even though they lowered the effective rate at which they expropriated. Intuitively, the proposition resembles the much-maligned Laffer curve of a century later: By limiting the rate at which they taxed the economy, the Meiji oligarchs increased the tax base enough to increase their tax revenues. In an irony several recent scholars have noted, perhaps by limiting their political power they increased their financial returns.[10]

Whether the theory explains democratization elsewhere, it does not explain it in Imperial Japan. For one thing, the oligarchs did not establish institutions that seriously limited their ability to expropriate. Although they created a judiciary and an elected legislature, they left room to circumvent them. For another, the oligarchs designed electoral institutions that promoted inefficient investment, not efficient growth. Although they did create competitive electoral markets, they designed rules that gave the elected politicians incentives to enact inefficient policies – policies that badly skewed investments (Chapter 4).

Second, perhaps the oligarchs hoped competitive electoral institutions would extend their tenure in office by giving them information about the policies they needed to adopt (Bendor, 1985; Miller, 1992: 79–82). Because the oligarchs lived well, they had insulated themselves from the populace. Absent elections, maybe they thought they could not obtain the information they needed about the policies Japanese citizens wanted. Absent those policies, maybe they thought they could not stop a revolution. By letting their rivals run political campaigns, they would learn what policies they needed to enact to preserve their control.

This theory works no better than the first. Like the first, it does not explain the institutions the oligarchs actually adopted. The oligarchs enacted electoral rules that – far more than in most societies – led political entrepreneurs to promise voters private goods such as pork (Chapter 4). Through the elections, therefore, the oligarchs obtained information primarily about the private goods the voters wanted. Yet that information

8

they could easily learn from economic markets. What they could not readily learn was what public goods the citizens wanted: what macro-economic policies they hoped the government would implement, for instance, or what infrastructural investments they hoped it would make, and what foreign policy initiatives they hoped it would adopt. They could not obtain that information from economic markets. Given the institutions they created, neither could they obtain it through the electoral market.

Last, perhaps the oligarchs wanted information not about what policies the citizens wanted, but about which political entrepreneurs posed the greatest threat. Maybe, in other words, they introduced competitive electoral markets to locate their most effective rivals. Once they knew who they were, they could coopt them with government posts. Unlike the other two hypotheses, this one fits the facts. The oligarchs did establish electoral markets that let them identify the men who could most credibly challenge their regime. Many of these men were extraordinarily sophisticated and politically astute, and the oligarchs plied them steadily with the perquisites of government office.

Nonetheless, this hypothesis by itself does not explain why regime change occurred, and for that reason we couple it with our earlier hypothesis about the instability of the oligarchic cartel. Fundamentally, the two hypotheses work in tandem: (a) The need to identify political entrepreneurs explains why the oligarchs used electoral markets, given the devolution of power; it does not explain that devolution. (b) The instability of the oligarchic cartel explains that devolution; it does not explain why any devolution took electoral form. Fundamentally, the two hypotheses address different phenomena: The need to identify competitors explains the shape that the devolution of power took; oligarchic instability explains why that devolution occurred at all.

2.2. Bureaucrats, judges, and the military (Chapters 5–7)

Bureaucrats and judges. Although scholars routinely claim that imperial bureaucrats independently masterminded Japanese policy, nothing of the sort occurred (Chapter 5). Just as modern Japanese bureaucrats answered to the majority party for nearly four decades (Ramseyer and Rosenbluth, 1993), so too did imperial bureaucrats answer to other masters. During the early decades, they answered to the oligarchs; during the middle years, they answered to party politicians; and during the last pre-war decade they answered to the generals and admirals. The same probably holds for judges: They too seem to have answered, in succession, to oligarchs, politicians, and the military leaders (Chapter 6). Ultimately, bureaucrats and judges were not principals. They were agents.

The politics of oligarchy

Oligarchic rhetoric disguised this relationship. The oligarchs claimed to have insulated bureaucrats and judges from themselves. With respect to both, they did institute rules that prevented cabinet ministers from hiring and firing them at will. Crucially, however, they did not prevent cabinet ministers from promoting them at will. Through promotions, of course, a principal can easily induce an agent to comply. From time to time, the oligarchs used their power over promotions for just that purpose. When the party politicians took power in the 1920s, they regularly did the same.

During the 1920s, the Seiyūkai and Kenseikai/Minseitō parties alternated in power. Although the politicians in each could promise not to intervene in personnel matters, they could also break that promise. Suppose that they had expected democratic government to continue indefinitely, and that their gains from judicial and bureaucratic independence had been high. If so, then maybe their expected future gains from that independence could have enabled them to make their promises about independence credible (Klein and Leffler, 1981). In 1920s Japan, however, they could not make the strategy work. They knew both that military leaders could engineer an effective coup any year (many military leaders had both access to the requisite technological resources and significant public support), and that soon they likely would. Because they knew that their political role could soon end, they could not commit themselves to cooperative strategies even had they wished. They faced an end-game, and they knew it. Accordingly, they adopted end-game strategies and flaunted their control over judges and bureaucrats.[11]

The military. The military was different (Chapter 7). To keep it independent from party politicians, the oligarchs required that Army and Navy ministers be active-duty military officers, let those ministers report directly to the emperor, and made the Army and Navy chiefs of staff independent even of those ministers. Over the years, the oligarchs sometimes found themselves forced to let party politicians form cabinets. Because active-duty soldiers and sailors did not run for electoral office, and because the oligarchs informally controlled access to the emperor, they could thereby keep the military for themselves even while they gave politicians the cabinet.

More than any other oligarch, Yamagata Aritomo ran the military. Unable to settle the distribution of power among themselves, the oligarchs had never clarified (much less institutionalized) who among them controlled the emperor. As a result, even though they created rules that made it clear that they as a group controlled the military, those rules did not clarify which of them controlled the military. Ironically, that was how Yamagata wanted it. For Yamagata had personal, non-institutional means of running the military. He had organized the new Army on a Prussian model. From the start, he had stacked it with people who were personally loyal to him. Over the decades, he had continued to reward their personalized loyalty.

Yamagata carefully preserved this control. As an oligarch without charisma, he could not cheaply organize mass support, and could not jockey for advantage by playing the democratic game. To compete with his oligarchic rivals, he used the military instead. By implicitly threatening to use it against the government, he could protect his own power from his more charismatic rivals.

To the oligarchs, a military subject to Yamagata's personalized control – even if not a first-best strategy – was better than many alternatives. The oligarchs did not want cabinet control over the military, for party politicians might control the cabinet. They did not institutionalize their own direct control, for they could not agree on the shape that such control would take. But provided they stayed alive, the structure they created did ensure both (1) that (through their control over the emperor) they controlled the military indirectly, and (2) that Yamagata himself controlled the military more directly. In the process, they prevented the two worst-case outcomes: (a) that the military might run itself, or (b) that the party politicians might run the military. Unfortunately, by 1931 almost all of them were dead, and the military was independent. With no one over them save a puppet emperor, the military officers took charge. Soon, they overran China.

Crucially, the oligarchs never collectively discovered how to bequeath their power to chosen successors. By now the reason should be obvious. Collectively, they never institutionalized their succession for the same reason they seldom did anything else collectively: They could not cooperate. The puzzle – one we do not satisfactorily answer – is why they did not bequeath their power individually. Some did try to pick their successors, but none succeeded, and few besides Yamagata even came close.[12]

Gambling apparently on their abilities to pick successors, the oligarchs had kept the military institutionally independent. They lost the gamble. Even if shrewd ex ante, gambles (probabilistic calculations that they are) sometimes produce catastrophies ex post. In Japan, this one did. The actors involved chose their individually rational moves, nature played its randomized hand, and collective disaster ensued.

2.3. Regulatory consequences (Chapters 8–10)

This institutional structure produced distinctive economic consequences, and we explore them through three industries: banking (Chapter 8), railroads (Chapter 9), and cotton textiles (Chapter 10). Although we could have chosen a variety of others, we chose these industries for two reasons. First, all three are industries that scholars usually argue played a major role in Japanese economic development. According to most observers, the banking and railroad industries formed crucial parts of the infrastructure. The textile industry was one of the largest of all modern industries.

Second, in several ways the three industries together present a diverse mix. They represent different sectors of the economy: finance, transportation, and light manufacturing. They implicate different ministries: the Ministry of Finance, the Ministry of Railroads, and the Ministry of Commerce and Industry. Two are service industries, and one a manufacturing industry. Two are industries where most scholars find positive externalities, and one an industry where they do not. Two are industries that hired men, and one an industry that hired women. Two are industries where most scholars applaud the way the government regulated the industry, and one an industry where the government did not much intervene.

Banks. To date, most Japanologists argue both that the banking industry provided significant positive externalities, and that government regulation contributed to that beneficial role. Take the *Cambridge History* again (Crawcour, 1988: 391):

A substantial contribution to economic growth both at this time [1885–1913] and later, . . . was made by the heavy investment in infrastructure such as ancillary services like banking . . . . With the experience of the advanced industrial countries in front of them, Japan's leaders anticipated and provided for future needs for such infrastructure.

The banking system did not, it explains, "develop in response to the needs of economic growth." Rather, it "was created in advance of demand and played a positive part in facilitating economic development" (id., 393).

Not so. In the early oligarchic years, the government did little more than let entrepreneurs form banks when they wished, and create a few special-purpose banks of its own. Under the politicians, it did begin to intervene in the 1920s – mostly to close the smaller banks. In doing so, however, it pursued decidedly political ends. At the time, the party in power (the Kenseikai/Minseitō) relied for support on the big urban banks, while its competitor relied on the smaller rural banks. In 1925 the parliament had just passed a universal manhood suffrage law and a set of electoral rules (multi-member districts and a single-non-transferrable vote – see Chapter 4) that forced the parties to divide the vote within each district. Within this political world, institutions (such as banks) that could help a party divide a community took on added importance. By closing pivotal rural institutions, the Kenseikai/Minseitō thus could badly penalize the Seiyūkai. Perhaps for just that reason, it closed the smaller banks.

Railroads. The railroad industry too supposedly provided crucial spillovers and benefited from shrewd government policies. Again according to the *Cambridge History* (Crawcour, 1988: 394, 396):

Before World War I, this [railroad] sector absorbed more public and private investment than did any other single industry. The development of railways and shipping services provides good examples of how government and private groups combined in various ways to perform tasks of national importance.

The contribution of the railways to Japan's economic development, both then and later, was enormous. They greatly reduced transport costs, thus promoting geographical specialization and mobility of labor and benefiting all sections of the population in the areas they served.

Here too the standard accounts mislead. Note first that railroads were not as indispensible as most scholars assume. Implicitly or explicitly, most scholars compare them with palanquins rather than with their more realistic alternative. Just as canals would have provided most of the gains attributed to American railroads (Fogel, 1964), coastal shipping would have provided cheap and effective freight (not passenger) transportation for most (not all) Japanese commercial centers.

Second, railroads produced few externalities. Although they did generate economic gains, most of those gains accrued either to the railroads, to parties contracting with the railroad directly (for example, a shipper), or to parties contracting with the railroad indirectly (for example, a hotel catering to train passengers). So long as such direct or indirect ties exist, the railroads will internalize most of the spillovers. Much of the benefit to government involvement then disappears.

Third, by the time party politicians began to play important roles, the government followed a distinctly political logic in its railroad policies. When it nationalized firms in the early twentieth century, it paid the highest price to the firms that supported the party in power. When it subsidized construction and repairs in the 1920s, it routed its money primarily to its electoral supporters. Necessarily, elected politicians are more responsive to popular pressure than unelected oligarchs. Under the party politicians, in other words, an electoral – not economic – logic governed Japanese railroad policy.

Textiles. This political logic to economic regulation reappears in the textile industry. Here too the government did little to promote the industry, and when it did intervene (primarily under the party politicians) it pursued distinctly political aims. When it banned night work in the factories, for example, it did so in a way that helped the party in power compete under the new electoral rules. When it cartelized the weaving firms in the 1920s, it chose a scheme that helped the party in power. And when it cartelized the spinning firms in the 1930s, it now answered to military masters and anticipated the regulation they wanted for a wartime economy. Throughout, a political logic prevailed.

3. THE PROJECT

Ideology matters, readers will complain. Culture matters, philosophy matters, religion matters. People explain what they do by the way they imagine the world, and their collective "discourse" describes how they imagine it. We agree. But in this book we have a more limited goal – to outline the strategies that Japanese leaders pursued and the principal results that ensued. Toward that end, we adopt a far more parsimonious approach. We explain institutional development and regime change through an unadorned rational-choice model: Political actors maximize their tenure and economic actors maximize their wealth. We do not deny that this misses much of the richness of human experience. We do not deny that it becomes reductionist. Instead, that it does all that is exactly the point. To the extent that we succeed, the very simplicity of the model clarifies the basic dynamics at stake.

2

The collapse of oligarchy:
Failed attempts at cartel-maintenance

1. INTRODUCTION

"Revere the emperor, throw out the barbarians" and "Rich country, strong army" were their refrains. But a more fundamental concern of the Meiji oligarchs[1] – and a more self-serving one than they cared to advertise in their rhetoric – was to avoid the fate they had visited upon the Tokugawa family in 1868. As with all political leaders, the oligarchs had first to remain in office before they could achieve any other goals they might have had – whether those were increasing their own wealth or that of their countrymen or anything else.

The Meiji oligarchs ultimately failed to retain the monopoly grip on power they had collectively won; but their loss was not for lack of trying. This chapter recounts the rounds of internal bargaining and institutional adjustments among the oligarchs between 1868 and 1881. There was a palpable tension throughout the period: On the one hand, the oligarchs knew they had to cooperate to protect their regime. On the other hand, each oligarch struggled to rise above his fellow oligarchs. The result was a continuing pattern of alliance-shifting and coalition-building. Some oligarchs – Ōkuma Shigenobu, Itagaki Taisuke, and later Itō Hirobumi – eventually threw in their lots with the political parties to boost their relative power within the oligarchy. It was this jockeying for power among themselves and bringing in support from outside the circle that destroyed the oligarchy's exclusive control of Japan's political system.

This chapter explores how the oligarchs went about shoring up their tenure in office and how their choice of governmental institutions reflected that objective. We also examine how the institutions they chose reflected problems peculiar to their situation. Because they were an oligarchy – a group of strong-willed leaders not led by a single dictator – they tried to devise institutional arrangements that enabled them to work with each other. And because they were self-appointed rather than

15

elected, they tried to find non-electoral ways of discerning the minimum level of public service the citizenry would tolerate before rising up in revolt.

Not surprisingly, the process of institutional adjustment in the early Meiji period involved considerable trial and error. We review the events of the years leading up to 1889. That was the year, with the promulgation of the Meiji Constitution, that the oligarchs decided to commit their plan for government to paper and to throw procedural roadblocks in the way of institutional change.

For readers even passingly familiar with subsequent Japanese history, all of this prompts the question of why, if the oligarchs were as clever and self-interested as we suggest, they devised institutions that ultimately destroyed the very empire they created. Perhaps our hindsight makes us unfair critics, for gambles that come out badly ex post are sometimes good deals ex ante.

The oligarchs, in choosing institutions to solve one set of problems, eventually brought on another problem that proved, for Japan if not for the oligarchs themselves, far larger. Their eagerness to protect themselves from each other and from the rise of political parties gave rise to a military more powerful and independent than they might have wanted. It was their distrust of one another that also prevented them from solving their succession problem. Even if they chose unwisely for Japan, however, the oligarchs did manage to do quite well for themselves.

This chapter is organized as follows: Section 2 explores who the oligarchs were and what they wanted. Section 3 outlines the earliest negotiations and settlements among the oligarchs, and traces the path toward the Meiji Constitution. Section 4 concludes by explaining the discord within the Meiji government in the light of modern cartel theory.

2. THE CAST OF CHARACTERS

2.1. Introduction

As Carol Gluck (1985) has elegantly argued, imperial sovereignty was one of the most vacuous of Meiji's modern myths. Had the emperor actually wielded the powers of a classic dictator, the political institutions of Meiji Japan would have looked quite different and Japanese history would likely have taken another course. A powerful emperor, wishing to remain so, might have delegated varying amounts of discretion to his advisers and even conceded some perquisites to his competitors. But as the final arbiter of all disputes not resolved farther down the chain of authority, he would have unified the realm under his rule. His agents would have acted in anticipation of what he wanted, hoping to raise their

16

own stature. The resulting system would have been not one of checks and balances, but of centralized control.

An oligarchy, by contrast, consists of leaders competing with each other for supremacy, even as they may seek to secure a common goal. Because none alone was strong enough, the leaders of the Meiji Restoration had to band their forces together to overthrow the Tokugawa shogunate. But once collectively in power, each individually had an incentive to wrest more power from the others for himself.

One might ask why the Meiji oligarchs invoked the imagery of the emperor at all. Ōkubo Toshimichi – an early member of the oligarchy who died within a few years – commented soon after the Restoration that the coalition between the two domains that had led the Meiji Restoration, the Satsuma and the Chōshū, was more powerful than the imperial court. The building of the Imperial House, he argued, would thus depend on the cooperation of the oligarchs (Ōkubo ke, 1928: III-347–58). By all indications, Ōkubo was not exaggerating. Indeed, when the Satsuma and Chōshū men first discussed the matter of overthrowing the shogunate, they considered keeping the shogun as titular head. They opted for imperial restoration to make a cleaner break with the past, to eliminate more vestiges of the old system (Tōyama, 1973: 285).

At a minimum, the emperor served as a unifying device for the Meiji oligarchs since all policies had to be cleared through him and the somewhat bizarrely named "Keeper of the Privy Seal."[2] Perhaps – though we table the issues of ideology and symbolism for another occasion – the rhetoric of benign Imperial rule also served as a focal point for the Japanese public, and established an (admittedly vague) standard for assessing the quality of the Meiji regime. In giving the public some measure by which to evaluate their performance, perhaps the oligarchs collectively disciplined themselves.

To win support from a wide variety of sources, the leaders had to be able to convince the public that they would not turn the new government into a private rent-extracting machine for themselves and their progeny. They had to be able to commit themselves to limiting their own take. Perhaps – again, we table these issues – ostensibly fighting for someone else as monarch helped them do that. Perhaps the oligarchs were trying (however imperfectly) to tie their hands to their private advantage.

The other institutions of Meiji government evolved as the more successful of the oligarchs gained power relative to the others and shaped the rules to suit their interests. Oligarchs who found themselves being eclipsed typically objected vociferously, usually extracting concessions in exchange for their renewed cooperation. The rules were quite fluid, as we will point out, until the underlying power balance became more established.

17

The politics of oligarchy

2.2. The historical context

The oligarchs made the best of an inhospitable international environment. During the dying years of the Tokugawa shogunate, all of the major Western sea-going powers had taken advantage of Japan's weakened state to forge "unequal treaties" with Japan. Japan was forced to accept imports from these countries at low tariff levels, and to allow these countries extra-territorial legal jurisdiction in Japan.[3]

The foreign powers had encroached on Japan in a way that ominously resembled the early stages of their dismantling of China. Although this gave the oligarchs something to worry about, the oligarchs eventually freed themselves of unwanted foreign interference by building up a sizable conscription Army and Navy. It was their domestic situation that proved the harder to manage. The fiercest competition, as it turns out, was among themselves.

2.3. The oligarchs

For the most part, the oligarchs were low-ranking but ambitious samurai dissatisfied with their lot in the disintegrating Tokugawa regime. They hailed disproportionately from the southern domains of Chōshū, Satsuma, Tosa and Hizen – but not because these areas were most economically disadvantaged. Historian Thomas Smith (1988) points out that the economies of these areas were flourishing, in part because the Tokugawa's guild regulations were implemented most weakly in the outer reaches of the realm. Farthest from the Tokugawa's watchful eye, they could also mobilize for war undetected.

Itō. Itō Hirobumi, generally regarded as the most powerful Meiji leader, was actually the son of a poor farmer. Itō's father left his farm before Itō was born and worked for a samurai family in the southern domain of Hagi, part of Chōshū. That family eventually adopted Itō's father, enabling him to pass their samurai status to his descendants (Hani, 1956: 311).

Itō was as enamored of Western power as he was angered by its use against Japan. He and his fellow-Chōshū clansman, Inoue Kaoru, had been anti-foreign activists in their youth, torching the foreign legation in Gotenyama, Tokyo, in January 1863 (Satow, 1983: 71). But later that same year, at the invitation of the Hong Kong-based trading firm, Jardine Matheson, young Itō and Inoue Kaoru traveled to England.[4] There they studied law, though their stay was cut short when, six months later, relations between Japan and Britain became strained over British demands for access to more Japanese harbors.[5]

18

Yamagata. Yamagata Aritomo, in time to become Itō's most powerful colleague and rival, also was born to a low-ranking samurai family in Chōshū. Yamagata inherited his father's post as financial manager and construction contractor for his domain. In time he took on a variety of other managerial positions in his domain, including rice collector, and gendarme in charge of gauging the popularity – or lack thereof – of the feudal lord. Eventually, he became commander of the domain's army. Here he led his first real battle against foreigners, and was notoriously unsuccessful. Yet it was those battles against the British, American, French and Dutch naval forces in 1864 that then led him to oppose continued isolationism.[6]

Ōkuma. Ōkuma Shigenobu was the eldest son of a retainer in the service of the daimyō of Hizen in southern Japan. Rewarded for his role in the Restoration, he was a member of the new government from the start, and was named Vice-Minister of Foreign Affairs in 1869. In 1870, at the age of 33, he already presided over several government ministries. After the death of Ōkubo in 1878, he and Itō assumed the leading positions in government.[7]

The Restorationist samurai appealed to merchants, farmers, and outer-domain lords for support to overthrow the Tokugawa. But the interests of the various members of this motley coalition were at odds on numerous scores. Rich farmers were not interested in the land redistribution that peasants wanted, and the samurai wanted maximal compensation from everyone else.[8] Building a national constituency from this shaky basis would be the Restorationists' biggest challenge, one they would meet with mixed success.

3. THE FIRST ATTEMPTS AT INSTITUTIONAL DESIGN

The leaders of the Meiji Restoration lost little time subduing the country militarily. One of their first orders of business was to wrest power from the feudal domains and establish exclusive control over taxation. In 1870, they sent one of their most senior members, Iwakura Tomomi, on a mission to the feudal domains that were holding out from joining the new regime. Iwakura convinced leaders of the remaining domains to abandon their resistance in exchange for high positions in the Meiji government.[9] By the following year, scarcely four years after overthrowing the Tokugawa shogunate, the government managed to abolish feudal domains altogether, merging several at a time into prefectures instead (*hai han, chi ken*) (Ōshima, 1972).

The oligarchs still had to deal with the vast majority of the samurai, and the last thing they needed was a rebellion by all the weapons-wielders in the country. Since they could not buy off all the samurai with government positions, they decided to reduce the risk of revolt in two other ways. First, they would eliminate the samurai class's centuries-old monopoly on weapons and institute nationwide conscription for military service in its place.[10] Second, to soften the blow of lost income and status, they issued each samurai family government bonds (*chitsu roku kōsai*) in December 1873 as a severance payment.

In another step to restructure the configuration of power in Japan, the oligarchs introduced – in the name of the emperor, of course – a peerage system in 1876. Despite its stuffy sound, the new aristocratic system may have been a shrewd device. To the extent people valued the prestige associated with the new regime, it gave the oligarchs a cheap way to buy off opponents and reward supporters. To the extent people did not value the prestige, it was a low-cost experiment. Within this new system, the imperial family enjoyed the highest rank (*kō shaku*), in keeping with the emperor's ostensible role as sovereign. Next, samurai who had contributed importantly to the Restoration (for example, the oligarchs themselves) would receive the second highest title of count (*haku shaku*), for all posterity. Less illustrious samurai, who had served for ten years or more in a high government post, would also be eligible for appointment with the title count. Their appointment, however, would last for their own lifetime (Tōyama, 1988: 540).

In his capacity as director of the government's legislative affairs bureau, Itō Hirobumi added more ranks to the peerage in 1878. Borrowing from the European system of labeling aristocrats, he created the category of marquis (*kō [sōrō] shaku*) above count for all former daimyō, and viscount (*shi shaku*) and baron (*dan shaku*) below count to reward loyal bureaucrats and various others (Tōyama, 1988: 541).

3.1. Resistance to central control

The Meiji leaders' early attempts to form a strong government met with prolonged resistance and repeated failure. In 1873, the fledgling government nearly fell apart over whether or not to attack Korea. Unemployed samurai were putting considerable pressure on the government to launch a military campaign; Korea was merely a convenient target (Fujimura, 1961; Akamatsu, 1967: 275).

More fundamentally, a schism was emerging in the oligarchy along old domain lines.[11] The oligarchs from Tosa and Hizen were troubled by what appeared to them to be a growing concentration of power in the hands of a few oligarchs from Satsuma and Chōshū.[12] Etō Shimpei, a leader of the Restoration from Hizen, was so infuriated by the Satsuma-Chōshū cabal that he raised an army of his own in 1874, and fought government forces for two months before dying in battle along with many of his men. The next year, the government was again embroiled in an internal dispute along the same fracture lines. This time the ostensible reason for the split was disagreement over whether or not to attack Taiwan, but given the flairing tempers, the impetus could just as well have been anything else (Osadake, 1930: 103; 232).

The last and most serious military challenge to the government from within its own ranks came in early 1877 when Saigō Takamori, one of the most charismatic leaders of the Restoration, took on government forces with a contingent of nearly 30,000 soldiers and volunteers from his native Kagoshima (Satsuma). Although himself a Satsuma oligarch, Saigō had not found his way into Itō's and Yamagata's inner circle, and instead threw in his lot with the renegades of Tosa and Hizen. Along with Etō, Saigō favored war with Korea, and left Tokyo to found a network of military schools in Kagoshima. The "mainstream" oligarchs tried to undermine Saigō's movement first by sending spies into Saigō's schools. Then, in January 1877, when the government tried surreptitiously to remove ammunitions from Saigō's base, Saigō's forces attacked. Saigō and his men fought for six months before losing to the government's far larger conscription army, led by Yamagata. Over 5,000 of Saigō's men died in action, and another 1,488 were convicted of war crimes following the insurrection (Konishi, 1968). Saigō himself died in the final battle.

As the bloody confrontation with Saigō's forces makes clear, the government had to deal with sharp differences of interest within its own ranks. Paying off resisters with government positions had its risks, but so did shutting mavericks out. To reduce these risks, the oligarchs strove to make credible their threats to punish defectors. Their willingness to put the lives of their soldiers on the line was, no doubt, a potent deterrent. But it was a deterrent with inherent limitations.

Yamagata probably deserves his reputation as the most hard line of the oligarchs. As supreme military advisor to the emperor, he stood at the helm of the nation's new military by age forty (Hackett, 1971: 83). Several months after his successful campaign against Saigō's errant forces, he presided over the shooting of fifty-three of his own soldiers who protested salary cuts. He had another 300 or so soldiers punished less severely for their involvement in the protest (Hani, 1956: 313).

3.2. The first institutions

The oligarchs knew that domestic military control, while essential to the survival of their regime, was not enough. They had also to govern. If the citizens were too unhappy with the state of public affairs, after all, their disaffection would make military suppression more difficult and costly.

The politics of oligarchy

No amount of military might could match a nationwide rabble of aroused and angry peasants, should matters come to that.

It was no easy task to forge a coherent government from the leaders of the twenty-three feudal domains that together toppled the Tokugawa forces (Osadake, 1930: 54). This was an unwieldy group with few common interests and many disparate ones, as the frequent institutional re-shuffling testified. The first Meiji government, instituted in January 1868, consisted of three "branches": a president (Arisugawa Taruhito Shinno, an obscure and otherwise powerless member of the imperial family), a council of 30 (the leaders of the rebellious feudal domains), and a body of 106 "advisors." The advisors – who were the real activists in the Restoration – presided over seven "departments" that were to implement the policies decided in the council: imperial, internal, foreign, military, fiscal, judicial, and structural affairs.[13]

The Meiji leaders reorganized themselves three times in the next four months. In 1869 they streamlined their government into a more hier-archical system. The government was to be led by two councils: the Imperial Affairs Bureau, which was to be paramount, and the General Governance Bureau. Below these were six ministries to handle the day-to-day tasks of government: Public Affairs, Finance, Military, Justice, Imperial Household, and Foreign Affairs (Tōyama and Adachi, 1961: 1; Tōyama, 1973b: 286).

Although streamlining may have been one concern, the oligarchs also reorganized themselves to maintain coalitions of convenience among themselves and to keep their rivals off balance. In 1871, for example, they reversed the 1869 merger between the Ministry of Finance and the Ministry of Public Affairs. Itō and Ōkubo had apparently decided that the Minister, Kido Takayoshi, had become too powerful.[14] In 1873, Ōkubo became head of the Ministry of Home Affairs, a new ministry with wide-ranging jurisdiction. It was no coincidence that this occurred when he enjoyed the support of Itō (Tōyama and Adachi, 1961: 1–2). In 1880, Itō undermined Ōkuma Shigenobu's influence over the Finance Ministry with a "reform" that removed the councilors' authority over ministries. Itō's intentions were no secret – as soon as Ōkuma left the government in 1881, he reversed the "reform" (Tsuji, 1944).

In 1871, in a plan somewhat reminiscent of separation of powers, the oligarchs established three councils under the General Governance Bureau to oversee better the growing government apparatus. The "Council of the Left" would draft and pass laws; the "Council of the Right" would implement policy; and the "Council of the Center" would arbitrate disputes within bureaucracy.[15] In fact, these councils held no independent veto. All were subordinate to the Imperial Affairs Bureau, later called the Council of Elders (*Genrō in*).

22

The collapse of oligarchy

Despite some consolidation by the early 1870s, strategic differences among the oligarchs continued to plague their efforts to hold their regime together. Kido and Ōkubo claimed that a repressive, top-down government would generate widespread popular unrest. At root, they seem to have feared that the Itō-Yamagata alliance effectively excluded them from power. Electoral regimes, they apparently hoped, might break that grip. Toward that end, they urged their colleagues in 1873 to include the scholar Fukuzawa Yukichi in a committee that would plan a new government structure. A well-known advocate of democratic institutions and popular elections, Fukuzawa would have supported their point of view.

Leery of unnecessary concessions to the populace – let alone of institutional changes that could weaken their standing relative to rival oligarchs – Itō and Yamagata blocked Fukuzawa's participation (Hani, 1956: 313). Itō and Yamagata agreed that they needed to forestall national uprising with some form of parliamentary government. But they insisted on moving slowly.

By 1874, oligarch Itagaki Taisuke, whom Itō and Yamagata had excluded from power, decided to fight back. That January he recruited a small band of disaffected Tosa samurai and formed the Patriotic Party (*Aikoku kōtō*). As its first political act, this new party petitioned the Meiji government for an elected national assembly. When the other oligarchs ignored the request, Itagaki extended the geographical reach of his party. In February 1875 he organized disgruntled former samurai in Osaka, one of the commercial centers of Japan. This new group, the Patriotic Society (*Aikoku sha*), would soon become a hub for regional clubs of former samurai across the country.

Within three weeks of the club's founding, Itagaki dissolved the Patriotic Society. He disbanded it not because it failed to reach its aims; quite the reverse. He disbanded it because he had achieved the most important part of his aims: The other oligarchs had invited him back into the government, this time with elevated status. In February 1875, at what historians call the "Osaka Conference," Itagaki, Kido, and Ōkubo reached a compromise with Itō Hirobumi. They agreed, as a transitional measure toward a parliamentary system, to structure the Council of Elders as a quasi-legislative body. Although the elders would not be elected, they would include Itagaki, Kido, and Ōkubo. The Councils of the Right and of the Left would be abolished, leaving only the Council of the Center (by 1879 renamed the Cabinet) in the General Governance Bureau. Finally, a new Supreme Court (*Daishin in*) would serve as a judicial body.[16]

Within a year, Itagaki again resigned from the government strategically. If the other oligarchs continued to hoard the best government positions and perquisites, he apparently found it more advantageous to resort to political entrepreneurship beyond the confines of the oligarchy. By 1878 he had revived the Patriotic Society. Soon he had transformed it into the center of a national movement for "popular rights" – by which, however, most members of the group meant a broader-based oligarchy rather than popular sovereignty (Naitō seichō, 1968: 48–49; Mason, 1969: 7–9).

In due course, what began as a movement of disaffected former samurai encompassed the entire wealth-holding strata of Japanese society (Inoue, 1956). In October 1881, Itagaki founded the *Jiyūtō* (Liberal Party). Although samurai continued to hold key positions in it, particularly in the early years, the backbone of the party's constituency came to be the tax paying landowners. Land taxes had made landlords into a clear group of agitated citizens for Itagaki to court (Satō, 1954: 31–38).

The following April, Ōkuma Shigenobu established the *Rikken kaishintō* (Constitutional Progressive Party). Among his followers were several talented young bureaucrats who had resigned their posts in sympathy with him at the time of his 1881 ouster. Because the Jiyūtō was preoccupied with the interests of the rural landholders, the urban leaders of the emerging large businesses also lent Ōkuma their support. Iwasaki Yatarō, for example, who headed what soon became the Mitsubishi conglomerate, was an early supporter of the Rikken kaishintō.[17]

By bringing in public sentiment on their side, the non-mainstream oligarchs attempted to strengthen their positions within the oligarchy. Their readiness to cease their entrepreneurial activities as soon as the mainstream made them concessions suggests that they were more interested in improving their status within the oligarchy than in destroying the group's monopoly on power. Yet the nature of their strategies – inviting players outside the oligarchy into the fray – would eventually destroy the arrangements they hoped to build.

Meanwhile, the "insider" oligarchs made it clear they were not interested in the general public's opinion on these – or any other – matters. By censoring newspapers in 1876, the oligarchs declared their collective intention to silence dissenters (Hani, 1956: 313). They soon found that keeping the public ill-informed was no easy task, particularly when some among them would leak news to the press. In an attempt to skew political outcomes, disaffected oligarchs routinely contacted newspaper writers. It was a cheap way to cheat on the power cartel, and it worked. In 1881, for example, despite heavy media censorship the public learned of a huge kickback scheme. It seems that a private entrepreneur, Godai Tomoatsu from Satsuma, had arranged with cabinet member Kuroda to purchase government assets in Hokkaido at prices far below their market value, all with a thirty-year interest-free government loan (Itō, 1930: 152–160).

Untouched by the scandal, Ōkuma Shigenobu was delighted. Itō and Yamagata felt compelled, by dint of the bad publicity, to concede to his demands for parliamentary government sooner than they would have

24

liked. Whether or not the citizens expected representative government to be less corrupt, they at least wanted the right to throw out embezzlers.

In what presaged the beginning of the end of oligarchic rule, the oligarchs arranged for the Meiji Emperor to issue an Imperial Rescript in October 1881 pledging a National Assembly by 1890.[18] But they also relieved Ōkuma of his government post. Their pretext was that Ōkuma had not secured revised treaties with the West. The real reason was transparent: Ōkuma had not been a team player (Osadake, 1930: 387).

Why did the oligarchs capitulate to demands for a representative assembly? The short answer is that it was their best option for ensuring their own political survival. Their first choice would have been to retain their collective monopoly on power. But the enthusiasm of the public for representation presented them with a continuous incentive to cheat on each other. They were, in other words, in a classic prisoner's dilemma. Punishment – throwing the offending oligarchs out of office – ultimately failed to maintain cooperation because the punished mavericks simply reverted to their political-entrepreneurial activities.

4. THE DEMISE OF OLIGARCHY

Although the Meiji oligarchs maintained a cartel, it was only a tacit cartel: They had no higher authority that could monitor their actions and punish cheaters. Therefore, to maintain their grip on power they had to devise schemes that were self-enforcing. They may have had a variety of other goals, including policy preferences, but they first had to stay in office to achieve these other goals. Successful collusion, then, entailed an agreement to limit political decisions to themselves. Allowing any outsiders to have a say in decisions that would affect an oligarch's tenure in office thus became a breach of the agreement.

Note that the oligarchs were always jostling among themselves for more power relative to each another. Nothing in the literature on cartels suggests the market share of cartel participants had to be the same. Some oligarchs could be more influential than others (have larger market share). Yet they could all ensure their joint welfare by agreeing to exclude all non-oligarchs from political decisions.

Ex ante, how successful should the oligarchs have expected to be in preserving their collective job security? All oligarchs had an incentive to cheat. By organizing non-oligarch support for his position at the expense of the other oligarchs, each oligarch could increase his own influence and security. But as in any prisoner's dilemma, if all oligarchs did that the result would be disastrous: They would destroy the very oligarchy within which they were trying to advance.

Tacit cartels have a potent tool with which to sustain their collusion: So long as they can monitor cheating, even if indirectly, they can punish the offender(s) by cutting prices to market prices or even below for some period. All cartel members suffer (and earn lower rents), but at least the offenders learn that cheating does not pay.[19] Likewise in oligarchies: If the members of the oligarchy learn that a colleague panders to the unrepresented public (if a cartel member is cheating), they can all pander. In the process, the cheater will learn that even political cheating does not pay. Suppose, for example, that oligarch A discloses graft by oligarchs B and C. B and C could then disclose fraud by A. Suppose A incites disaffected landlords in prefecture X. B and C could then incite anti-landlord sentiment among tenants in X. Two or more can play most political games, and that makes retaliation possible – so long as cheating is observable.

Borrowing from the literature on cartels, we suggest three reasons why the oligarchs' cartel failed to hold together in Meiji Japan. First, tacit cartels disintegrate where members cannot observe cheating. Ōkuma had secret ties with newspapers, for example, and could leak damaging information to them. Saigō Takamori maintained a chain of unorthodox "schools" in his native Kagoshima, and could secretly encourage revolt. In both cases, the oligarchs initially responded conservatively. They squelched the media in Ōkuma's case and spied on the Kagoshima schools in Saigō's case. Yet they found it hard to silence the papers effectively, and hard to draw the line between personal loyalty to Saigō and treason. In both cases, they eventually decided that they observed cheating, and opted to punish the offenders directly – but only after significant delays.

Note that one difference between an oligarchy and a cartel in homogenous products is that oligarchs can expel or kill cheaters. As we know from history, members of oligarchies and juntas do use these methods from time to time in their power struggles. However, they take risks when they do, particularly when the renegades have cultivated public support. In turn, those risks explain why the Meiji oligarchs killed each other so rarely.

The oligarchs had to calculate the likelihood that their retaliatory punishment would increase the public demand for their ouster. They faced a dilemma: Because much of the cheating was unobservable, they could not identify cheating mavericks until those mavericks had already raised outside support. Once they had cultivated personal support through their entrepreneurship, killing them was dangerous. In the case of Saigō, the oligarchs took the risk; in the case of Ōkuma and Itagaki, they did not. Even for oligarchs with exclusive control over the military and police, an alarmed and aroused public could be a dangerous weapon in the hands of a political entrepreneur.

This suggests the second condition under which collusion is difficult to sustain: high levels of market demand for the cartel's product (Rotemberg and Saloner, 1986). Cheating Meiji oligarchs could sell the public political participation. If citizens (the consumers) had low levels of demand for such participation, the oligarchs (the sellers) would have little incentive to cheat because even the short term gains from undercutting the other cartel members would be small.

Obviously there is no precise measure for the popular demand for political participation. Consider, however, the steady spate of popular uprisings in the latter years of the Tokugawa period (White, 1988), and the explosive energy of the popular rights movement in the Meiji period (Inoue, 1956). Together the phenomena suggest that many Japanese citizens badly wanted participatory rights. Knowing that the popular response would be strong, and knowing that the other oligarchs had reason to worry about the latent power of the masses, Itagaki and Ōkuma had stronger incentives to cater to the public than otherwise.

Note too that once the public is organized, political entrepreneurs incur few costs to rally them to political action (Olson, 1982; Taylor, 1988). Having once expended the high initial fixed costs of establishing political organizations, Itagaki and Ōkuma faced ongoing temptations to cheat. Each time they renegotiated a truce with the other members of the oligarchy, they continued to find themselves tempted by the low-cost opportunities of upping the ante once more.

A third market condition that lowers the likelihood of successful collusion is the presence of cost-asymmetries among cartel participants. This phenomenon, too, weakened the Meiji oligarchy. When the cost structures for all members of the cartel are the same, all members maximize profits at the same price. As a result, firms can relatively easily settle on an equilibrium price. When firms produce a good with different levels of efficiency, however, their preferred prices will differ. They lack, then, a focal equilibrium price on which they can agree as the cartel's monopoly price (Tirole, 1989: 150).

Unfortunately for the Meiji oligarchy, the oligarchs were asymmetrically endowed in their ability to deal with popular political participation. Itagaki and Ōkuma could not successfully compete in closed-room dealings with their fellow oligarchs, but were charismatic and wildly popular among the Japanese public. Hence they seemed to think they could improve their prospects for job security in a system with some level of popular participation.

Other oligarchs – and in particular Yamagata Aritomo whose power base was in the military and whose taciturn disposition ill-suited him for popular campaigning – strongly opposed Itagaki's and Ōkuma's visions of the future. Yet with unobservable cheating, strong public demand for representation, and asymmetric endowments among the oligarchs, hold-

27

ing the line on the status quo was untenable. Now that Itagaki and Ōkuma had already established, much of it surreptitiously, the basis for nationwide political mobilization, punishing or even killing them would hardly accomplish anything. More likely it would incite the public to revolt en masse. Instead, the oligarchs hoped to hold Itagaki, Ōkuma, and others like them in check, by establishing political institutions that would sufficiently constrain the opportunities for mass political participation. The Meiji Constitution, to which we turn in the next chapter, was just such an institution.

5. CONCLUSION

In this chapter we outline the choices of the early Meiji oligarchs, and use modern cartel theory to interpret them. Although the oligarchs had a collective interest in keeping the reins of government to themselves, they voluntarily agreed to share power with an elected assembly. After just over a decade in office, they did not do so because they had had their fill of governing an unruly country. Rather, they did so because from the start they faced circumstances hostile to collusion.

The oligarchy eventually went the way of many tacit cartels: It collapsed under the weight of massive cheating from within its own membership. The multitude of ways in which the oligarchs could cheat on each other undetected, the strength of popular support for that cheating, and the large variance among the oligarchs in their ability to take advantage of the popular support doomed the oligarchy long before the military took over the Japanese government in the early 1930s. By the time the oligarchs drafted a constitution in the 1880s, their differences of view were so profound that they failed even to enshrine their own power in the document.

3

Concession or facade: The Meiji Constitution

1. INTRODUCTION

Consider why the oligarchs established a representative assembly. In many ways, the choice they faced resembled decisions made by any autocratic government in any era. But crucial to their choice, we argue, were their numbers. Modern cartel theory suggests that an oligarchy should act fundamentally differently from a dictatorship.

We consider four reasons for the oligarchs' acquiescense to a legislature. First, perhaps the oligarchs hoped to maximize their personal income, and decided that constructing an efficient economy would be the best way to do so. Establishing a legislative check on their power would send a credible signal to investors that they would not use their power to confiscate private property. In the process they would encourage economic growth, and growth in turn would generate more cream for them to skim off.

Second, perhaps the oligarchs were so insulated in the upper stratum of Japanese society that they lacked information about the source of discontent in other social tiers. Recognizing the danger of this predicament, they may have decided to hold regular elections. Through the elections, citizens would choose from among candidates who offered a variety of reformist policy portfolios. In the process the oligarchs would learn what concessions would most effectively and cheaply forestall revolution.

Third, perhaps the oligarchs thought it necessary to share power with entrepreneurs from the political parties before those entrepreneurs launched a full-scale revolution. If so, they may have been acting more urgently and more defensively than either the wealth-maximization or information-maximization hypotheses would suggest. By giving their competitors the right to participate in some limited governance, perhaps they simply hoped to extend their own tenure.

Fourth, as we suggested in Chapter 2, it may have been the oligarchs' inability to resolve their own differences that led to representative government. Dissatisfied with their share of that power, some of the oligarchs themselves may have invited supporters outside of the oligarchy to participate.

In Sections 2 through 4, we describe how the oligarchs perceived the democratic threat, and retrace the steps they took to ensure they would enter the legislative era from a position of strength. In Section 5 we evaluate our four hypotheses for why the oligarchs might have decided to share power in light of the empirical evidence. We conclude that the instability within the oligarchy made power-sharing inevitable.

Although the oligarchs collectively would have preferred to relinquish as little power as possible, ultimately they could not hold their ranks together. By 1881 they had already promised to share power in a representative assembly. In doing so without enshrining their own succession in the constitution, they began a process that increasingly placed power up for grabs as they died off.

Military leaders were in a strong position to take advantage of the power vacuum. In order to insulate the military from the politicians, the oligarchs had given those leaders the power to write their own ordinances, and to bring down cabinets by refusing to supply active-duty officers as armed service ministers. As we note later in Chapter 7, the military almost destroyed itself too during the 1920s and 1930s. Unlike the oligarchs, however, it solved its coordination problem. It did so simply by giving the Army China and the Navy Southeast Asia.[1] Ultimately, of course, the military's own successful cooperation was the nation's undoing.

2. THE ROAD TO THE CONSTITUTION

The oligarchs had decided to make a significant concession to political entrepreneurs, but they made it grudgingly. Determined to limit the level of public agitation, Itō and Yamagata tightened restrictions on public gatherings. In the four years between 1881 and 1884, authorities prohibited 193 proposed speeches, broke up 569 political meetings, and denied permission for 2,814 proposed speech topics. Granted, it would be nicer to know the percentage of speeches and meetings these figures represented. Nonetheless, they at least suggest that the government leaders did censor meetings. In 1883 they augmented their censorship provisions, and banned the publication of about eighty newspaper issues and even closed forty-seven newspaper companies entirely (Hani, 1956: 314).

Despite the muzzling of the publishers, demonstrators continued to stage anti-government rallies. People rioted across the country – in

Fukushima in 1882, Takada in 1883, Gumma, Kawayama, Chichibu, Iida and Nagoya in 1884, Osaka in 1885, Shizuoka in 1886 – demanding lower taxes and political representation.

The oligarchs seem not to have been moved. They frequently sent in troops, and Yamagata ordered those troops to use brutality "as necessary" to quell the revolts. Newspapers (not always reliable, of course) reported hundreds killed or wounded (*Tokyo nichinichi shimbun*, Nov. 6, 1884).

In December 1887, Yamagata, as Minister of Home Affairs, drafted a Peace Preservation Order that further restricted political activities.[2] The Order forbade all secret societies and assemblies (§1), gave police the authority to disburse any political meeting (§2), and empowered the Home Minister to expel any "disruptive person" from within a seven and a half mile radius of the Imperial Palace (§4). In time, the government used this order to expel over 570 people from the capital (Hackett, 1971: 105–106).

The heightened level of public agitation was the bane of the oligarchy, for it enhanced the opportunities for political entrepreneurship. Effectively, it forced the oligarchs to reassess the value of their lock on power, for with some help in mobilizing, the populace potentially could overthrow the Meiji regime altogether. Itagaki's and Ōkuma's fledgling political parties were gaining adherents with every rally, all on variants of an anti-oligarchy platform. Better to allow elections as a mechanism to select the most effective political entrepreneurs. Having identified the entrepreneurs, the mainstream oligarchs could then pay them off with money or other favors and thereby neutralize them as political threats.

The mainstream oligarchs began work on a constitution that made as many concessions as necessary, but as few as possible. The maverick oligarchs, with their latent power to mobilize the rebellious masses, had forced them to retreat from autocratic rule. The oligarchs now had committed themselves to elections and a representative legislature. But they wanted to design a parliamentary system that would preserve substantial power for themselves.

Itō traveled with a few associates throughout Europe in 1882 to study various constitutions already in place, particularly in Germany and Belgium.[3] Upon his return, he established the Institutional Research Bureau (*Seido torishirabe kyoku*) to coordinate intra-governmental negotiations over the shape of the new constitution.[4] He and his fellow oligarchs also spent the next few years bracing themselves for the changes to come.

As director of the Institutional Research Bureau, Itō amended the classification of the aristocracy in 1884.[5] He undoubtedly had the new constitution in mind, and was preparing the way for a friendly House of

Peers. It would, he hoped, serve as a counterweight to the less predictable House of Representatives.[6] Using the amended criteria, he appointed 505 new Peers in 1884, doubling the Peerage to 1,016.[7]

The following year (1885) the government adopted a "cabinet system" in anticipation of parliamentary government.[8] Rather than share responsibility with the rest of the cabinet for the performance of the government as a whole, however, each minister was responsible only for the performance of his own ministry. This foreshadowed the oligarchs' determination to insulate the cabinet from the legislative attacks they anticipated.[9]

Also in preparation for the parliamentary era, the oligarchs instituted an examination system for the civil service in July 1887.[10] It seems they were willing to forego some discretion in selecting candidates for office in exchange for withholding those prerogatives from future elected officials. Only graduates of Tokyo Imperial University were exempted from the stringent exams. Why they exempted the Imperial University graduates is unclear. Of course, they may have thought the graduates well-qualified. They may also have reasoned that the graduates came predominantly from aristocratic families and would more likely sympathize with the oligarchs than with representatives (Tsuji, 1944: 117). Years later, the cabinet's power to select bureaucrats became a point of contention between the politicians and the oligarchs, as we discuss in Section 4 and in Chapter 5. But it was a struggle the oligarchs had foreseen and for which, to some extent, they had prepared.

In 1888 the oligarchs transformed the Council of Elders (*Genrō in*) into the Privy Council (*Sūmitsu in*) and authorized it to preside over the drafting of the constitution.[11] Itō Hirobumi became president of this Privy Council, and did much of the drafting of the constitution himself, along with his close associates, Inoue Kowashi, Itō Miyoji, and Kaneko Kentarō.[12] As powerful as he was, however, Itō knew the constitution would need the support of the other oligarchs. Toward that end, they envisioned the Privy Council as a way to institutionalize their power. The Council would continue into the parliamentary era as the oligarchs' protective institution. In Itō's words, it would be "the highest body of the emperor's constitutional advisors."[13]

Through the Imperial House Regulations of 1889, the oligarchs gave the Privy Council control over imperial succession. Under Section 9 of those regulations, the Council, in conjunction with the imperial family, could change the order of succession either in the event of an incurable disease of mind or body or, more ominously, for "other sufficient cause."[14] While a progressive, activist emperor could hypothetically have claimed powers rightly his under the Constitution for himself, the Privy Council would likely not have permitted such hubris. In any case, no such emperor appeared in pre-war Japan. As political scientist David Titus

(1974: 11) put it, "[i]n the prewar decision-making process, . . . the emperor was an institution, not an autonomous personality exercising an arbitrary individual will in politics."

3. THE DIET UNDER THE CONSTITUTION

By the time the oligarchs had promulgated the Meiji Constitution in 1889 (effective 1890),[15] they left few surprises but abundant ambiguities. They issued the Constitution in the name of the Emperor, and reaffirmed him as sovereign. Because they intended him to be their front man, however, the Constitution did not establish the autocratic monarchy that a superficial reading might suggest.

Although many government institutions existed before the Constitution ratified them, the Diet was new. This bicameral legislature was to contain both a House of Peers and an elected House of Representatives. According to Article 5 of the Constitution, "[t]he Emperor exercises the legislative power with the consent of the Imperial Diet." As Itō explained (somewhat misleadingly, as we note later), the Diet "takes part in legislation, but has no share in the sovereign power; it has power to deliberate upon laws but none to determine them."[16]

The new House of Peers included members of the Imperial Household, other Peers, and assorted citizens of "high achievement," of "learning," or with substantial tax liabilities. The details appeared in an 1889 Imperial Order.[17] Under this order, men in the Imperial House became unpaid life members of the House of Peers at the age of twenty (§2).[18] Princes and marquis became unpaid life members at thirty.[19] And because there were so many counts, viscounts, and barons, these men elected roughly one in five of their cohorts as Peers for seven-year terms (§4).[20]

The House of Peers also contained a sizeable group of men not born to nobility, though many received titles with their Diet posts. According to the 1889 Imperial Order, the emperor selected 125 members on the basis of their service to the nation.[21] In addition, members of the Imperial Academy (*Teikoku gakushi in*) elected four members for seven-year terms. Finally, taxpayers with the heftiest tax payments elected an unspecified number of their colleagues for seven-year terms.[22] Itō himself – he had named himself count by that time, and would eventually become a prince – served as the first Speaker of the House.

The Constitution described the House of Representatives only in the broadest terms (Art. 35): "The House of Representatives shall be composed of Members elected by the people, according to the provisions of the Elections Act." The details it left to statute.[23] It gave neither House the right to initiate constitutional amendments. According to Article 73, "[w]hen it has become necessary in the future to amend the provisions of the present constitution, a notice to that effect shall be submitted to the Imperial Diet by Imperial Order." As Itō explained, "[t]he right of making amendments to the constitution must belong to the emperor himself, as he is the sole author of it."[24]

As another precaution against politicians usurping government control, the Constitution did not make the cabinet accountable to the Diet.[25] Indeed, it does not even mention the cabinet, though Article 55 provides for ministers of state. The 1889 Imperial Order spelling out the functions of the cabinet[26] did not specify how the Prime Minister was to be chosen, presumably because Article 10 of the Constitution states that the emperor appoints and dismisses all government officials. In practice, the oligarchs appointed the Prime Minister, in the name of the emperor, as long as they were alive. And for the first decade or so after 1890, they mostly appointed themselves.

The Privy Council, as the highest advisory group to the emperor, was the government organ to watch. The rest of the Constitution represented guarded, hedged concessions to the public or rhetorical flourish. The Privy Council, however, was the oligarchs' remaining grip on the Japanese government. That grip continued to be tight, even over legislative functions nominally in the realm of the legislature. But it is important to note – particularly in order to understanding the subsequent course of events – that the Privy Council's influence was not institutionally based. Rather, it rested almost entirely on the personal stature of the oligarchs who were its first members.

4. RULE-MAKING UNDER THE CONSTITUTION

Legislation (*hōrei*) under the new Constitution included statutes (*hōritsu*), orders (*meirei*), and a variety of other regulatory provisions. The oligarchs had already been using statutes and orders for several years.[27] Why they or anyone else bothered with the distinction before the Constitution is not clear. Until then, the oligarchs seem to have promulgated both, pretty much on whim.[28]

Even under the new Constitution, the scope of statutes and orders continued to overlap. The Constitution provided that taxes (Art. 62) and various specified civil rights (Arts. 18–32) could be changed only by statutes. It further required that a statute could be amended only by another statute (Art. 9).[29] At the same time, it placed other matters, including the Imperial Household (Art. 74) and Peerage (Art. 15), beyond the ambit of statutes. Most issues, however, it let the government handle either by statute or by ordinance. Reflecting more concern for practical politics than for theoretical niceties, Itō noted at the time that "the politi-

cal development of each country determines what comes within the
sphere of law and what within the sphere of ordinance" (Itō, 1889: 69).

Under the Constitution, a bill became law (*hōritsu*) through a process
that gave a bit more power to the Diet than Itō's deprecatory comments
would suggest. It became law only if both houses of the Diet passed it in
identical form by majority vote (Arts. 5, 37, 47). A cabinet minister
would then submit it, with his advice, to the Emperor. If the Emperor
approved it (Arts. 5,6), a minister would then countersign (*fukusho*) it
and it would become law (Art. 55).[30] In principle, then, this procedure
gave both houses of the Diet a veto.

If the Constitution gave both houses equal power over statutes, it
seemed to give the House of Representatives greater control over the
budget.[31] But even this advantage was dubious. In June 1892, following a
collision between the Lower House and the cabinet over the budget, the
Privy Council issued an imperial edict giving the House of Peers the right
to reinsert items of the government budget stricken by the Lower
House.[32] Furthermore, because the budget was considered an administrative program subordinate to law, the Diet could not refuse to appropriate
funds required for the execution of laws.[33] As an extra safeguard against
political control, the Constitution empowered the cabinet to use the previous year's budget (Art. 71). This, combined with the cabinet's ability to
deflate the currency, gave it substantial spending power beyond the control of the Diet.[34]

Not surprisingly, given the divergence between the Diet's and the cabinet's interests, the Diet took care to specify spending requirements in its
laws and to deny the cabinet the power to pad the budget. Japan's pre-
war government was in many ways more similar to the "divided government" of a presidential system with different parties in control of the
legislative and executive branch than to the parliamentary system of post-
war Japan.

Although the Diet may have tried to ensure that laws were highly
specific and gave the oligarchs little room for maneuver, Article 70 gave
the cabinet another loophole: "When the maintenance of the public safety requires it and the Diet is not in session, the government may raise
funds beyond that allowed in the budget through Imperial Orders." The
article required the government to submit the Imperial Order to the Diet
for ratification in the next Diet session. Once the government had spent
the money, however, the Diet's protests were often in vain. As we shall see
in Chapter 4, the ambiguities inherent in the Constitution's budget provision led repeatedly to rancorous negotiations between the Lower House
and the cabinet.

The Privy Council had an effective right to comment on certain bills, though not explicitly to veto them. The Constitution itself did not specify this right. Instead, it stated that the scope of the Privy Council's role would be specified in an Imperial Order.[35] By order, the Privy Council was to comment both (a) on disputes over statutes "relating to" the Constitution, and (b) on proposed statutes "relating to" the Constitution.[36] But note that the Privy Council retained an effective veto by way of its advisory role to the emperor. This much had not changed with the new Constitution: Whoever controlled the emperor could halt the legislative process.

The Privy Council also wielded a comparable check over Imperial Orders (*chokurei*). The Constitution stated that the emperor could issue these orders without consulting the Diet. Once he had done so, with certain qualifications, the orders acquired the same legal effect as statutes.[37] A proposed Imperial Order took effect as follows. Initially a minister would propose it to the cabinet. If the cabinet passed it, the Prime Minister would then submit it to the emperor with his advice. Provided the emperor approved it, a minister would countersign it and it would become law.[38] As with statutes, the Privy Council could block any ordinance as long as the Privy Council controlled the emperor. In practice, as we would expect under these circumstances, the cabinet cleared bills with the Privy Council before submitting them to the emperor.[39]

Through the Meiji Constitution the oligarchs undeniably made significant concessions to the public – and to the mavericks who threatened to galvanize the public. Not only did they permit political entrepreneurs to mobilize voters, they paid these men to do so.

In many ways, however, the oligarchs stopped short of giving voters and their representatives a full veto. Although they buried the mechanisms in a variety of provisions, they retained for themselves several ways to circumvent uncooperative legislatures. They could often avoid statutes through Imperial Orders, and the House of Representatives could not change the status of the Constitution, the Privy Council, or the House of Peers even if it wished.[40] The oligarchs could often keep even the budget beyond real legislative control. Should the legislature prove particularly intransigent, the oligarchs could simply dissolve it (Art. 7). By doing so, they could then impose huge expenses on the political parties.

The oligarchs did not use these ploys at every opportunity. Inciting the fury of political entrepreneurs was precisely what they hoped to avoid through the Constitution. But for the politicians, the cost of confrontation with the oligarchs was greater than any damage they could inflict in return. The oligarchs could legislate through Imperial Order, use the previous year's budget, and deflate the currency to increase that budget if necessary. The equilibrium under the Meiji Constitution may have been one where each side obtained less than what it ideally wanted, but it was one where the parties found the situation less advantageous than the oligarchs.

5. EXPLAINING POWER-SHARING

Consider then why the oligarchs shared power at all. The first hypothesis for the oligarchs' decision to adopt a legislative assembly, introduced at the beginning of this chapter, points toward economic efficiency. Economists Yoram Barzel (1992) and Douglass North and Barry Weingast (1989) argue that rational autocrats will generally want efficient economies. Efficient economies generate the most surplus from which the rulers can extract rents. But to generate confidence in the economy, they need to convince their subjects that they will not confiscate their wealth. Rational autocrats will thus share power with others because by sharing power they limit their right to confiscate; by reducing the likelihood of confiscation, they increase economic production and the economic rents they ultimately extract.

The efficiency argument falls short of explaining the Meiji oligarchs' choices. First, the oligarchs did not actually give the politicians a full-fledged veto. Instead, they gave them something considerably more anemic than that. As a result, they left ample room for their own backroom rent-extraction, to which a long list of oligarch-implicated scandals attests.[41] Second, the oligarchs drafted electoral rules that gave politicians perverse incentives, if the goal was economic efficiency. A single non-transferable vote in multi-member districts (SNTV-MMD), as we discuss in more detail in the next chapter, resulted in tremendously corrupt campaign practices and funds-for-favors politics.

The second hypothesis blames information asymmetries for the oligarchs' insecurity in office. Were the oligarchs aware of everything about every potential threat to their regime, they would be unlikely to vest political power in their competitors. But "without omniscience, omnipotence might be dangerous" (Miller, 1992: 79).

Jonathan Bendor (1985) suggests an information-based reason for why the oligarchs might voluntarily have relinquished some of their power to a legislature. Arguing that "two relatively independent heads are better than two relatively dependent heads" (1985: 47) at identifying and solving problems, Bendor suggests that oligarchs should relinquish some power to independent competitors out of self-interest. In relinquishing that power, they would create the means (elections) by which citizens would tell them the policies they most wanted. They could then choose the most cost-effective way to maintain their own tenure. In thus institutionalizing the channels through which they could acquire the information they needed, the oligarchs could actually strengthen their own hold on power.

The politics of oligarchy

This second hypothesis fares as poorly as the first, and for much the same reason. If the oligarchs had wanted to improve the quality of information they received about popular preferences, they would not likely have written the Constitution and statutes that they did. The system of incentives they created for politicians could hardly have been more poorly suited to discover the sources of dissatisfaction within the country.

The information the oligarchs needed was information about the portfolio of public goods that the population wanted. Government leaders typically provide citizens with some combination of public and private goods (Cain, Ferejohn and Fiorina, 1987). For leaders trying to stay in office, information about the public and private goods the populace wants is crucial. But those leaders do not need an electoral market to obtain information about the preferences their subjects have for private goods. Economic markets already provide that information efficiently. What they find hard to discover is the portfolio of public goods the populace wants.

The oligarchs could have designed an electoral system that would have elicited that information, but they did not. As we explain in Chapter 4, the MMD-SNTV electoral system that they created instead elicited information only about the private goods voters wanted. Effectively, they designed a system that extracted information about preferences they could have discovered more simply by looking at the market (the portfolio of private goods wanted), but that did not extract the information they most needed (the portfolio of public goods wanted).

The third hypothesis is logically simple. To lessen the likelihood that their political competitors would overthrow them in a revolution, the oligarchs decided to give their competitors a stake in the existing regime. They could have done that either through an electoral system, or by making their competitors powerful bureaucrats. They chose the former because the electoral system operates as a screening device – it forces applicants for powerful positions to demonstrate first that they can indeed be a political threat.

Of these three hypotheses, this third comes closest to the historical record. Although the oligarchs constructed a system that was economically inefficient and gave them noisy signals about the populace's preferences, the late Meiji political system did seem to identify talented political entrepreneurs and then tame them. But this hypothesis too leaves out an important dimension to the decision to adopt a new form of government. As we described in the previous chapter, the oligarchs' ongoing rivalry among themselves prevented them from making any unified decision as to the seriousness of the public threat.

The oligarchy's disunity, rather, is the key to understanding the Meiji Constitution. Some oligarchs, despite vain importuning from the others, had courted personal support in the public and had established political parties. The oligarchs eventually agreed to a representative assembly rather than face a possible revolution led by these renegade oligarchs. The oligarchs' own rivalries, then, were the agents of new entry in the political system.

Had the oligarchs been able to act as a single dictator, chances are the Meiji Constitution would have been a very different document. Not burdened with internecine rivalry, they may not have needed the unifying imagery of the emperor. If they had not faced the constant possibility of betrayal from within their own ranks, they might have institutionalized the powers of the Privy Council. Without fear of double-cross from other oligarchs, they might have committed themselves to succession rules. Although a band of mutually distrustful leaders may have a powerful incentive to create binding rules, their conflicting interests can also make it harder for them to do so.

Instead of establishing an institutional framework that ameliorated their disagreements, the oligarchs institutionalized the suspicion with which they viewed one another. An essentially defensive document, the Meiji Constitution left more questions than answers. The emperor would rule in name, but who would in fact govern? Voters would elect representatives, but how much authority would the legislature wield? Who would succeed the oligarchs when they passed from the scene? And who would control the military? The Constitution answered none of these questions.

Ultimately unable to hold their own ranks together, the oligarchs lost their monopoly on power. Some oligarchs, to the consternation of the others, established their own political parties. In so doing, these maverick oligarchs bolstered their positions at the cost of the oligarchy itself. In self-defense, other oligarchs strengthened the military and controlled it through personalized loyalty. The oligarchy's own internal rivalries, then, allowed the new competitors to enter the political system. Effectively, these rivalries also set the stage for the battle between the political parties and the military. That, however, was a battle the Meiji Constitution did not prepare the parties to fight.

6. CONCLUSION

By the time the oligarchs adopted a Constitution in 1889, they had collectively achieved a great deal in consolidating their regime. They had made few concessions to local government, and almost none to feudal autonomy. They had eliminated the samurai class, and in its place had established a tier of aristocratic ranks that had little continuity with the past. Through these new nobility classifications, they now rewarded themselves and their supporters with the titles and perquisites of high office.

The politics of oligarchy

Several crucial ambiguities, however, remained in the new Constitution. These ambiguities reflected the oligarchs' failure to settle their internecine disputes. Contrary to the underlying configuration of power at the time, the oligarchs named the emperor as the sovereign – indeed, divine – ruler of the land. They institutionalized their own voice in the Privy Council. Yet, to prevent any one of their cohort from seizing dictatorial powers for himself, they gave the Council only advisory powers. As they died off, they thus left sovereignty in the hands of a puppet leader. In doing so, they created a vacuum and brought about an unruly, violent quest for power. The rest of the story is well known: The military wrested the reins of government and led the nation to disastrous war.

The oligarchs may have had less choice at the time they drafted the Constitution than many suppose. Had they resolved their own rivalries, they probably could have postponed the day of representative government longer than they did. But like all cartels without a supra-cartel enforcement mechanism, oligarchies are inherently unstable creatures. The Japanese oligarchy too was unstable, and like most cartels eventually caused its own disintegration.

4

Electoral rules and party competition:
The struggle for political survival

1. INTRODUCTION

The Meiji Constitution left a crucial element in the political process unspecified: the selection of Diet representatives. In the last chapter we outlined the logic behind the devolution of power from the oligarchs. In this chapter we explore how the shifting configuration of power influenced the choice of electoral rules. The choice of those rules – and the rules were adjusted several times – involved protracted negotiations among the oligarchs and the Peers, the political parties, the voters and indirectly the disenfranchised. Because electoral rules are at the very heart of political accountability, their evolving shape tells us something about who had power in the system, how much they had, and how they obtained it.

Although the oligarchs gave the Diet only limited powers in the Constitution, they remained concerned that the party politicians would gain popular support. Lest the politicians then demand more concessions, they established electoral rules that encouraged intra-party competition and thereby kept the parties weak. The party leaders mitigated this fratricidal competition by providing voters private goods, but the consequence was widespread corruption and in time voter disenchantment.

In this chapter we first describe the oligarchs' experiments with various electoral rules. We consider the consequences those rules had for the politicians and for their relationship with the oligarchs and the voters. In Section 2 we explore the initial choice of one- and two-member districts in 1889, and the switch to multi-member districts in 1900. In Section 3 we explain how the Seiyūkai used its legislative majority and electoral arguments to persuade Yamagata to approve single member districts in 1919. By then, neither the parties nor the Privy Council wielded absolute power, and both had to make concessions.

In Section 4, we account for the decision to extend the suffrage to all adult men. The government leaders expanded the electorate for the same reason that they agreed to a legislature initially: They could not cooperate enough to maintain their collective hold on power. The two major political parties and the voters they represented probably preferred to keep the franchise limited. For the existing voters, universal suffrage would mean having to share the government's largesse with the general public. For the parties, it would mean far more expensive campaigns and greater electoral uncertainty. But the party politicians were no more able to collude effectively than the oligarchs had been four decades earlier.

In Section 5 we explain why the legislature passed a bill reinstating multi-member districts. With no party commanding a Diet majority, the bill reflected a compromise among three parties: Multi-member districts would give each of them a chance to win seats in most districts. In Section 6 we consider the consequences of those multi-member districts for electoral strategy. Finally, in Section 7 we review the historical record of elections under single non-transferable vote (SNTV), multi-member district (MMD) electoral rules.

2. THE INITIAL RULES

2.1. The first Elections Act

The oligarchs dealt cautiously with democracy. Although they had promised a House of Representatives in the Constitution, they did not explain how any elections would take place. Nowhere in the Constitution did they specify electoral rules. That task they left to the Elections Act of 1889, promulgated in the same year as the Constitution.[1]

The Elections Act enfranchised 453,000 voters out of a total population of 42 million. According to Section 6 of the Act, a voter had to be a male subject over twenty-five years of age, registered and residing for more than a year in his electoral district. A further requirement, disqualifying all but a tiny swath of the population, was that the voter had to have paid ¥15 in national land taxes for at least a year or in income taxes for at least three years prior to the election.[2]

The Elections Act provided for 300 representatives elected to serve four year terms. It divided the 47 Japanese prefectures into 257 electoral districts, and assigned each district one or two representatives depending on its population. The notion was that the Act would allot one representative to every 120,000 people or so, regardless of the number of qualified voters. Districts with a population of between 100,000 and 200,000 received one seat in the House, and those with a population of over 200,000, two seats.

One might imagine that the system instituted an urban bias: Rural areas with many wealthy landowners returned a smaller percentage of representatives to the House than urban areas with large populations but few eligible voters.[3] Because the tax requirement disqualified almost everyone but wealthy farmers, however, the urban bias meant only that landowners in densely populated areas were over-represented compared with landowners in rural areas.[4] It seems the oligarchs took care to ensure that the first Diet, representing only property owners, would be conservative.

Even having taken some precautions, the oligarchs were not willing to leave electoral outcomes to chance. They stacked the deck in favor of their own candidates in a number of other ways. In a rule that was probably designed to intimidate the electorate, voters were required to sign their ballots in the presence of election officers (Elections Act, §38). They also used the police freely to harass party candidates and to break up political meetings.[5]

Despite repression, anti-government politicians won a legislative majority of 171 in the first election. Prime Minister Itō and the other oligarchs were peeved, and without waiting for the new Diet to convene passed an ordinance further restricting the activities of political parties. The ordinance forbade parties to solicit members, distribute fliers, or contact other parties.

Once the Diet convened, the oligarchs faced an obstreperous opposition. But the parties' powers and resources were limited, making them vulnerable to propositions from the government. When a legislative majority threatened to revise the cabinet's budget, the oligarchs lured away from the majority – reportedly with ample remuneration – over forty party representatives (Hani, 1956: 315).

In 1892, the oligarchs dissolved the Diet in the face of renewed legislative truculance. The ensuing election was among the most violent in Japanese history. Party candidates tested the limits of the government's tolerance for campaign activism, convening rallies around the country. The police – both the regular police and the hated security forces (*kempei tai*) – rose to the challenge, killing 25 and wounding over 400. Notwithstanding the government's heavy-handed tactics, the political parties once again won a legislative majority (Kishimoto, 1990: 42–43; Hani, 1956: 316).

In the early years of Japan's constitutional government, relations between the legislatures and the oligarch-dominated cabinets were strained, at best. Some Diets lasted only days before the oligarchs dissolved them. The Diet was vulnerable to dissolution and to the government's divide-and-conquer tactics, but the oligarchs were still learning what price they would have to pay to hold together a majority coalition. That price, as it turns out, was control of the cabinet. Nonetheless, that concession would come piecemeal.[6] Consider first a brief – and necessarily somewhat chaotic – account of the early Diets.

The politics of oligarchy

In 1895, Itō Hirobumi as Prime Minister responded to a vote of no confidence by suspending the Diet and in the meantime forging a deal. Former oligarch Itagaki Taisuke had formed the Jiyūtō, and with 107 seats that party was now the largest in the Diet. In exchange for the party's cooperation, the oligarchs agreed to name Jiyūtō members to cabinet posts. The result was the first coalition government in Japanese history. But the cabinet fell as a result of internal squabbling. Count Matsukata, with the support of Count Ōkuma Shigenobu and his Shim-pōtō (heir to the Rikken kaishintō, and with 94 seats) organized the next cabinet. This cabinet too fell after a year and four months in the face of a no-confidence vote. Itō became Prime Minister again in January 1898, but he needed additional revenue and even he could not raise land taxes. Rather than compromise, he dissolved the Diet and resigned after only six months in office.

In what was to prove a brief alliance, Itagaki and Ōkuma merged their parties into the Kenseitō in 1898, and formed an overwhelming Diet majority of 260.[7] When the Itō cabinet fell later that year, the oligarchs invited the two to form a cabinet. Until then, the cabinet had been a line of self-defense the oligarchs had refused to breach. Now, Ōkuma became Prime Minister, and Itagaki Minister of Home Affairs.[8] By preventing the cabinet from functioning, the party politicians had found a way to scale even that barrier to power.[9]

Alarmed by these concessions to the politicians, Privy Council Chairman Yamagata urged his protege, Army Minister Katsura Tarō, not to comply with Ōkuma's cuts in the military budget. At this time, in 1898, Yamagata had not yet issued an ordinance requiring that Army and Navy Ministers be active duty officers. Even without the backing of that rule, however, Yamagata had enough influence over the Army to control Army Minister appointments. Firing Katsura without getting anyone to replace him would have left Ōkuma with an incomplete, and therefore invalid, cabinet. Outmaneuvered, Ōkuma resigned.[10]

Again Prime Minister, Yamagata dealt with the Diet in two ways. On the one hand, he used government resources liberally to buy off legislative opposition. On the other hand, he insulated the military further from political control. In a revision of the Imperial Order on the Army and Navy Ministries, Yamagata required that all Army and Navy Ministers and Vice Ministers be high-ranking active-duty officers.[11] In Chapter 7 we explore the consequences of an independent military for Japan's political fate.

2.2. Multi-member districts and the SNTV

The Diet continued to resist the oligarchs' fiscal policies.[12] The oligarchs' appetite for more revenues and the Diet's refusal to provide them prompted the oligarchs to adjust the electoral rules again in February 1900.[13] First, they gave cities of 30,000 or more people electoral districts of their own, distinct from the surrounding countryside.[14] Second, they eased the suffrage requirements. To qualify to vote, a person had to have paid ¥10 in land tax, down from ¥15, or an income tax of ¥10 or more for at least two consecutive years (1900 Act, §8). Both provisions – the introduction of urban districts and the relaxation of the tax criterion – were designed to dilute the representation of wealthy farmers and to pave the way for higher land taxes.[15] Although wealthy farmers were conservative, they also resisted tax increases. Through the 1900 Act, the oligarchs more than doubled the electoral base to 983,000 voters, or 2.2 percent of the population.[16]

A third aspect of the 1900 electoral revision had even more profound consequences for electoral competition: the adoption of 97 multi-member districts in the place of existing small-member districts (1900 Act, Appendix). Yamagata worried about the advantage single-member districts conferred on large parties. As Maurice Duverger would express many years later, but as Yamagata apparently already recognized, single-member districts tend to eliminate small parties until two large parties emerge.[17]

Japan had imported its first set of electoral rules, the single-member district system, directly from Britain. The oligarchs had considered other electoral rules used in Europe. The leaders of the two principal political parties knew about the range of possibilities as well, and stated their clear preference for single-member districts, followed by medium-sized districts with closed lists.[18] Impeding the rise of small parties was clearly in their interests. As second best, closed lists in a multiple member district would at least give party leaders control over their own party's candidates and thus facilitate party discipline (Uchida, Kanehara, and Furuya, 1991: 226–29).

Yamagata's designs ran directly counter to the parties' interests. To keep parties as weak and fractious as possible, Yamagata devised a brilliant combination of electoral rules: multi-member districts (MMD) in which voters had a single non-transferable vote (SNTV) (1900 Act, § 45). The idea was to force any party seeking to win or maintain a legislative majority to field multiple candidates in most districts (Soma, 1986: 41–42). Parties would face severe intra-party competition and thus be less likely to act coherently in the Diet. An SNTV-MMD system would not necessarily prevent a large party from gaining a solid majority (witness the Liberal Democratic Party of the 1950s and 1960s); it would, however, make such consolidation much harder.

Given Yamagata's aims of fragmenting the parties, the puzzle is why the Diet passed his bill. It did, after all, have a veto over legislation. The answer apparently goes to Yamagata's ability to piece together a barely sufficient alliance through promises and cash. In 1900, the "progressive" political parties together formed a bare majority in the House of Representatives. With no single party commanding a legislative majority, Yamagata could "divide and conquer." To pit the parties against each other, he promised favorable treatment in the future and cash now. By buying just enough votes to earn a majority, he passed the bill that would cause the parties problems for nearly two decades.

To deal with the political parties, Yamagata badgered, stonewalled, sabotaged, bribed, and repressed. Itō, by contrast, used the parties. To him, they were another way to play the political game. Over Yamagata's strong objections, in August 1900 Itō recruited Jiyūtō members, formed the Seiyūkai, and became its president. In so doing, he diversified his political portfolio without relinquishing his power as an oligarch.

While Itō's move was clever from his own point of view, it underscored the fragility of the oligarchs' coalition. Even the new Constitution had not effectively bound the oligarchs into a united front against their subjects. Because the most powerful oligarchs continued to compete among themselves for power, they were unable to maximize their collective power. Itō's defection presaged the oligarchs' failure to solve their succession problem.

3. A RETURN TO SINGLE-MEMBER DISTRICTS

The costs of electoral campaigns under the MMD-SNTV electoral rules placed a serious financial and organizational burden on the political parties (Tomita, 1986: 91). Given that members from the same party competed against each other in elections, party leaders had trouble maintaining discipline within their ranks. Lacking the resources with which to ensure each member a relatively secure niche, the leaders had to resort to cajoling and pleading to maintain party unity on important legislative votes. Often they did so to no avail.

The Seiyūkai, by now the largest political party, never abandoned its quest for smaller districts. In 1911, under the cabinet of Prime Minister Saionji Kimmochi, Seiyūkai politician and Home Affairs Minister Hara Takashi established a working group to study electoral reform. Composed of five Diet members from each of the two houses and ten bureaucrats from the Ministry of Home Affairs, the group recommended the return to single-member districts. The bill based on the group's proposal passed the Seiyūkai-controlled Lower House, but ran into overwhelming opposition in the Upper House and therefore did not pass (Masumi, 1986: 44–46).

In 1918, in what is typically called the first true party cabinet, Hara himself became Prime Minister. Hara played on Yamagata's fears of the burgeoning forces of socialism. By 1919, Yamagata knew that the Bolsheviks had engineered a coup and massacred the Romanovs, that the Prussian monarch William II had abdicated and fled to the Netherlands, and that the Japanese urban poor had been rioting en masse (Lewis, 1990). Later in 1919, the Comintern would launch its campaign for world revolution. And, increasingly, disaffected Japanese laborers were turning to the fringe-left "proletarian" political entrepreneurs. Given the widespread pressure for universal suffrage, Yamagata realized that these men would soon vote. When they did, even he recognized, they might vote socialist.

It was in this politically polarized world that Hara convinced Yamagata to adopt smaller electoral districts.[19] With Yamagata's imprimatur, the House of Peers gave its assent as well, and the single member district rules took effect on March 18, 1919. Under the new Act, voters chose representatives within 295 single-member districts, 63 two-member districts, and 11 three-member districts.[20]

Yamagata and the Diet also further broadened the electorate. According to the Elections Act of 1919, adult men could vote if they had paid ¥3 in taxes.[21] This group now included 8 million people – over 5 percent of the population.

The tumultuous saga of the pre-war Diet up to 1919 is a tale of intrigue, posturing, and mutual concessions between the oligarchs and the political parties. The defection of Itagaki and Ōkuma to party politics in the 1870s was the initial impetus for adopting the Constitution. Itō's founding of the Seiyūkai in 1900 dealt a further blow to the oligarchs' collective grip on power. For Yamagata, the most distressing defection of all was when his handpicked successor, Army General Katsura Tarō, joined the Rikken dōshikai in 1911. Some of the oligarchs still resisted desperately. Increasingly isolated in his hard line opposition to representative government, Yamagata and his followers threw every obstacle in the path of representative government that they could. Although Yamagata had failed to solve his succession problem, unable to convince even Katsura of the viability of ongoing oligarchic rule, he used his clout in the Privy Council to muzzle the Diet for as long as he lived (until 1922).

4. THE ROAD TO UNIVERSAL SUFFRAGE

Political parties had two battles to fight. One was with the hardcore oligarchs who were trying to stifle their role. The other was with the vast majority of Japanese subjects, who were disenfranchised under the existing electoral rules. Political parties, in other words, found themselves in much the same situation as the oligarchs of a generation or two earlier: They faced cracks in their tacit collusion against the broadening of power.

If even the oligarchy was unstable as a cartel, the parties and the upper-class voters they represented did not have a chance. Because the parties directly competed against each other, they took every opportunity to improve their relative positions. Hypothetically, they would all have been better off if they could have limited the franchise and hence their campaign expenditures. The upper-class voters would have been better off keeping government representatives accountable only to their, and not the wider public's, interests. But the parties faced ample possibilities for unobserved cheating (secret ties with the news media), asymmetries in political advantage (the Seiyūkai was most strongly identified with the land-holding minority of voters), and strong public demand for political participation. Accordingly, most party leaders reluctantly concluded that all-out electoral competition and universal suffrage were inevitable.[22]

The parties played a complicated political game to obtain the maximal benefit from the suffrage issue. Leaders of the Kenseikai and smaller Kokumintō publicly criticized the Seiyūkai's reservations about universal suffrage, but themselves cut deals to forestall the day when they would face an expanded electorate. In turn, the Seiyūkai had a public relations field day in 1922 when it discovered that the Kenseikai's president, Katō Takaaki, had accepted corporate contributions in exchange for gutting the then-circulating universal suffrage bill. In 1924 the Seiyūkai conspired with the small Shimpōtō (Progessive Party) to topple Katō's Kenseikai cabinet by introducing an even more reformist bill than the one the Kenseikai publically supported. Their goal, though unsuccessful, was to engineer a crisis in the cabinet's relationship with the Privy Council.[23]

Adopting universal suffrage in a tumultuous age carried risks for the old-line leaders of Japan. Yamagata Aritomo, the parties' staunchest enemy, had died in 1922. Among the Restoration-vintage oligarchs, he left Matsukata Masayoshi and Saionji Kimmochi. The oligarchs had picked the Privy Council members carefully, however, and those members shared the oligarchs' uneasiness about political parties. Male factory workers and tenant farmers – not groups known for their quiescence in pre-war Japan – comprised the bulk of the 9 million new voters. Yet that is precisely why the conservative Privy Council took this calculated gamble: It reasoned that it was safer to forfeit some power to the masses before they seized more for themselves. Moreover, to reduce the risk this entailed, they combined electoral reform with the passage of new police powers with which to harass the fringe-left parties.[24]

Koizumi Sakutarō, a Seiyūkai strategist in the House of Representatives, tried to build opposition to universal suffrage in the House of Peers as a way of toppling the Kenseikai government (Matsuo, 1989: 318–

319). Although his plan had some supporters, most of the Peers shared the concern that delaying universal suffrage indefinitely could incite more public anger than the government could handle.[25] The only amendment the House of Peers attached to the bill was the proviso that people receiving "public or private assistance or relief for their livelihood on account of poverty" be disqualified from voting (1925 Act, §6(c)).[26]

When the suffrage bill finally passed both houses in 1925,[27] elections would become far more expensive for parties, especially the still largely rural Seiyūkai. With universal male suffrage, candidates would have to woo all eligible males aged twenty-five or more instead of the wealthy few (Act, §5). By 1928, when the first election under these rules was held, the electorate encompassed 12.5 million voters, or 21 percent of the population (Soma, 1986: 87).

5. BACK TO MULTI-MEMBER DISTRICTS

More vexing still than the suffrage issue for the political parties was the issue of districting. Each party wanted rules that would give it an advantage relative to the others. But in 1924 when the parties were negotiating the terms of the suffrage bill, no single party had a Diet majority with which to control the legislation. The Kenseikai cabinet thus not only had the usual hurdles of the Privy Council and House of Peers, but had also to cobble a working coalition with the other parties to clear any new law through the Diet.

The interest among the parties in single-member districts had all but disappeared. At least initially, the small districts had worked like a charm for the Seiyūkai. At the time the 1919 Act took effect, the party held 162 (42 percent) of the 379 seats. In the first election under the new rules, it won 278 (60 percent) of the 464 seats (Seisen, 1930: 617). This was the first time in Japanese history that a single party controlled both the cabinet and a legislative majority. As we discuss in later chapters, the Seiyūkai made ample use of their opportunity to allocate budgetary and other regulatory favors to their constituents.

Within the party, the small-district system gave the party leaders new power, for party endorsement now mattered more than ever before. Elections, moreover, were cheaper than before for large parties because single-member districts eliminated intra-party electoral competition. No longer forced to field multiple candidates in most districts, large parties could consolidate their resources in each district behind their chosen candidate.

Unfortunately for the Seiyūkai, small districts also helped consolidate the Kenseikai, the leading opposition party. As voters abandoned fringe parties without a chance of winning, the Kenseikai itself began to grow strong.

49

The politics of oligarchy

A more serious problem for the Seiyūkai was that a splinter group left in 1924 to form its own party. The new party, the Seiyūhontō, not only destroyed the Seiyūkai's majority, but was large enough to vie for a majority on its own (Kawato, 1992: 220). In single-member districts, as the parties seemed to understand, two parties tend to emerge as the main competitors, while smaller parties atrophy. So long as the Seiyūkai was assured of being either the largest or the second largest party, it had preferred single-member districts. Now the Seiyūkai faced the prospect of being eclipsed altogether.

The general elections of May 1924 reinforced the Seiyūkai politicians' fears. The Seiyūhontō won 116 Diet seats, second only to the Kenseikai's 151 and more than the Seiyūkai's 101. Seiyūkai leaders began to reevaluate the old multi-member district system: They would at least have a better chance of winning seats in the event that the Seiyūhontō remained a potent rival (Matsuo, 1989: 309). Multi-member districts, in other words, might serve as insurance against the risk of being shut out of the legislature.

Following the election, oligarch Saionji appointed Kenseikai president Katō Takaaki to head the new cabinet. Although the Kenseikai too lacked a majority, Home Affairs Minister Wakatsuki Reijirō established a three-party working group between his own Kenseikai, the Seiyūkai, and the small Kakushin Club to draft a new election bill. Wakatsuki bypassed the upstart Seiyūhontō, but by forging a majority coalition to work on the bill, ensured smooth passage through the House of Representatives (Matsuo, 1989: 309). The Kenseikai and Kakushin Club too favored new electoral rules. With the establishment of the Seiyūhontō, the Kenseikai now also had reason to fear being the third-party out in a single-member district system. Should the Seiyūkai merge with some small party, the Seiyūkai and Seiyūhontō could establish themselves as the two dominant parties and hurt the Kenseikai's chances for resurgence. And as the small party in the coalition, the Kakushin Club had a clear interest in abolishing single-member districts. Multi-member districts would give it a more secure competitive niche: With fewer resources than the larger parties, it was more likely to win one of three or four or five seats in a district than a district's only seat.

The 1925 Elections Act reflected this altered political landscape. The law established 53 three-member districts, 38 four-member districts, and 31 five-member districts (Act, Appendix). From the standpoint of the three parties drafting the bill, medium-sized districts would give each of them a chance for at least one seat in most districts, and more than one seat in many districts.[28] This medium-sized district magnitude suited the Privy Council and House of Peers as well, since the districts were too small to leave much of an opening for socialist candidates.

50

6. THE POLITICAL LOGIC OF MULTI-MEMBER DISTRICTS[29]

The parties had not abandoned their respective quests for a Diet majority, but the new electoral rules changed their strategy for obtaining one. Recall the electoral logic discussed earlier. Under the 1925 electoral rules, as under those of 1900, electoral districts each returned several representatives to the Diet. Although each voter had only one non-transferable vote, the voters in each district collectively elected three to five representatives. As a result, to obtain a majority in the House of Representatives a party had to elect more than one representative from most districts.

To elect multiple representatives per district, a party necessarily had both to pit its own candidates against each other and to ensure that no one of them dramatically overpowered the others. After all, if any one candidate captured significantly more votes than rivals from the same party, the weaker ones could easily trail opposition candidates they would otherwise have beaten. As a consequence, the party would have elected one representative from a district that could have supported two or more if the party had but divided its supporters more evenly.

To divide its supporters among multiple candidates, a party like the Seiyūkai could have tried several strategies. For example, it could have given its supporters cues about how to vote in ways that maximized the party's electoral success. In a district where it hoped to elect two candidates, for instance, it could have told supporters to vote for candidate A if their address ended in an odd number and to vote for candidate B if it ended in an even number.[30] Unfortunately for parties like the Seiyūkai, such cue-giving schemes could work only if supporters identified strongly with the party. For most of the pre-war period (just as in contemporary Japan), however, Japanese voters did not strongly identify themselves with the mainstream parties.[31]

Second, a party could let its candidates distinguish themselves from each other ideologically. Left-of-center supporters would vote for the leftish candidates, right-of-center supporters for the rightish. Alas for the party, at least two problems would present themselves.[32] First, the politicians would jeopardize the party label. Candidates closest to each other politically tend to be their fiercest competitors. If candidates from the same party attacked each other's platforms, voters would obtain confused signals about the party's collective plans. Candidates left to their own devices could reduce total votes for the party, as American parties often discover during their primary campaigns. The second problem with ideologically based vote-division is that the party leaders would find it harder to foresee (and plan for) electoral outcomes. Particularly in electoral markets (as in pre-war Japan) without sophisticated polling techniques, they would find it hard to predict just who would vote for whom over time. Unable to predict, they would find it hard to adjust for changes at the margin.

In order to avoid these problems, the pre-war centrist parties such as the Seiyūkai adopted strategies like the one the post-war Liberal Democratic Party (LDP) adopted: They divided their supporters by using private goods (generally pork or bribes) to induce them to join personalized support groups for individual candidates. The party controlling the Prime-Ministership, in other words, would use its control over the government to build its candidates' personal networks and thereby divide its votes. In post-war Japan, the ruling LDP used government-dispensed pork, cash and in-kind gifts, and bureaucratic services. In pre-war Japan, the leading parties used much the same tactics, if perhaps with more bribes than the LDP used.[33]

The political power of the business community in pre-war Japan followed from this need for cash among the leading parties. To divide the vote, the parties needed cash. To obtain the cash, they needed the goodwill of the business community. To keep that goodwill, they had to dispense advantageous regulatory schemes. Despite the legal ceiling of ¥10,000 on campaign expenditures, politicians spent as much as ¥100,000 under the 1900 Elections Act.[34] Faced with the vastly expanded electorate under the 1925 Act, they spent much more.[35] Most of that money came from the business community.

The Seiyūkai had its roots in rural Japan, whereas the Kenseikai was relatively stronger in urban districts (Sakairi, 1932: 239–245). Given the parties' different constituencies (Chapter 9), it is not surprising that the Kenseikai began espousing a relatively left-leaning labor policy as soon as it recognized the inevitability of universal suffrage (Garon, 1987: 55–68). Both parties sought Diet majorities, and both forged ties with businesses to help pay for those majorities. Although many businesses hedged their bets, giving to both the Seiyūkai and the Kenseikai, each party had a coterie of firms with which it had especially close relations. Mitsui was called "the Seiyūkai's zaibatsu." Also backing the Seiyūkai, though reputedly with less fidelity than Mitsui, were the Yasuda and Sumitomo zaibatsu, along with the Asano, Ōkura, Kawasaki, Ōsaka Shōsen, Furukawa, Kuhara, Fujita, Hattori, Ōkawa, Fukuzawa, and Nakahashi groups. On the other hand, the Mitsubishi zaibatsu, and the Shibusawa, Yamaguchi, Nezu, and Hara groups as well as the Tōhō Electric Power and Japan Electric Power companies supported the Kenseikai.[36] Political favoritism left many firms out of the loop, prompting them to decry both parties and to press the government to eschew interference in industry.[37]

The pre-war political system struck many observers as corrupt (Minobe, 1930; Rōyama, 1930). Ozaki Yukio, leader of a small, "progressive" party, spoke for many in the voting public when he quipped, "The only difference between the Seiyūkai and Kenseikai is that one is a robber and the other a thief" (quoted in Colegrove, 1928: 402). But note here that the corruption was institutionally driven: Multi-member districts forced the major parties to divide their votes; the parties could divide their votes more competitively if their candidates cultivated personal support networks; and those candidates could cultivate those networks most effectively if they could manipulate the party's control over the government to extract cash contributions from the business community and the government itself.

7. ELECTIONS UNDER SNTV, MMD RULES

All parties – the Kenseikai, the Seiyūkai, the Seiyūhontō, and the Kakushin Club – dreaded the first election under the new electoral regime. For the parties, multi-member districts and universal suffrage were a particularly expensive mix. Each party would have to divide the vote within each district among several of their own members, all when the electorate had become suddenly larger and less predictable. Although the parties advertised their policy differences vociferously in public, the Kenseikai cabinet struck a quiet, backroom deal with the other parties to undermine a no-confidence vote against it in 1927.[38] The parties were clinging to a common interest in forestalling the elections for as long as possible before the Diet's four year term expired in May 1928 (Colegrove, 1928: 401).

As the mandatory end of the legislative term began to approach, each party prepared for the first mass election with the variety of resources available to them. In March 1927 the Kenseikai and Seiyūhontō decided to merge to create a more powerful Minseitō. In addition, this new Minseitō had hoped to be in the cabinet at the time of the election to compete from a position of strength. But Wakatsuki's Minseitō cabinet fell in April 1927 following a clash with the Privy Council. The confrontation was ostensibly over Wakatsuki's plan to bail out the ailing Bank of Taiwan and Suzuki shōten. As we discuss in greater detail in Chapter 8, however, Privy Council minutes suggest that an anti-Minseitō coalition had formed in the Council that wanted his cabinet out of office before the election.[39]

The Seiyūkai, dwarfed by its rival party but now in control of the cabinet and the Ministry of Home Affairs, fired almost all the prefectural governors – particularly those installed by the previous Kenseikai (Minseitō) government (see Table 5.2 on p. 66). As earlier elections had shown, the parties found local governments invaluable in allocating the vote in each electoral district. Local governments also controlled police regiments, and the parties could induce the police to be selective in enforing campaign laws (see Chapter 6).[40] Both major parties employed spies to report on the infractions of their rivals, but in 1928 the police caught the Minseitō candidates more often.[41] As if that were not enough, the Justice Ministry, also now under the Seiyūkai, had discretion over which infractions to prosecute.[42]

Half a dozen peasant and labor parties and a group of independents campaigned against both the status quo powers of the Privy Council and House of Peers and the two large, "bought-and-paid-for" political parties. Uncomfortably for the two large parties, the anti-establishment parties had large stores of corruption stories to tell about the Seiyūkai and the Minseitō. Nevertheless, the two large parties had huge campaign war chests, and the Seiyūkai had the police. These were far more potent campaign tools, as it turns out, than a cause or integrity.[43]

The proletarian parties won a mere eight seats among them in the House of Representatives in the 1928 election. The real competition was between the two political behemoths, the Seiyūkai and the Minseitō. Although the Minseitō had come into the election with a large Diet majority, the Seiyūkai made full use of its control of the cabinet to squeak past its larger rival.[44] But the result was that, once again, no party commanded a Diet majority.[45] The marriage of convenience between the Seiyūhontō and Kenseikai, which had together formed the Minseitō in 1927, fell apart a few months into the new Diet session. Now the Seiyūhontō could do much better for itself as part of the new cabinet party, and returned to the Seiyūkai from which it had split in 1924.[46]

The two largest parties, the Seiyūkai and the Minseitō, took turns at the helm of the cabinet, at the suffrance of Saionji Kimmochi, the last Meiji oligarch. That also meant they took turns winning elections. Despite the defection of the Seiyūhontō to the Seiyūkai in August 1928, which shrank the Minseitō's Diet presence, the Minseitō won a majority of seats on its own in the February 1930 election.[47] Soon after a Seiyūkai cabinet replaced the Minseitō cabinet, the Seiyūkai won a resounding election victory.

The end of the political era was not far behind. Below the surface of all the parties' money-grubbing and electioneering, more sinister events were overtaking Japanese history. Assassinations and coup attempts by one military group or another splashed onto the headlines with growing frequency, warning of the rise of military power. In the next chapters we ask why only the military was apparently so well-positioned to survive the political turmoil in pre-war Japan.

8. CONCLUSION

The oligarchs, we have argued, agreed to a representative assembly as their last best hope: As long as the oligarchy was disintegrating, they found it safest to discover who the entrepreneurs were, and then buy their acquiescence. In due course, the political parties adopted the same logic and supported universal suffrage. Unable to collude tacitly among themselves, members of the political parties voted to make their lives miserable. At least then they might be able to stay in office.

Even before universal suffrage, the oligarchs had designed electoral rules to make politicians suffer. By dint of the MMD-SNTV rules, parties were forced to divide the vote among multiple candidates in many districts. The oligarchs, it seems, hoped that parties would collapse in a welter of internal dissension. Instead of falling apart, however, parties tried to lessen the effect of the rules by selling enough favors to constituents to smooth the way for all of their candidates.

The two largest parties survived, but their money-grubbing and scandal-ridden pork-based politics alienated voters en masse. Parties occupied themselves with raising enough money for the next election. To do so, they forged incestuous ties with the businesses they regulated.

The oligarchs never intended to give the Diet a full veto. So long as they controlled the cabinet, they often had ways (like Imperial Orders) to circumvent the Diet's influence over statutes. Yet eventually they lost that control over the cabinet. When they did, they lost control over the judiciary, the police, and the rest of the bureaucracy as well. Granted, the Privy Council and House of Peers remained forces with which the party politicians had to reckon. As the oligarchs died and failed to name powerful successors, however, those institutions lost their control over the emperor. With it, they lost their hold over the political process as well.

5

The bureaucracy: Who ruled whom?

1. INTRODUCTION

Scholars make much of "bureaucratic control" in Japan, particularly in the pre-war era. We find their discussions misleading, and in this chapter explain why. Simply stated, bureaucratic governance describes pre-war Japan only if one considers the Meiji oligarchs – those entrepreneurs who overthrew a shogunate and launched their own experiment – to be bureaucrats.

Even were the oligarchs bureaucrats, the pre-war Japanese government was not consistently under oligarchical control. Within twenty years of their reign, the oligarchs began to lose their monopoly on power. Never able to quell their internecine rivalries, they struggled to maintain what amounted to a classic failed cartel. Some of them enlisted the aid of "new entrants" in their struggles against each other. For a brief period in the 1920s the political parties founded by these renegade oligarchs were on center stage.

Some oligarchs, particularly Yamagata, gave the military a high degree of independence precisely because they were afraid of the encroachment of representative government. This too, in our view, was an outgrowth of intra-oligarchy rivalry. An independent military, Yamagata reasoned, would preserve his power from hostile political forces for at least as long as he was alive.

To the Japanese people, granting the military political independence was the oligarchs' greatest disservice. But the criticism may be beside the point. Whatever the rhetoric, the oligarchs were in the business of protecting themselves. Promoting the larger interests of Japan (an issue at the heart of this book) seems to have been at most a secondary goal.

In Section 2 of this chapter we address the issue of bureaucratic behavior in theoretical terms. Through standard principal-agent theory, we explore the circumstances under which bureaucrats may behave autonomously from their political overseers, and to what extent. We particularly note the danger of concluding that bureaucrats are autonomous simply because they are active while politicians are passive.

In the remainder of the chapter we examine the evidence of bureaucratic discretion in pre-war Japan. In Section 3 we consider why pre-war politicians wanted to control bureaucrats. In Section 4 we analyze how they did so. Specifically, we examine how laws and regulations structured the incentives of bureaucrats. Who promoted them? Who had the power to fire them? Under what circumstances? The law, we find, gave the cabinet, if not the legislative majority, some room for maneuver in manipulating bureaucratic loyalties. As the oligarchs' grip on power began to slip, the political party in control of the cabinet increasingly used its influence over bureaucrats.

In Section 5 we turn to the statistical record on bureaucratic placement and advancement. We find, at least during the cabinet-government period of 1918 to 1932, that the political parties wielded considerable power over bureaucratic careers. During those years, the politicians apparently found ways to circumvent the oligarchs' power over policymaking and implementation. Because politicians competed with Privy Council members for the control over the bureaucrats, bureaucrats had a plethora of overseers, not a lack of them.

2. POLITICIANS AND BUREAUCRATS: A PRINCIPAL-AGENT ANALYSIS

The notion that bureaucrats – because they are the first and the last people to have their hands on the law – must be the ones who rule, is not unique to scholarship on Japan. Much of the "state and society" literature in comparative politics (Skocpol, 1979; Schmitter, 1979) and the "decline of Congress" literature in American politics (Lowi, 1969; Neustadt, 1964; Sundquist, 1969) is a eulogy to representative democracy as it might have been. These theorists find no government by voter-sensitive legislators. Instead, they find politicians who have, voluntarily or not, abdicated their authority over policymaking to countless unaccountable bureaucrats.

Scholars first noted the problems with these abdication theories in industrial organization rather than political science. For years, economists and lawyers had been making the same arguments about corporate governance that political scientists made about democracy. We had entered an age of "managerial capitalism," they declared, where managers had effectively wrested control of firms from the hands of the shareholders (Berle and Means, 1932).

Ultimately, these arguments about managerial capitalism did not make sense. Ostensibly independent managers steadily maximized the returns they paid the ostensibly powerless shareholders; ostensibly powerless shareholders happily placed their money with the ostensibly independent managers. To understand how shareholders induced managers to maximize their (shareholders') profits, economists eventually developed the conceptually and empirically sophisticated literature known today as principal-agent theory: how principals (for example, owners) ensure that their agents (for example, managers) behave as they ought (Alchian and Demsetz, 1972; Jensen and Meckling, 1976).

In recent years, political scientists and legal scholars have turned to this principal-agent theory to sort through the arguments about bureaucratic control in government. In doing so, they note that the appearance of bureaucratic autonomy (a common phenomenon) need not imply that bureaucrats are actually independent from their political overseers (a rarer phenomenon). Why political scientists for so long thought they saw independent bureaucrats is straightforward. In a wide range of political systems, bureaucrats draft laws, implement them, and possess sophisticated information about the economy. They may even have a substantial voice in the personnel affairs of their respective bureaus. At least by appearances, politicians seem simply to rubber stamp what the bureaucrats do.

Such an appearance is deceptive. That bureaucrats are active and politicians passive need not mean that bureaucrats govern. Consider how the world would look if politicians could have their druthers. They would hire bureaucrats who would look for policies that would help them win reelection, who would draft the policies into bills, and who (after they had enacted those bills) would implement those policies. Because the bureaucrats would do exactly as the politicians wanted them to do, the politicians would need do nothing more than rubber stamp. Bureaucrats, in this unreal world, would seem to be in control – but in fact would not. They would be servile agents to their political principals, faithfully working to ensure that those principals win reelection.

To determine whether passive politicians actually control outcomes, one must instead ask whether politicians can cheaply monitor and effectively veto their bureaucrats. These elements, in turn, will disclose whether bureaucrats will anticipate the preferences that politicians hold. Suppose politicians can veto what bureaucrats do – that they can fire, promote selectively, or overturn a bureaucrat's actions. If they can do all this, rational bureaucrats will anticipate what the politicians want. They will do so because, if they do anything else, the politicians will reject their programs and possibly even punish them to boot. Bureaucrats, in this world, will appear autonomous. But the appearance will result from effective, but invisible, political control.

The bureaucracy

Suppose now that monitoring costs are high – that politicians find it hard to detect bureaucratic subterfuge. Real political markets, according to many observers, are markets where monitoring costs are indeed high. Bureaucrats, these observers argue, usually have access to superior information. Even if politicians have information directly relevant to their campaigns, they have little else. Absent information about policy, however, politicians will be unable to monitor their bureaucratic agents.

For two reasons, these observers exaggerate the problems that monitoring costs pose. First, even politicians without significant information about policy can establish competitions among bureaucrats for promotions or budgetary allocations. They will then reward the bureaucrats who win and punish those who lose. In turn, in order to convince politicians to reward them, ambitious bureaucrats will provide politicians with positive information about their own proposals and negative information about everyone else's. Such politicians can run the competitions because they hold a veto over bureaucratic careers and budgets. In effect, their veto itself reduces monitoring costs.

Second, politicians can mitigate monitoring costs by delegating monitoring to their constituents. Without paying enormous sums for auditors or whistle-blowers, they can receive a steady stream of information about the performance of bureaucrats from the voters and interest groups that care most about the policies in question.[1] This, of course, is precisely the sort of information that vote-maximizing politicians need.

Introducing multiple principals complicates the principal-agent logic. What is an ambitious bureaucrat to do when he has several bosses, each of whom tells him to do different things? For at least part of the pre-war period, this seems the situation in which most bureaucrats found themselves: They answered to oligarchs, politicians, and the military. This situation, however, resembles the quandary in which American bureaucrats find themselves. Operating in a world of divided government, they find their actions constrained by the potential vetoes of all principals. The result is not that bureaucrats become independent. It is rather that they find themselves more limited in their ability to act autonomously.

Note, further, that the relative strength of the various principals changed over time. Astute bureaucrats knew that at first the oligarchs were their sole principals. Later, political parties became additional principals, at least when they controlled the cabinet, and the power of the oligarchs waned. In due course, the military eclipsed the party politicians. With each shift, ambitious bureaucrats had to change the policies they provided. In the section that follows, we examine the nature of the vetoes that each principal possessed, and explain why their potency waxed and waned.

3. BUREAUCRATS AND POLITICIANS
IN PRE-WAR JAPAN

Traditionally, scholars of pre-war Japan focused on two groups contending for power: the politicians and the bureaucrats. By politicians, they referred to the members of the political parties. What they referred to as "the bureaucracy" was a much more heterogeneous group. We have no quibble with classifying career civil servants as part of the bureaucracy. We see no reason, however, to group them with oligarchs who rose through the ranks as bureaucrats in the fledgling Meiji regime before leading the government as autocrats. These were quintessential politicians, competing for power in a non-electoral setting.

It is true that many of the oligarchs began their political life as bureaucrats. But to climb as far as they did, and to become the rule-makers themselves, they had to be ambitious entrepreneurs. The lines between the rulers and implementers can be fuzzy in an autocracy, of course. No electoral process ferrets out the legislators as it does in a democracy. Yet these oligarchs were men who had won internal struggles for power, who were sometimes even the residual claimants of the system, and who presided over teams of subordinates who implemented their rules.

As we explained, scholars first applied principal-agent theory to politics in the context of American government, with all its checks and balances. There they found that the theory helped unfurl the conceptual complexities of divided government, where different political parties sometimes controlled the executive and the legislative branches. Under divided government, bureaucratic agents potentially answer to two principals: the president in one political party and the legislative majority in another. In parliamentary systems, by contrast, a single line of authority runs from the legislature to the bureaucracy, and more straightforward delegation results. In that context, political principals can more effectively oversee their bureaucratic agents, which is why the monitoring is harder to observe. With fewer instances of failed oversight, politicians less often intervene overtly to straighten things out.

Pre-war Japan was not a presidential system, but neither was it a purely parliamentary one. The Diet's majority party did not automatically secure the Prime Ministership, as it would in a parliamentary system. Neither could it use a vote of no confidence to force the cabinet to step down or to dissolve the Diet. As long as the oligarchs remained on the scene, they were able to shape bureaucratic incentives: They could credibly threaten to torpedo legislation, and they could offer bureaucrats aristocratic titles and post-bureaucratic careers in the Privy Council. By contrast, the party politicians merely possessed a much weaker motivator: the legislative veto. For several decades, then, Japan had a complicated divided government, with the electorally unaccountable oligarchs as the executive, and party politicians in the Diet.

Until they wrested control of the cabinet, party politicians had an incentive to draft legislation as specifically as possible to constrain bureaucratic behavior. At the same time, the oligarchs had an incentive to choose top bureaucrats who would implement the laws in ways they, the oligarchs, wanted. The oligarchs, moreover, possessed a veto of their own by way of their "advice" to the emperor.

By the 1920s, the party politicians had eclipsed the oligarchs in political influence, only to encounter another problem: competition with each other for money and votes. In this competition, they found their oversight over bureaucrats problematic. The more tightly they controlled the bureaucracy, the more tightly their successors controlled it as well. The more their successors could undo their policies, the less effectively could they promise their constituents policies that would last. The less stability they could promise, the less they could induce their supporters to pay for policy favors.

Given this trade-off between bureaucratic control and policy stability, the politicians had some incentive to insulate the bureaucracy from themselves. To ensure higher contributions, they might have tried to maintain a bureaucracy over which no one would have political control. They did not try that, for the Meiji Constitution gave them no easy way to try: It provided no institutional distance between the cabinet and the bureaucracy.[2]

The dilemma was one of "credible commitments" (Williamson, 1985). With the Constitution as it was, party politicians had no way credibly to commit to leaving the bureaucracy alone. They could promise ex ante – but if they did they would have an incentive to renege ex post. If none of the leaders of party A could credibly promise the leaders of party B that A would keep the bureaucracy independent as long as A controlled the cabinet, and if B leaders could not promise A leaders the same – then each party potentially had an incentive to manipulate the bureaucracy when it could.[3]

4. THE BUREAUCRACY: WHOSE SERVANT?

On paper, at least, the bureaucrats were independent of the political parties. The oligarchs had instituted civil service exams for low- and mid-level bureaucrats (*sōninkan* and below) in 1887 (see Chapter 3).[4] Apparently, they had hoped to prevent politicians from using bureaucratic posts for political patronage. Although they had initially exempted Tokyo Imperial University graduates from the exam, by 1893 they canceled even that exemption.[5] All would-be low- and mid-level bureaucrats now had to pass a stringent examination.

Crucially, the 1887 order exempted the highest level bureaucrats from the exams. When Ōkuma became Prime Minister in 1898, he appointed friends and supporters from his political party to those posts. As Privy Council chairman, Yamagata quickly drafted another Imperial Order to close this loophole too.[6] Under this new order, only people who had passed the civil service exam could now take any of the civil-service positions, even the highest. Only cabinet positions were exempt.[7] To augment this bureaucratic independence, Yamagata drafted additional Imperial Orders that made it hard for a cabinet to fire bureaucrats for any reason other than professional misfeasance or incompetence.[8]

Eventually, however, the party politicians found ways to control even these supposedly independent civil servants. Even if they could not fire a bureaucrat, they could refuse to promote him. Bureaucrats who wanted to climb the career ladder thus had little choice but to do as they said.

Still, ambitious bureaucrats who wanted to answer to political principals had to discover who those principals were. Where parties alternated in power, they would not find the task easy. They could try to play both sides. In many parliamentary systems, bureaucrats do exactly that: They serve loyally whomever is in office (Moe, 1990). Alternatively, they could stay loyal to one party exclusively. A fair number of bureaucrats in prewar Japan chose this route instead, as we shall see in the next two sections (see also Spaulding, 1967).

Apparently, bureaucrats identified themselves with one party because party politicians demanded – and rewarded – such exclusivity. For the bureaucrat, it was a risky gambit. He would thrive only during his patron's tenure. If he preferred a smooth career with regular promotions, he would not consider this a first-best strategy. Pre-war Japanese elections, though, placed a premium on bureaucratic loyalty. To win these elections, politicians needed to be able to control local governments and use them to dispense money and harass political opponents. In such a politicized environment, perhaps politicians hesitated to promote bureaucrats who tried to swing both ways. In any case, many bureaucrats chose not to try.[9]

5. THE EMPIRICAL RECORD ON BUREAUCRATIC ADVANCEMENT

To examine how successfully the oligarchs insulated the bureaucracy from the politicians, we used two techniques. First, we examined the roster of senior bureaucrats (section chief [*kachō*] or higher) for three key ministries: the Ministry of Home Affairs, the Ministry of Finance, and the Ministry of Railroads (we examine the Ministry of Justice roster in Chapter 6). Second, we looked for autobiographical reports from the bureaucrats themselves to obtain a sense of their subjective view of events. On the basis of these investigations, we answer the question of how insulated bureaucrats were in one phrase: "not very."

5.1. Evidence from bureaucratic rosters

We examined the personnel records from the entire pre-war period for the Ministries of Home Affairs, Finance, and Railroads to see whether career success correlated with changes in the parties governing the cabinets. Consider first the Ministry of Home Affairs. It had a wide range of responsibilities, many of which bore on the parties' electoral success. For example, it housed the Bureau for Internal Affairs and the Police Agency. The two organizations supervised elections. The ministry also was responsible for local government, including the appointment of governors for each of the forty-seven prefectures. These governors controlled a prefectural government apparatus that politicians could, and would, mobilize to canvass voters. Other bureaus in the Ministry included the Health Bureau (*Eisei kyoku*), the Society Bureau (*Shakai kyoku*), the Shrines Bureau (*Jinja kyoku*), and the National Land Bureau (*Kyokudo kyoku*).

The personnel records disclose a deep and wide-ranging connection between bureaucratic appointments and cabinet control. Beginning with Katō Takaaki's Kenseikai cabinet in the mid-1920s, the bureau directors, section chiefs, and senior police personnel, routinely changed hands when a new party took office (Table 5.1). The turnover appears particularly swift and systematic for the positions with the closest link to elections. Politicians manipulated the governorships with special ferocity. They typically replaced almost every governor within a few days of a change in party cabinet (Table 5.2).[10]

Take the aggregate figures for the annual turnovers in Home Affairs Ministry posts. In 1924 (the first year of Katō Takaaki's cabinet after Kiyoura's cabinet of oligarchs and court officials), the data show a quantum leap of more than 50 percent over the number for any previous year. The number of posts vacated went back to the usual level during the next year, but thereafter, each time another party took over the cabinet, it leapt back up to the 1924 high (Table 5.3). An apolitical ministry this was certainly not. Bureaucrats forced to compete in this way for partisan patronage should have been singularly unsuccessful in acting either independently or on the advice of the oligarchs against the wishes of party politicians.

The data from the Finance Ministry show considerable political influence as well, even if perhaps less than in Home Affairs. In the Ministry of Finance, the Administrative Vice Minister (*Ōkura jikan*) seemed to have been a political appointment from at least around 1924 (Table 5.4). Prime Minister Katō Takaaki immediately replaced his Vice Minister. Each suc-

Table 5.1. *Turnover in the Ministry of Home Affairs and Police Agency, 1924–1931*

	6/11/24 Katō Kenseikai	6/30/26 Wakatsuki Kenseikai	4/20/27 Tanaka Seiyūkai	7/2/29 Hamaguchi Minseitō	4/14/31 Wakatsuki Minseitō	12/13/31 Inukai Seiyūkai
Date / Cabinet / Party						
Bureau chiefs						
Health	X (1 day)	—	—	X (2 mos.)	—	X (1 wk)
Internal Security	—	—	X (2 days)	X (1 day)	X (1 day)	X (1 day)
Society	—	—	—	X (2 wks)	X (3 wks)	X (1 wk)
Shrines	—	—	X (3 wks)	X (3 wks)	—	—
Local Government	—	—	—	X (3 days)	X (1 day)	X (1 wk)
National Lands	—	—	X (1 mo.)	X (3 days)	X (1 day)	X (1 wk)
Section chiefs						
Internal Security						
High-Level Section Chief*	NA	NA	NA	X (1 wk)	X (1 wk)	X (1 wk)
Inspection	—	—	X (1 mo.)	X (1 wk)	—	X (2 wks)
Security	—	—	X (1 mo.)	X (1 wk)	—	X (1 wk)
Local government						
Administration**	NA	—	X (1 wk)	X (1 wk)	—	—
Finance**	NA	—	—	—	—	—

Police agency						
Police Chief	X (1 day)	—	X (1 day)	X (1 day)	X (1 day)	X (1 day)
Secretariat	X (2 wks)	X (1 mo.)	X (2 days)	X (1 wk)	X (2 wks)	X (1 wk)
Judicial Affairs	X (2 wks)	—	X (2 days)	X (1 wk)	—	X (1 wk)
Police Affairs	X (2 wks)	—	X (2 days)	X (1 wk)	—	X (1 wk)
Security	—	—	X (2 days)	X (1 wk)	X (2 wks)	X (2 wks)
Special Police Affairs	—	—	X (1 mo.)	X (2 wks)	—	—
Fire Dept.	—	—	—	—	—	—
Health Bureau	X (2 mos.)	—	—	X (1 wk)	X (2 wks)	—

Notes: An X indicates that the cabinet appointed a new bureau director general or section chief. We indicate in parentheses the amount of time the cabinet waited before making the appointment. We do not record new appointments after lapses of more than two months following the formation of a new cabinet.

* The Tanaka cabinet created the Internal Safety Bureau high-level section chief (*Keiho kyoku kōtō kachō*) position in July 1928.

** The Katō cabinet created the Administration and Finance sections of the Local Government Bureau in December, 1924.

Source: Compiled on the basis of data found in Ikuhiko Hata, *Senzenki Nihon kanryōsei no seido, soshiki, jinji* [*The System, Organization, and Personnel of the Pre-war Japanese Bureaucracy*] (Tokyo: Tokyo daigaku shuppan kai, 1981), pp. 327–332.

Table 5.2. Turnover in prefectural governors under changing party control of cabinets

| Date | 6/11/24 | 6/30/26 | 4/20/27 | 7/2/29 | 4/14/31 | 12/13/31 |
| Cabinet | Katō | Wakatsuki | Tanaka | Hamaguchi | Wakatsuki | Inukai |
Party	Kenseikai	Kenseikai	Seiyūkai	Minseitō	Minseitō	Seiyūkai
Prefectures						
Aichi	X (2 days)	—	X (1 mo.)	X (3 days)	—	X (1 wk)
Akita	X (2 wks)	—	X (1 mo.)	X (3 days)	—	X (1 wk)
Aomori	X (2 wks)	—	X (1 mo.)	X (3 days)	—	X (1 wk)
Chiba	X (2 wks)	—	X (1 mo.)	X (3 days)	—	X (1 wk)
Ehime	X (2 wks)	—	X (1 mo.)	X (3 days)	—	X (1 wk)
Fukui	X (2 wks)	—	X (1 mo.)	—	—	X (1 wk)
Fukuoka	—	—	X (1 mo.)	X (3 days)	X (3 wks)	X (1 wk)
Fukushima	—	—	X (1 mo.)	X (3 days)	X (1 day)	X (1 wk)
Gifu	X (2 wks)	—	X (1 mo.)	X (3 days)	—	X (1 wk)
Gumma	X (1 mo.)	—	X (1 mo.)	X (2 mos.)	—	X (1 wk)
Hiroshima	—	—	—	X (3 days)	X (3 wks)	X (1 wk)
Hokkaidō	—	—	X (10 days)	X (3 days)	—	—
Hyōgo	—	—	X (1 mo.)	X (3 days)	—	X (1 wk)
Ibaraki	—	—	X (1 mo.)	X (3 days)	—	X (1 wk)
Ishikawa	X (2 wks)	—	X (1 mo.)	X (3 days)	—	X (1 wk)
Kagawa	X (2 wks)	—	X (1 mo.)	X (3 days)	—	X (1 wk)
Kagoshima	X (2 wks)	—	X (1 mo.)	X (3 days)	—	X (1 wk)
Kanagawa	X (2 wks)	—	X (1 mo.)	X (3 days)	—	X (1 wk)
Kōchi	—	—	X (1 mo.)	X (3 days)	—	X (1 wk)
Kumamoto	X (2 wks)	—	X (1 mo.)	X (3 days)	—	X (1 wk)
Kyōto	—	—	X (1 wk)	X (3 days)	—	X (1 wk)
Mie	X (2 wks)	—	—*	—	—	X (1 wk)
Miyagi	X (2 wks)	—	—	—	—	X (1 wk)

Prefecture					
Miyazaki	—	X (1 mo.)	X (3 days)	—	X (1 wk)
Nagasaki	X (2 wks)	X (1 wk)	X (3 days)	—	—
Nara	—	X (1 mo.)	X (5 wks)	X (5 wks)	X (1 wk)
Niigata	—	X (1 wk)	X (3 days)	—	X (1 wk)
Ōita	X (7 wks)	X (1 mo.)	X (3 days)	—	X (1 wk)
Okayama	—	X (1 mo.)	X (3 days)	—	X (1 wk)
Okinawa	X (2 wks)	X (1 mo.)	X (3 days)	—	—
Osaka	—	X (1 mo.)	X (3 days)	—	X (1 wk)
Saga	X (7 wks)	X (1 mo.)	—	X (1 day)	X (1 wk)
Saitama	X (2 wks)	X (1 mo.)	X (3 days)	—	X (1 wk)
Shiga	—	X (1 mo.)	X (2 mos.)	—	X (1 wk)
Shimane	X (2 wks)	X (1 mo.)	X (2 mos.)	X (2 mos.)	X (1 wk)
Shizuoka	X (2 wks)	X (1 mo.)	X (3 days)	X (3 wks)	X (1 wk)
Tochigi	X (2 days)	X (1 mo.)	X (3 days)	—	X (1 wk)
Tokushima	X (2 wks)	X (1 mo.)	X (3 days)	—	X (1 wk)
Tokyo	—	—	X (3 days)	—	X (1 wk)
Tottori	X (2 wks)	X (1 mo.)	—	—	X (1 wk)
Toyama	X (7 wks)	X (1 mo.)	—	X (1 day)	X (1 wk)
Wakayama	X (2 wks)	X (1 mo.)	X (3 days)	—	X (1 wk)
Yamagata	X (2 wks)	X (1 mo.)	—*	—	X (1 wk)
Yamaguchi	X (2 wks)	—	X (3 days)	—	X (1 wk)
Yamanashi	X (2 wks)	X (1 mo.)	X (3 days)	—	X (1 wk)

Notes: An X indicates that the cabinet appointed a new governor; the number in parentheses indicates the amount of time the cabinet waited before appointing a new governor. We do not record new appointments after lapses of more than two months following the formation of a new cabinet.

An asterisk (*) indicates that the cabinet replaced the governor just before an election, although more than two months had elapsed since the cabinet had been formed.

Source: Compiled on the basis of data found in Ikuhiko Hata, *Senzenki Nihon kanryōsei no seido, soshiki, jinji [The System, Organization, and Personnel of the Pre-war Japanese Bureaucracy]* (Tokyo: Tokyo daigaku shuppan kai, 1981), pp. 333–349.

Table 5.3. *Turnover in the Ministry of Home Affairs, 1918–1932*

Date	Cabinet change	Number of turnovers
1918	Terauchi(N) to Hara(S), 9/29/18	14
1920	—	54
1921	Hara(S) to Takahashi(S), 11/13/21	13
1922	Takahashi(S) to Katō (N), 6/12/22	51
1923	Katō (N) to Yamamoto(N), 9/2/23	48
1924	Yamamoto(N) to Kiyoura(N), 1/7/24, and Kiyoura(N) to Katō (K), 6/11/24	80
1925	—	38
1926	Katō(K) to Wakatsuki(K), 6/30/26	46
1927	Wakatsuki(K) to Tanaka(S), 4/20/27	73
1928	—	39
1929	Tanaka(S) to Hamaguchi(M)	77
1930	—	27
1931	Hamaguchi(M) to Wakatsuki(M), and Wakatsuki(M) to Inukai(S)	116

Notes: (N) refers to non-party cabinet; (S) refers to a Seiyūkai cabinet; (K) refers to a Kenseikai cabinet; and (M) refers to a Minseitō cabinet.
Source: Compiled on the basis of data found in Ikuhiko Hata, *Senzenki Nihon kanryōsei no seido, soshiki, jinji [The System, Organization, and Personnel of the Pre-war Japanese Bureaucracy]* (Tokyo: Tokyo daigaku shuppan kai, 1981).

cessive cabinet involving a party change promoted a new man to the job, sometimes bringing back Vice Ministers who had served previously. Nonetheless, a number of bureau chiefs did manage to hold their positions through cabinet changes. Perhaps for bureaucrats implementing policies not intensely election-related, the occasional dismissal of one of their peers was sufficient to keep them from sabotaging the intent of the cabinet. As we would predict, there were more of these apparently partisan turnovers concentrated in the relatively important – from a political standpoint – bureaus of the budget (*shukei kyoku*) and tax (*shuzei kyoku*).[11] Note, however, that the aggregate figures for the number of posts vacated in the Ministry of Finance tell the same story as for the Ministry of Home Affairs: bureaucratic turnover jumps every time the cabinet changed parties (Hata, 1981).

The rosters for Ministry of Railroads too show some partisan-motivated turnover – more like the Ministry of Finance, perhaps, than like the Ministry of Home Affairs. Many of the bureau chiefs were reassigned with shifts in cabinet government. As with the other ministries, the

Table 5.4. *Turnover in the Ministry of Finance, 1924–1931*

Date Cabinet Party	6/11/24 Katō Kenseikai	6/30/26 Wakatsuki Kenseikai	4/20/27 Tanaka Seiyūkai	7/2/29 Hamaguchi Minseitō	4/14/31 Wakatsuki Minseitō	12/13/31 Inukai Seiyūkai
Administrative Vice Minister	X (1 day)	—	X (2 days)	X (2 days)	—	X (2 days)
Bureau chiefs						
Budget	X (2 mos.)	—	—	X (2 days)	—	—
Tax	—	—	X (1 mo.)	X (2 days)	—	X (1 wk)
Banking	—	—	—*	—	—	—
Trust Fund	X (2 mos.)	—	—	X (2 days)	—	—
Government Monopoly	—	—	—	X (2 days)	—	—
Finance	—	—	—	—	—	—
Currency Printing	X (2 mos.)	—	—	—	—	—

Notes: An X indicates that the cabinet appointed a new person to the position in question; we indicate in parentheses the amount of time the cabinet waited before making the appointment. We do not record new appointments after lapses of more than two months following the formation of a new cabinet.

An asterisk (*) indicates that the cabinet replaced the bureau chief before an election.

Source: Compiled on the basis of data found in Ikuhito Hata, *Senzenki Nihon kanryōsei no seido, soshiki, jinji [The System, Organization, and Personnel of the Pre-war Japanese Bureaucracy]* (Tokyo: Tokyo daigaku shuppan kai, 1981), pp. 355–359.

pattern began in the mid-1920s, and repeated itself with every party shift in the cabinet (Table 5.5). Not surprisingly, these personnel shifts show up as increases in the number of positions vacated every time the party controlling the cabinet changes (Hata, 1981). Ultimately, they suggest that railroad routing and maintenance were important items in the parties' respective pork barrels (a point we confirm in Chapter 9).

Slicing the data from another angle, we considered the changes in the length of time all civil servants held their positions. Between 1868 and the first party cabinet of 1918, the oligarchs maintained a relatively tight control over the government. During that time, 28 percent of the bureaucrats kept their assignments for more than three years. In the ensuing period of party cabinets (1918 to 1932), only 10 percent of the bureaucrats stayed in a job that long. From 1868 to 1918, 47 percent of the bureaucrats switched assignments within 18 months. During 1918 to 1932, that number climbed to 60 percent (Table 5.6).

5.2. Self-reported evidence

If the aggregate personnel data suggest advancement within the ministries was not random from a partisan point of view, consider the lives of a few of the bureaucrats as they and their peers saw them. Take first the case of Yamaoka Mannosuke.[12] Yamaoka was a young public prosecutor who became affiliated with Seiyūkai mentors early in his career. We will return to his story in the next chapter, when we consider the independence of the Japanese judiciary. For our purposes here, note that he lost his job as the chief of the Prosecutorial Bureau in the Justice Ministry in 1925 when a Kenseikai cabinet replaced a Seiyūkai cabinet. He spent the next two years or so as a "private scholar" (read, unemployed) until, to his good fortune, Seiyūkai politicians once again took the reins of government in late 1927. They then appointed him chief of the Internal Security Bureau (*Keiho kyoku*; the secret police) in the Ministry of Home Affairs (Hosojima, 1964: 87).

As Security Bureau chief, Yamaoka was in a position of crucial political importance for the Seiyūkai, for his bureau monitored the electoral laws. In that capacity, its officers consistently favored the party in power in investigations, precisely because partisans like Yamaoka oversaw their activities.[13] Yamaoka's job was especially important in 1927 because the new universal suffrage act, which had altered the nature of electoral competition, made the Seiyūkai more defensive than ever.

When the election finally took place in January 1928, the Minseitō, predictably, accused Home Affairs Minister Suzuki Kizaburō and his protege Yamaoka of harsh and biased surveillance of electoral campaigns (for example, *Tokyo asahi shimbun*, January 25, 1928; January 27, 1928;

Table 5.5. *Turnover in the Ministry of Railroads, 1924–1931*

Date	6/11/24	6/30/26	4/20/27	7/2/29	4/14/31	12/13/31
Cabinet	Katō	Wakatsuki	Tanaka	Hamaguchi	Wakatsuki	Inukai
Party	Kenseikai	Kenseikai	Seiyūkai	Minseitō	Minseitō	Seiyūkai
Positions						
Transport	—	—	X (1 mo.)	X (1 wk)	—	—
Management	—	—	X (1 mo.)	X (1 wk)	—	—
Facilities	—	—	—	X (1 wk)	—	X (2 wks)
Engineering	—	—	—	X (2 wks)	—	X (2 wks)
Electricity	—	—	X (1 mo.)	X (2 wks)	—	—
Construction	—	—	—	—	—	—
International Tourism*	NA	NA	NA	NA	—	—
Research Center	—	—	—	—	—	—

Notes: An X indicates that the cabinet appointed a new person to the position in question; we indicate in parentheses the amount of time the cabinet waited before making the appointment. We do not record new appointments after lapses of more than two months following the formation of a new cabinet.

* The Hamaguchi cabinet created the International Tourism Bureau.

Source: Compiled on the basis of data found in Ikuhiko Hata, *Senzenki Nihon kanryōsei no seido, soshiki, jinji [The System, Organization, and Personnel of the Pre-war Japanese Bureaucracy]* (Tokyo: Tokyo daigaku shuppan kai, 1981), pp. 384–386.

Table 5.6. *Changes in length of bureaucratic tenure,*
1868–1932

	Percentage turnover			
Periods	1–6 mos.	6–18 mos.	1.5 to 3 yrs.	Over 3 yrs.
I. 1868–1917	15	32	25	28
II. 1918–1931	17	43	30	10

Source: Calculated from data found in Ikuhiko Hata, *Senzenki Nihon kanryōsei no seido, soshiki, jinji [The System, Organization, and Personnel of the Pre-war Japanese Bureaucracy]* (Tokyo: Tokyo daigaku shuppan kai, 1981).

January 29, 1928). To quell the partisan furor that ensued, both Suzuki and Yamaoka resigned their posts (Hosojima 1964: 93; *Tokyo asahi shimbun,* May 4, 1928). Although the episode ended Yamaoka's Home Affairs career, he had earned the respect and trust of the Seiyūkai leaders. Less than a year later, they rewarded him by appointing him to the House of Peers.[14] Taking a few hard knocks from the opposition in the name of political loyalty, by all accounts, had paid off handsomely for Yamaoka.[15]

Next, consider Aoki Tokuzō, a Ministry of Finance (MOF) bureaucrat. Aoki first became involved in politics in 1914, when, as a 30-year-old MOF official, he served as Finance Minister Wakatsuki's secretary (Ōkurashō, ed., 1977: 228, 232).[16] That connection to the Dōshikai – and later to the Kenseikai and Minseitō, as the party changed names – would stay with Aoki throughout his career.[17] Aoki received his next big promotion within the MOF when the Kenseikai once again controlled the cabinet, in 1924. Hamaguchi Osachi, who had served as Wakatsuki's Vice Minister in 1914 and who was now Finance Minister himself, smoothed the way for Aoki's promotion to section chief of the Legislative Affairs Section of the Ministry's Secretariat (*Ōkura daijin kanbō bunsho kachō*) (Endō, Katō, and Takahashi 1964: 137).[18] According to Aoki, it was not unusual for Ministers to become involved in promotion decisions all the way down to the section chief level (Ōkurashō ed., 1977: 252).[19] For a position with as much political importance as the Secretariat's Legislative Affairs Section, the personal interest of the Minister hardly seems remarkable.

Aoki's next big break came in 1929, when his mentor Hamaguchi Osachi headed a Miniseitō cabinet. Aoki was promoted to one of the Ministry's most prestigious jobs, director general of the Tax Bureau, at the early age of forty-six. But that was to be his last job within the Ministry of Finance. When the Seiyūkai took over the cabinet in December 1931, the new government assigned Aoki to be the chief of the Tariff Office in Yokohama. Aoki resigned rather than to accept the demotion. Aoki's political patrons would not return to power, and Aoki spent the rest of his professional life teaching economics (Ōkurashō, 1977: 200).

6. CONCLUSION

In both conceptual and empirical terms, we question the view that bureaucrats dominated pre-war politics. Bureaucrats answered first to the oligarchs, and later to the political parties. So long as they hoped for promotions, they had no choice but to do as their principals demanded. The evidence, both from aggregate personnel data and from biographical reports, confirm this. Bureaucrats did well if their patrons controlled the cabinet, and poorly if anyone else did. The same, we find in Chapter 6, eventually became true for judges. Only military officers (Chapter 7) escaped that fate.

6

The courts: Who monitored whom?

1. INTRODUCTION

On the independence of the imperial Japanese courts, most scholars turn a bit agnostic: The courts were sort of independent, they conclude, and sort of not. Political scientist Chalmers Johnson captures the mood. The Tsuda incident (described at Section 3.1) accomplished "the legitimation of judicial independence in Japan," he writes (1972: 29). But "the judiciary still came under intense pressure to insure that the interests of the state . . . and the interests of justice were never incompatible" (id., 160).

Legal scholars show a similar ambivalence. Kenzo Takayanagi insists that turn-of-the-century judges "scrupulously guarded their independence" (1964: 10), but suggests that the "rule *of* law" never took hold before the war (id., 14). Hiroshi Oda (1993: 65–66) argues that "the independence of the court was guaranteed to a certain extent," but concludes that "the Ministry of Justice was in charge of the overall administration of the courts."[1]

By contrast, on the probability of judicial independence in the abstract, most scholars are more positive. Some suggest, for example, that rational politicians will keep courts independent so that they can credibly promise contributors rent-extracting statutes (Landes and Posner, 1975). Others suggest politicians will keep courts independent so that they can use them to monitor their bureaucrats (McCubbins and Schwartz, 1984). Even to autocrats, some scholars champion judicial independence. Without independent courts, they explain, autocrats will be unable to make any promises they give credible.[2]

Because of the regime changes that occurred between 1868 and 1945, Japan potentially tests two hypotheses: (a) that democratic governments will likely offer independent judges, and (b) that autocrats will likely offer them. Ultimately, it contradicts both: Neither democratic nor autocratic governments maintained independent courts in imperial Japan. At the

74

outset, we outline the institutional structure of the courts (Section 2). We then study how nineteeth-century oligarchs treated the judiciary (Section 3), and how the later elected politicians treated it (Section 4). We conclude by proposing an alternative postitive theory of judicial independence (Section 5), and explain why politicians treated judges somewhat differently than they treated bureaucrats (Section 6).

2. THE INSTITUTIONAL STRUCTURE

2.1. *The pre-constitutional equilibrium*

Even before their 1889 Constitution, the oligarchs took a few steps ostensibly to insulate the courts from themselves. At least partially, these measures resembled those they took to insulate the bureaucracy (Chapter 5). In 1886, for instance, they issued an Imperial Order that prevented them from firing judges at will. Absent a criminal or disciplinary trial, they could no longer discharge or punish a judge.[3]

As insulation, it was tenuous at best. New Imperial Orders trumped old, and no rule prevented the oligarchs from revoking the 1886 order and firing a judge. Provided they could cooperate with each other enough to obtain a new Imperial Order, they still could constrain judges as they pleased.

Nonetheless, to conclude that the revocable 1886 order did not matter would miss the problem that the oligarchs together faced: Collectively, they gained by sharing power with each other; individually, they gained by cheating on each other. Consequently, they needed to protect themselves from each other as much as from any politicians. To prevent each other from trying to manipulate the courts in these fratricidal disputes, they passed the 1886 Imperial Order. So long as no oligarch could change an Imperial Order alone, even a revocable order added stability.[4] Even a revocable order, therefore, might protect them from each other.

2.2. *The constitutional equilibrium*

The 1889 Constitution helped stabilize this initial equilibrium. In it, the oligarchs included a clause much like the one they had included in the 1886 order: "No judge shall be dismissed from work except through a criminal conviction or disciplinary disposition."[5] Because they retained the fiction that the Emperor issued Imperial Orders, they had never fully specified the rules for issuing them (Chapter 3, Section 4). Never having specified them, under the 1886 order they never could ensure that their rivals would not collectively use Imperial Orders to stack the courts against them. Harder to amend, the Constitution more fully protected them from such ploys.[6]

Through the 1890 Judicial Organization Act,[7] the oligarchs specified the detail to this constitutional mandate. They placed judges squarely within the Ministry of Justice,[8] and gave the Minister some disciplinary power over them (though less than Ministers had over ordinary bureaucrats). If judges misbehaved egregiously, for example, the Minister could bring disciplinary charges before panels of either the High Court (the intermediate appellate court) or the Supreme Court. He could then obtain penalties ranging from pay cuts to impeachment.[9]

Nonetheless, the oligarchs did seem to insulate judges from political control in several ways. First, by failing to specify a mandatory retirement age, they effectively gave judges life tenure.[10] Second, they prohibited anyone from transferring a judge against his will or forcing him to retire (Act, §73). Crucially, though, they added a proviso: "this rule shall not apply when a judge has been transferred in order to fill a vacancy" (id.; for its application, see Section 3.3). Last, they let the Minister of Justice order a judge to retire only if the judge no longer could do his work and the en banc High Court or Supreme Court approved (Act, §74). They let him independently place a judge on inactive status at half pay, however, if he had no post for the judge (Act, §75).

The oligarchs did not extend these protections to prosecutors. Rather, they treated prosecutors much the way they treated other bureaucrats.[11] Under the Judicial Organization Act, the Minister of Justice could force prosecutors to follow orders (§82). Although he could not fire a prosecutor without a disciplinary hearing (§80), he could transfer him or order him to retire. If fired, the prosecutor lost his pension. If retired, he kept it.[12] In either case, he lost his job.

This institutional framework made it harder than otherwise for the oligarchs to manipulate the judiciary. Several decades later, it would also make it harder for the politicians who followed them. Notwithstanding that difficulty, the oligarchs soon decided (collectively) to override this framework. Several decades later, the politicians did the same.

3. OLIGARCHIC MANIPULATION

3.1. Kojima and the oligarchs[13]

The oligarchs tried to manipulate their judges barely a year after promulgating the Judicial Organization Act. The soon-to-be-Czar Nicholas II had come to East Asia to break ground for the Trans-Siberian Railway, and decided to visit Japan. It was not a prudent move. While returning to Kyoto after a sightseeing trip in May 1891, he chanced upon a small-town policeman named Tsuda Sanzō. Tsuda concluded that he came as a spy and, in a fit of imperial zeal, turned and stabbed him.

All this greatly worried the Russians, and in worrying the Russians greatly complicated Japanese diplomacy. To satisfy the Russians, the oligarchs wanted Tsuda executed. Unfortunately for them, Kojima Iken was Supreme Court Chief Justice. He reminded them that the law provided the death penalty for murder and attempted regicide, but not for attempted murder.[14] As badly slashed as he was, Nicholas did not die. As impeccably royal as he was, he was not Japanese, and the rules for regicide applied, Kojima insisted, only to the Japanese imperial family. Within the courts, what Kojima said seemed to govern. According to the standard histories, Kojima used the occasion to save Tsuda and teach Japan the "principle of judicial independence" (for example, Takayanagi, 1964: 9–10; Saitō, 1985: 307).

Would that it were so simple. Oligarch Yamagata Aritomo became Minister of Justice in 1892. Although court structure prevented him from firing Kojima outright, he soon looked for other means. It seems Kojima and several of his fellow justices patronized the geisha quarters. Because the law licensed prostitution, they could legally have hired prostitutes (Ramseyer, 1991). Because it allowed mistresses, they could legally have kept as many young women as they wanted. Because it permitted debauchery, they could legally have been almost as lewd as they pleased.

Like many American Supreme Court justices, however, Kojima and his colleagues played cards. Because gambling was illegal,[15] Yamagata's prosecutors could apparently now impeach them. They tried, and brought fourteen of the geisha to testify. But their own move was worse than a crime, as Talleyrand would have had it. It was a blunder, for the law required them to impeach the gambling justices before their peers. As the other justices now sided with their colleagues, the prosecutors lost. They did not prove, the justices explained, that the justices had bet money on the cards. By appearances, Kojima had beaten Yamagata. He had preserved his right to stay in office. And within a few days he resigned.[16]

The puzzle is why Kojima quit. He was no fool, and he liked his job. Presumably he calculated that if he tried to stay, Yamagata would find a way either to oust him or to make judicial life miserable. Presumably, too, he could accurately assess what Yamagata wanted and what he could do. Although the former is obvious enough a century later, the latter is not. Alone, the case simply does not disclose what Kojima thought Yamagata could have done. What happened during the rest of the 1890s, however, does. To clarify the tactics that Yamagata and the other oligarchs could employ, we turn to several other conflicts of the 1890s.

3.2. Chiya and the oligarchs[17]

By January 1894, fifty-four-year-old Chiya Toshinori had been on the Supreme Court for a little over a year. Suddenly, the Ministry of Justice transferred him to an Okinawan district court.[18] By most Japanese indices of status, it was a move from the top of the system to very nearly the bottom. Instead of taking the transfer, he refused. To Minister of Justice Yoshikawa Akimasa, he explained that the Judicial Organization Act entitled him to refuse. To Chiya, Yoshikawa replied that the Act gave Chiya no such right, provided he transferred Chiya to fill a vacancy. Because he had just moved an Okinawan judge,[19] he needed Chiya for Okinawa.

When Chiya stayed in Tokyo, the oligarchs impeached him for ignoring his Okinawan duties. Rather than repeat the embarrassment of losing an impeachment trial, they counted heads. When they found a supporter of Chiya's on the panel, they fired him.[20] For all their care, however, they never learned whether they had counted correctly. Chiya died in September 1894, and the issue became moot.

3.3. Bessho and the oligarchs[21]

It was not moot for long. Another two years later, the oligarchs faced the very quandary Chiya's death had conveniently resolved. In May 1896, the Ministry of Justice transferred district judge Bessho Wakatsu to another district court. A friend of Chiya's, Bessho refused. When he did not appear at his new post, the Ministry impeached him. Unlike Chiya, Bessho stayed alive until the end of the proceedings to hear the results: He won. The oligarchs had blundered again. At issue was the priviso (see Section 2.2) to Section 73 of the Judicial Organization Act. According to the court, the clause let the Minister of Justice transfer a judge against his will only if no appropriate candidate volunteered for the job. Until he had solicited volunteers, he could not make Bessho move.

That Bessho won was not the only bizarre twist. Like Kojima, like Bessho: having won, he promptly quit. Having had his Warhollian fifteen minutes of fame, he disappeared. Decades later, his hometown newspaper would carry an advertisement from an "Attorney, Bessho Wakatsu." By then, he had joined one Yamanashi "Trust" Company. "No money up front. All cases taken on contingency fee," the copy proclaimed. "Background investigations, and preparations for criminal and civil litigation" were all fair game. Clients could even ask the firm for credit investigations.[22] Quite why he quit the courts, he never said.

3.4. Why the oligarchs fired judges

To see why Kojima and Bessho resigned, ask first what the oligarchs hoped to do. Kojima, Chiya, and Bessho were not the only judges they tried to oust during the 1890s. Instead, they were conducting a wholesale sweep. Take Table 6.1 – the number of judges ordered to retire during 1893–94 and 1898–99. During the nineteen months from July to March 1893–1894 and August to May 1898–1899, the oligarchs ousted 158 judges.[23]

Granted, motive is always hard to show and non-political motives seem particularly ingenuous here – yet by all odds the oligarchs sacked most of these judges (Kojima aside) for "technical" reasons. Legal technique mattered importantly since (then as now) the vast majority of cases involved no politically controversial issues. Instead, they concerned mundane "technical" issues like mortgages and accidents. In this context, the early judges posed a problem for the oligarchs. The oligarchs had appointed them in the stormy first years after their coup.[24] The universities being what they were, these early judges could not have found a legal education even had they looked.[25] As a result, many of them lacked any formal legal training.[26]

By the late 1890s, two important changes had occurred. First, the Diet

Table 6.1. *Forced judicial retirements*

	Jan.	Feb.	Mar.	Apr.	May	June	July	Aug.	Sept.	Oct.	Nov.	Dec.
1893	1	1	3	0	0	0	8	5	14	7	12	4
1894	4	3	4	2	2	0	1	0	0	1	1	1
1898	1	1	4	3	2	4	1	4	5	10	13	25
1899	17	6	6	4	7	3	2	1	2	5	3	4

Notes: The following served as Prime Minister during these years: Itō (August 8, 1892 through September 18, 1896); Matsukata (September 18, 1896 through January 12, 1897); Itō (January 12, 1897 through June 30, 1898); Ōkuma (June 30, 1898 through November 8, 1898); Yamagata (November 8, 1899 through October 19, 1900). In addition to the 133 judges ordered to retire during 1898 and 1899, 23 judges were placed on inactive status.

"Forced retirements" refers to judges officially ordered to retire – those for whom the notice "taishoku wo meizu" ("ordered to retire") appears in the official government gazette, the *Kanpō*.

Source: Seiichirō Kusunoki, *Meiji rikken sei to shihō kan [The Meiji Constitution and Judicial Officers]* (Tokyo: Keiō tsūshin K.K., 1989), pp. 72, 265.

had passed an avalanche of complex and mostly Western-inspired legislation: the Civil Code, the Commercial Code, the Code of Civil Procedure, and the Code of Criminal Procedure, for example.[27] Like the Internal Revenue Code, these were complicated documents beyond the grasp of the self-taught. Second, the universities had begun to offer a sophisticated legal education. If the oligarchs could fire the older judges, they now could replace them with university-trained men. Unlike their earlier hires, these new judges would both know the new codes and come with elaborate comparative law training. Not only could they work through the Japanese statutes, they could handle Western commentaries as well.

3.5. How the oligarchs fired judges

Such was why the oligarchs eliminated so many judges. Consider how they did so. Recall that the Constitution and Judicial Organization Act prevented the Minister of Justice from firing judges at will. If he ordered a judge to retire (or even moved him to an obscure provincial court), the judge could properly refuse. To force a judge to retire, he instead had to submit the matter to the High Court or Supreme Court. Notwithstanding, for most of the "forced retirements" in Table 6.1, he obtained no such clearance. Yet the judges dutifully quit (Kusunoki, 1989: 73). The puzzle is how he induced them not to contest his contestable order.

The Minister of Justice simply bribed many judges. He did so by promoting them to a prestigious court at high pay, in exchange for their agreeing to retire quietly thereafter. In doing so, he not only gave them the face-saving chance to resign from a high court. He also hiked their pensions. Under the rules in effect, a judge's pension depended on his total years of service and his *final* pay. Suppose he earned a high salary for a day; he then earned a highly paid judge's pension for the rest of his life.[28]

The Minister of Justice bribed judges with high pensions on a wide scale. Even the Supreme Court was fair game. During the last months of 1898 and early months of 1899, he appointed fifteen judges to the twenty-nine-member Supreme Court. They served terms of one day to three weeks each.[29] At stake was a deal – the Minister agreed to name them to the Court; they agreed to quit. Because the judges who quit under these agreements resigned "voluntarily," many may not even appear in Table 6.1 among the judges forcibly retired. In essence, the oligarchs may have intervened in the judiciary more substantially than the table shows.

With more recalcitrant judges, the oligarchs needed a way to act more forcefully. Assume they ordered a judge to retire, and he refused. They had two choices. If they could convince the full High or Supreme Court that he could no longer do his work, they could force him to retire.[30] If they could prove he had violated the duties of his office, was derelict in his work, or had betrayed the trust of his office, they could impeach him.[31]

In all these proceedings, the oligarchs might win but they also might lose. Effectively they had created a system that seemed to pose real barriers to their attempts to control the judiciary. Had the barriers been a matter only of Imperial Orders (as in 1886), they might collectively have dismantled them. After the Constitution, matters seemed harder.

In fact, the right Imperial Order still worked wonders. By controlling the orders, the oligarchs controlled the game. In 1898 they made sure the judges knew it. That year, they began their judicial house-cleaning with a minor trick that clarified just how they controlled it. Through an Imperial Order, they canceled the size specifications of the various courts.[32] Where an earlier Imperial Order had specified how big the different courts would be, in their new Order they specified only the total number of all judges. In effect, they could now pack the High and Supreme Courts largely as they pleased. If a judge refused to retire, they would submit the issue to the relevant court. Before it voted, though, they could now name as many loyalists as they needed to that court. After the Kojima and Bessho fiascoes, they made clear to everyone that they were taking no chances.

3.6. Politicians and judicial independence

In June 1898 and squarely in the middle of this battle, the most powerful oligarchs named their chief rival Ōkuma Prime Minister (see Chapter 4). Ōkuma had few qualms about firing the older informally trained judges (Kusunoki, 1989: ch. 5). He had aggressively appointed his friends to the other bureaucracies (Chapter 5), and in firing these judges he simply created more posts for more friends.[33]

Curiously, Ōkuma also fired the chief architect of these judicial reforms, Yokota Kuniomi. Born in 1850, by 1896 Yokota had climbed to the top of the judicial bureaucracy and become Administrative Vice Minister of Justice. Before leaving the Prime Ministership in June 1898, Itō had now named him chief national prosecutor. By October, Ōkuma had fired him.[34] Nominally he fired him for insulting the new Minister of Justice. Although the real reason was nothing of the sort, it also had nothing to do with any hostility toward Yokota's personnel policies. Instead, it concerned political debts. One of the judges Yokota fired had been an old friend of Ōkuma's and a founding member of his political party (Kusunoki, 1989: 188). Philosophy is one thing, patronage another. When his friend complained, Ōkuma sacked Yokota.

The strongest evidence of Ōkuma's support for the judicial "reforms" is Table 6.1 itself: Itō began the "reforms"; Ōkuma continued them.[35]

Other evidence confirms this support. The Minister of Justice whom Yokota allegedly insulted wrote to Ōkuma supporting the personnel reforms. Even Ōkuma's party newspaper backed the reforms (Kusunoki, 1989: 182–95). And Yokota himself recovered handily. By the next April he had been reappointed as chief prosecutor for the Tokyo High Court. By 1906 he was Supreme Court Chief Justice.

4. POLITICAL MANIPULATION

4.1. The oligarchic bequest

Such was the legacy the oligarchs left the professional politicians. It was a legacy that complicated any efforts to manipulate the courts, for the institutional constraints that the oligarchs had installed seemed formally to protect the judges from the party politicians. Yet the politicians had several reasons to want to control the courts. Most obviously, they did not want to entrust policy disputes to men who shared the political preferences of the turn-of-the-century oligarchs.

Less obviously, the politicians could use loyal judges to help them win elections. Granted, judges mattered less than police officers. By controlling the officers, politicians could aggressively harass their competitors. This (as noted in Chapter 5) they freely did. Five days before the 1928 general election, Tanaka Giichi's Seiyūkai government had already induced police officers to file electoral law charges against 638 people. Most were Minseitō and proletarian party supporters (*Tokyo Asahi Shimbun*, Feb. 15, 1928). "The police only reported the actions of the parties out of power," Seiyūkai leader Hara had noted a decade earlier. They largely "left the government party alone to do as it pleased" (Hara, 1965: IV-93, entry of March 28, 1915). Despite the importance of the police, however, prosecutors and judges also mattered. Loyal prosecutors mattered because they would prosecute the right suspects. Loyal judges mattered because they would convict them.

4.2. Pre-Inukai

Nevertheless, judicial personnel records show relatively few obvious traces of political involvement during the 1920s. Consider Tables 6.2 through 6.4. Only Prime Ministers Tanaka and Inukai replaced the Administrative Vice Minister of Justice, and only they replaced the Supreme Court Chief Justice (Table 6.2). No Prime Minister replaced either the Civil Bureau Chief or the Chief Prosecutor. None of the three Prime Ministers preceding Inukai who replaced a Prime Minister of a different

Table 6.2. *Major personnel changes in the Ministry of Justice*

A. *Major posts (months from cabinet change to personnel change, if within one year)*

	Katō 8/2/25	Tanaka 4/20/27	Hamaguchi 7/2/29	Inukai 12/13/31
Administrative Vice Minister		1		1
Political Vice Minister	1	1	1	1
Chief, Criminal Bureau	1			
Chief, Civil Bureau				
Chief Prosecutor, Supreme Court				
Assistant Prosecutor, Supreme Court		1		
Chief Justice, Supreme Court		4		1

B. *Subsidiary posts (number of reassignments within two months, followed by number of additional reassignments during subsequent ten months)*[*]

	Katō 8/2/25	Tanaka 4/20/27	Hamaguchi 7/2/29	Inukai 12/13/31
Chief Prosecutor, High Court (7 posts)	0,0	0,4	3,1	2,0
Chief Prosecutor, District Court (51 posts)	1,16	3,17	1,9	12,12
Section Chief, Supreme Court (8 posts)	0,0	0,1	0,0	0,1
Chief Judge, High Court (7 posts)	1,0	0,1	0,0	1,0
Chief Judge, District Court (51 posts)	3,19	0,14	3,12	2,14

Notes: Party affiliations of cabinets involved – Katō (Kenseikai); Tanaka (Seiyūkai); Hamaguchi (Minseitō); Inukai (Seiyūkai). Wakatsuki cabinets are omitted because they followed cabinets of the same party.
* Calculations end upon assassination of Inukai in May 1932.
Sources: Calculated on the basis of data found in Ikuhiko Hata, *Senzenki Nihon kanryosei no seido, soshiki, jinji [The System, Organization, and Personnel of the Pre-War Japanese Bureaucracy]* (Tokyo: Tokyo daigaku shuppan kai, 1981), pp. 359–65; Shihō shō (ed.), *Shihō enkakushi [A Documentary History of the Judiciary]* (Tokyo: Hōsō kai, 1939, repub'd 1960), pp. 557–836.

party appointed many supporters either to the top (the Supreme Court) or to the bottom of the hierarchy (forced retirement) (Tables 6.3 and 6.4).[36] Politicians intent on intervening in the courts might have replaced disloyal Supreme Court justices during their first months in office with

Table 6.3. *Judicial reassignments*

A. *Number of judges assigned to the Supreme Court during the four months preceding and following cabinet changes*

	Before	After
Katō (8/2/25):	5	3
Tanaka (4/20/27):	1	2
Hamaguchi (7/2/29):	0	2
Inukai (12/13/31):	3	13

B. *Number of judges forceably retired during the four months preceding and following cabinet changes:*

	Before	After
Katō (8/2/25):	16	8
Tanaka (4/20/27):	13	15
Hamaguchi (7/2/29):	9	10
Inukai (12/13/31):	7	29

Notes: "Forced retirement" refers to judges officially ordered to retire – those for whom the notice "taishoku wo meizu" appeared in the official government gazette, the *Kanpō*. Wakatsuki cabinets are omitted because they follow a cabinet of the same party.
Source: Compiled from the daily government gazette, *Kanpo [Government Gazette]* (Tokyo: Naikaku insatsu kyoku, various issues).

their friends. Katō seems not to have done so.[37] If Tanaka and Hamaguchi did, it barely shows.

Nonetheless, these tables probably understate the extent Seiyūkai politicians manipulated the courts.[38] Back in 1913, the Seiyūkai controlled both the cabinet and the Diet. That April it set out to remake the courts, apparently in its own image. To ease its job, it first amended the Judicial Organization Act.[39] Under the revised Act, the Minister of Justice could now transfer judges by a simple majority vote in either the High Court or Supreme Court. Through a similar vote, he could place as many 232 judges and prosecutors on inactive status. From April to June, he retired 98 judges and prosecutors, placed 131 on inactive status, and transferred 443 (Nomura, 1966: III-382).

When the Seiyūkai regained the Diet and Cabinet several years later, it instituted mandatory judicial retirement.[40] By doing so, it automatically

Table 6.4. *Prosecutorial reassignments*

A. *Number of prosecutors assigned to the Supreme Court during the four months preceding and following cabinet changes*

	Before	After
Katō (8/2/25):	2	3
Tanaka (4/20/27):	4	6
Hamaguchi (7/2/29):	0	1
Inukai (12/13/31):	7	16

B. *Number of prosecutors forceably retired during the four months preceding and following cabinet changes*

	Before	After
Katō (8/2/25):	6	5
Tanaka (4/20/27):	2	4
Hamaguchi (7/2/29):	6	3
Inukai (12/13/31):	1	21

Notes: "Forced retirement" refers to prosecutors officially ordered to retire – those for whom the notice "taishoku wo meizu" appeared in the official government gazette, the *Kanpō*. Wakatsuki cabinets are omitted because they follow a cabinet of the same party. The pre-Tanaka Supreme Court appointments were last-minute appointments made within four days of the new cabinet. *Source:* Compiled from the daily government gazette, *Kanpō [Government Gazette]* (Tokyo: Naikaku insatsu kyoku, various issues).

purged the oldest judges and created new vacancies for its loyalists. Through the reforms, Yokota Kuniomi – architect of the 1890s sweep and longtime Supreme Court Chief Justice – finally lost office. In the process, he symbolized the Act's impact: It purged the men appointed by the oligarchs, and let the Seiyūkai install its own.

During the dozen years after 1913, the Seiyūkai controlled the cabinet only about half of the time. Although the remaining years might have given the Kenseikai time to appoint its own sympathizers to the Ministry, it did not do so. During almost half its term, maverick Ozaki Yukio headed the Ministry (April 1914 – October 1916). Ozaki had little interest in personnel issues,[41] and soon quarreled with the party leaders anyway. Kiyoura was a non-party Prime Minister for a time, but even he appointed a Seiyūkai bureaucrat Minister of Justice.

Given this history, the Seiyūkai apparently dominated the courts without the sort of tactics that appear in Tables 6.2 through 6.4. Consider the career of one Justice Ministry bureaucrat, Yamaoka Mannosuke.[42] Upon finishing college in 1899, Yamaoka worked as a prosecutor's apprentice and then as a Tokyo judge. After a stint in Germany, he returned to Japan in 1910 as a prosecutor. By 1914 he had endeared himself to a Seiyūkai-affiliated senior bureaucrat. With his patronage, he moved into a series of important posts, and by 1925 headed the Criminal Bureau. Then, under a Kenseikai cabinet, the Minister of Justice summarily placed him on inactive status.[43] Legal commentators complained that politicians were politicizing the judiciary, but Yamaoka himself was graceful to a T[44]:

I do think I've been impartial, . . . but if you look at the Ministry of Justice from the Kenseikai's perspective, you'll see it's just about completely packed with Seiyūkai people. It's true that Mr. Ozaki was Minister of Justice for a while under the [1914] Ōkuma Cabinet, but he stayed almost totally aloof from these things. As a result, there's hardly any trace of the Kenseikai there.

4.3. Inukai

Whatever modest independence the judiciary had in the 1920s, it apparently lost completely when Inukai became Seiyūkai Prime Minister in 1931. Inukai dominated the judges and prosecutors outright.[45] Even before he took office, some observers predicted he would make massive changes (*Hōritsu shimbun*, 3352: 17 (1931)). He did indeed. Within four months of taking office on December 13, 1931, he appointed thirteen justices to the twenty-nine-member Supreme Court and fired twenty-nine judges (Tables 6.3 and 6.4). A day later (on April 14, 1932), he announced yet another massive series of personnel changes. The legal press called it "The Great Judicial Office Shuffle." In one day he transferred 213 judges and prosecutors (*Hōritsu shimbun*, 3396: 19 (1932)).

Inukai even more forcefully manipulated the prosecutors. Prosecutors enjoyed less institutional independence, and probably could more directly help politicians harass their competitors. As a result, within two months of taking office, Inukai named almost a quarter of the district court chief prosecutors. By the time he was assassinated some three months later, he had appointed nearly half the prosecutors (Table 6.2). The Supreme Court had posts for only thirteen prosecutors. Never mind, for within four months Inukai appointed sixteen men to the job (Table 6.4). Although he fired twenty-nine judges and twenty-one prosecutors, the comparison is misleading, for there were twice as many judicial posts as prosecutorial posts (Shihō shō, 1939: 563). Effectively, he had fired nearly double the percentage of prosecutors. Whatever independence judges and prosecutors may have had in the 1920s, they lost it by 1931.

5. A POSITIVE THEORY OF JUDICIAL INDEPENDENCE

This lack of an independent judiciary in Imperial Japan is less puzzling than it might appear, for the case for independent judiciaries is less compelling than we usually suppose. Granted, independent courts do deliver many of the advantages we commonly note. Yet they also interfere with the delivery of policies. They make it hard both for oligarchs to deliver the policies they want and for elected politicians to deliver the policies voters want.

To explore when politicians might find judicial independence advantageous, take two political coalitions, S and M. Although S is in power now, it expects to lose power periodically in the future. Although M is out of power, it expects to gain power periodically. In this situation, S and M may rationally adopt what amount to cooperative strategies in an indefinitely repeated game: Both parties will agree not to manipulate the courts to their partisan advantage (that is, will agree to keep courts independent) while in power.

In this world, notwithstanding any short-term advantage to monitoring courts, both S and M may find it profitable to keep courts independent. The reason derives from the way each coalition may rationally expect the other to reciprocate. If both coalitions expect that (a) their returns while out of office from this hands-off-the-courts strategy (the reduction in the losses they would otherwise suffer when out of office) will have a present value greater than (b) their returns to manipulating courts while in office, then both coalitions will have an incentive to keep the courts independent. Both will less effectively implement their policies while in office, but both will protect themselves against large losses while out of office.

If all this be true, then whether any coalition of rational voters will want independent courts will depend on whether it expects to alternate in power with other coalitions. Consider three possibilities.

I. S is in power but expects to alternate in power with M indefinitely. For reasons just explained, S may rationally decide to keep judges independent.

II. S is in power and expects to stay in power indefinitely. S may manipulate the courts. S earns a return from a hands-off-the-courts strategy only if it expects to be out of power periodically. If it does not expect to lose power, it has less incentive not to monitor and discipline its judges.

III. S is in power but expects soon to lose power indefinitely. Necessarily, M is about to take its place indefinitely. Since M (given the logic in (II)) may not find independent courts advantageous, S may expect M to manipulate the courts. Expecting M to manipulate them soon, S may find it advantageous anticipatorily to manipulate them itself.

The politics of oligarchy

In Imperial Japan, this dynamic applied both to the politicians and to the oligarchs. Take the politicians in 1931. By then, they knew that the military might soon usurp control. They may not have known quite when or how, but they knew it would likely take power soon. Because they expected to lose power permanently, they manipulated the courts (logic (III)).

Or take the oligarchs of the 1890s. They expected (incorrectly) that they and their designated heirs would remain in power for many decades. Granted they set in motion a process by which power devolved to the politicians – but they did so only against their collective better judgment, as they each cheated on their collective cartel. They may have planned to let politicians occasionally form cabinets, but at least initially they expected to keep the basic control to themselves. By the 1890s, they decided to replace some of their earlier hires – sometimes to replace the intransigent judges (for example, Kojima), sometimes to obtain better trained judges. Because they expected to stay in power indefinitely, toward these ends they manipulated the courts (logic (II)).

6. JUDGES AND BUREAUCRATS

By its own terms, this analysis applies to bureaucrats as much as to judges. The question is therefore why politicians began to manipulate some bureaucracies by the 1920s (Chapter 5) but may have waited to manipulate the courts until 1931.[47] Why, once politicians decided to constrain their agents, might they have chosen to constrain their bureaucrats before constraining their judges? Two answers suggest themselves.

First, the politicians faced stricter institutional constraints on how they could control judges. As noted earlier, the oligarchs had established a system that made it harder for political principals to interfere in the courts than in the bureaucracy.[48] Accordingly, party politicians found it cheaper to manipulate bureaucrats than to manipulate judges.

Second, the politicians earned lower returns from controlling judges. Recall from Chapter 5 that politicians did not treat all bureaucrats equally. The Ministry of Home Affairs they controlled tightly because of its electoral role. Ministries without electoral significance they largely left alone. Although not electorally irrelevant (see Section 4.1), the courts lacked direct electoral connections. Once politicians began to adopt endgame tactics, they attacked the electorally most important institutions (like the Home Ministry) first. The courts they turned to next.

7. CONCLUSION

The autocrats who ran Japan in the 1890s controlled the courts tightly. By 1931, the politicians who followed them did the same. The reason is simple: Rational government leaders are most likely to maintain independent courts when they expect to alternate in power indefinitely with others. If they expect to stay in power permanently, they may control the courts from the start. If they expect to lose power permanently, they may control the courts while they have the chance.

So too in Japan. The oligarchs apparently controlled the courts by making clear how they could manipulate judges – and thereby inducing judges to avoid decisions that would tempt the oligarchs to intervene. By 1931, the politicians apparently controlled the courts the way they controlled key ministries – by replacing people as soon as they obtained the cabinet. The autocrats controlled the courts because they expected to stay in office. The politicians controlled them because they expected to lose office. Because neither group expected to alternate in power with anyone else, neither group found independent courts advantageous.

7

The military: Master of its own fate

1. INTRODUCTION

For their civil bureaucracy and courts, the Imperial Japanese oligarchs built an institutional framework that let cabinet ministers monitor and control the men they hired (Chapters 5 and 6). Bureaucrats and judges thus answered to the cabinet. During the first Meiji decades, the oligarchs jockeyed to control that cabinet. During the 1920s, the professional politicians did the same.

For their military, the oligarchs built a radically different framework. They – but primarily Yamagata Aritomo – instead built an institutional framework that gave power to those (1) who retained access to the Emperor, and (2) who cultivated particularistic ties of loyalty within the military. Consider the detail. First, the Emperor maintained formal control over the military. As a result, to shape basic military contours, one needed to be able to manipulate the Emperor. This favored Yamagata and most of his fellow oligarchs over the politicians; it did not favor Yamagata over many of his oligarchic competitors.

Second, military leaders could bypass the cabinet in drafting regulations, in making operational command decisions, and in picking their ministers. Effectively this meant that a place in the cabinet did not give a man control over the military. Instead, to control it he needed personal ties within it. This favored Yamagata over most of his fellow oligarchs, for Yamagata had purged his opponents from the Army and stacked it with loyal men. As long as he lived, the Army was independent in theory, but not in fact. Rather, it did as he said.

In this chapter we explain why the Meiji oligarchs chose these institutions. We first outline their early struggles for control (Section 2), and detail the framework that they established (Section 3). We then turn to data from personnel records to investigate whether the professional politicians could manipulate military careers (Section 4). We conclude by

90

studying the influence the military had over political fortunes (Section 5) and by summarizing the strategic calculations that the oligarchs made (Section 6).

2. EARLY CONFLICTS

By the time of the Emperor Meiji's death in 1912, Yamagata dominated the Japanese Army. During the early Meiji years he had controlled it directly; during the later years he controlled it through the men he had installed within it. In crucial ways, therefore, the internal history of the Japanese Army is a biography of Yamagata Aritomo.

Yamagata needed the Army because he could not compete with his oligarchic competitors on their terms. Where men like Itō Hirobumi and Ōkuma Shigenobu could improve their own position within the oligarchic cartel by charming the politically dispossessed (Chapter 2), Yamagata had no charm. To maintain his position, he needed somehow to prove that he could profitably refuse to cooperate with his oligarchic competitors. He could not do that by holding political rallies. Instead, he did it by maintaining his personal control over the Army.

Yamagata had not always had that control. In the first years of the new regime, several oligarchs had maintained rival factions within the Army. Yamagata's strongest competitor was one Saigō Takamori. Saigō had helped build the Army from the start, and had assembled a loyal following within it. By some measures, he had amassed more power than even Yamagata himself (Matsushita, 1963a: 178–79; 1967: I-76).

Yamagata's chance to oust Saigō came early. In 1873, Saigō urged his fellow oligarchs to invade Korea (see Chapter 2). They refused. Perhaps to fortify his personal following, perhaps to sulk, Saigō retreated to his home province. There, through a network of private military schools, he built a formidable military machine. Correctly sensing a threat to their reign, the oligarchs triggered a civil war in 1877. In the end, 18,000 of Saigō's followers were killed or wounded, and Saigō himself died in battle. The oligarchs then had another 22 men executed, and over 1,000 more imprisoned. When it was all over, Saigō and many of his key lieutenants were dead.[1]

Through this war, Yamagata consolidated his strength. Granted, some raw numbers show only a modest advance. In 1875, for example, five Army officers with the rank of major general or higher had been from Yamagata's home province, and one was a lieutenant general or higher; from Saigō's province eight officers had at least the rank of major general, three were at least lieutenant generals, and Saigō himself out-ranked Yamagata. By 1879, Yamagata seemed to have made only modest progress. Seven officers from Saigō's province were still at least major gener-

91

als, and four were lieutenant generals; six from Yamagata's province were now at least major generals and four were at least lieutenant generals. These numbers understate Yamagata's progress, however, for within two more years, two of the remaining seven rival generals died, and one left for Hokkaidō.[2] Increasingly, the Army was Yamagata's own.

When new rivals challenged him, Yamagata purged them from the Army. In 1881, for instance, four powerful generals directly complained to the Emperor about an Army scandal (discussed in Chapter 2). It seems Army General Kuroda Kiyotaka had urged the government to sell facilities in Hokkaidō to others from his home province at bargain-basement prices. When the four generals disclosed the detail, many in the public were outraged. Although not personally implicated, Yamagata was outraged too – though for different reasons. The four generals had badly embarrassed the new regime by going over his head. He now ensured they lost their Army careeers. He removed two of them from active Army service immediately, and by 1888 had removed the rest. Even officers under their command found themselves demoted (Matsushita, 1967: I-108–25).

By the turn of the century, Yamagata's control over the Army was largely complete. For several years after Saigō Takamori's death, oligarchs Ōyama Iwao and Saigō Takamori's younger brother Tsugumichi had continued to compete with him for that control. From 1885 to 1896, Ōyama did serve as Army Minister in each of the six Cabinets.[3] Matters, though, soon changed. From 1898 to 1911, only Yamagata proteges held the post, and they dominated the post again in the 1920s.[4]

3. THE YAMAGATA REFORMS

3.1. Independent command

At the same time that he increased his personal control over the military, Yamagata institutionalized its independence from other political leaders. Toward that end, in 1878 he divided the military hierarchy into administrative and command units, and kept only the administrative functions under the cabinet.[5] Henceforth the military command could avoid the cabinet entirely.[6]

The man who detailed this new organization was one Katsura Tarō, a young Yamagata protege.[7] Under his new system, Katsura placed the Army administration (*gunsei*) in the Ministry of the Army (what would become the *rikugun shō*).[8] He placed the command (*gunrei*) under the Emperor in the Army General Staff (the *sanbō honbu*). On matters of administration, the Army brass would report to the Army Minister, who in turn would report to the Prime Minister.[9] On matters of command, they would report directly to his majesty. And as the first Army Chief of Staff (*sanbō sōchō*), Yamagata appointed himself (Nihon kindai, 1971: 142). The 1885 cabinet reforms continued this bifurcated system,[10] the 1889 Constitution seemed to enshrine it,[11] and the system itself lasted through the Second World War.

Quite what constituted command and what administration was something no one ever clarified. At the least, command included matters of military strategy and troop deployment. At the least, administration included questions of staffing and weapons procurement. As the line remained vague, Army leaders increasingly interpreted command broadly and administration narrowly.[12]

3.2. Active-duty requirement

In 1900, Yamagata strengthened his position further: He obtained Imperial Orders requiring that all Army and Navy Ministers and Vice Ministers be active-duty officers.[13] Effectively these orders often let him veto the Army's ministerial appointments.[14] If an officer were on active duty, he could accept a ministerial appointment only at the sufferance of the Army's personnel office. Through his control over the Army, Yamagata could now personally decide who would be the new Army Minister.

In fact, the 1900 Imperial Orders gave Yamagata much more: Potentially they let him and the other senior Army officers veto all cabinet decisions. Suppose, for example, that senior Army leaders objected to a given government policy. The Army Minister could resign, and the personnel office could refuse to appoint another officer to the post. The Prime Minister would be unable to field a cabinet, and under prevailing practice would have to resign. Indeed, any time a Prime Minister threatened to adopt measures the Army disliked, the Army could destroy his cabinet.[15]

Within the Army, senior officers consolidated their independence by requiring that the Army Chief of Staff (the head of command) approve all Army ministerial appointments. They imposed this internal rule to deal with the fact that Army personnel matters were issues of administration, not command – and thus potentially subject to cabinet control. Because only command was independent, they internally gave the Chief of Staff a veto over new Army Ministers (Inoue, 1975: 95).

3.3. Military orders

Yamagata also let the military bypass the cabinet in issuing administrative orders. Under the Meiji Constitution, the oligarchs could validly issue administrative orders in the name of the Emperor (the *chokurei*) (see Chapter 3). To do so, however, they needed first to submit the order to the cabinet.[16] Under Yamagata's 1907 reforms, the Army and Navy Ministers could now issue Imperial Orders without the consent of the Prime Minister. Instead, the Ministers could each submit the proposed orders to the Emperor himself, and promulgate them independently.[17]

3.4. The result

All this did not make an independent Army; instead, it made a powerful Yamagata. Yamagata was a career Army officer. From 1898 to his death in 1922, he was a member of the Supreme Military Command (the *gensuifu*), and at various times Army Chief of Staff and Army Minister. Together with the other oligarchs he controlled access to the Emperor. So long as he and the other oligarchs stayed alive, the institutional independence that he created merely kept the military independent from the party politicians and dependent on the oligarchs (and primarily on Yamagata himself). Once the oligarchs had died, however, most of the substantive checks on military power disappeared.

Yamagata never controlled the Navy. Into the first decades of the twentieth century, the Navy instead stayed under the influence of men associated with Saigō Tsugumichi and Yamamoto Gonnohyōe.[18] Yet the Navy was never as large or as important as the Army. Indeed, during the early years, Yamagata tried to control it simply by consolidating and controlling a combined Army and Navy command.[19] In that, however, he eventually failed: By the early 1890s, the Navy had its own independent command, and could directly appeal to the Emperor.[20] The Navy remained beyond Yamagata's control.

Although some observers objected to this institutional framework,[21] most observers were sanguine. Many even considered military independence part of an "immutable grand code" of the Japanese Empire (Nakano, 1936: 495–498; Fujii, 1940: 88). At least in theory, the code was far from "immutable." Yamagata had specified military independence only in Imperial Orders. New orders trumped old orders and statutes trumped orders.[22] As a result, the Diet might have tried to repeal the orders by passing a new statute. It did not try, and for two reasons probably would have failed even had it tried. First, the men who controlled the Emperor could veto proposed statutes (see Chapter 3). They were not inclined to let the military fall under the control of the party politicians. Second, as noted in Section 3.2, the military itself could destroy cabinets as it pleased. Should a cabinet threaten military autonomy, it could do just that.

94

4. AGGREGATE DATA

Military personnel rosters confirm this institutional independence. Changes in cabinet affiliation did not correlate with the advancement or dismissal of officers. New cabinets simply did not replace senior Army officials. A comparison of Tables 7.1 and 7.2 with the tables in Chapter 5 will make this clear. During the six cabinet changes from 1924 to 1931, on average the incoming administration replaced 2 of the 19 senior Army officials and 1.3 of the 15 most senior Navy officials. Given the institutional framework, this independence is exactly what one would expect. The politicians had no control over the highest ranking officers, and with no control over them, had little influence over lower-ranking officers either. The oligarchs knew how to make an organization independent if they wanted – and the military many of them wanted independent.

5. THE MILITARY IN POLITICS[23]

5.1. Cabinets

Having obtained this institutional power, the military used it. When Yamagata and the Army opposed oligarch Saionji Kinmochi's policies in 1908, they destroyed his cabinet (Izu and Matsushita, 1938: 353–55; Ritsumeikan, 1993: 61–79). The Army destroyed Saionji's second cabinet in 1912 as well, when its minister resigned over budgetary quarrels.[24] It helped bring down Wakatsuki Reijirō's Kenseikai/Minseitō government in 1927 over its "soft" policy toward China (Takahashi, 1981: 124–28). And the military prevented Kiyoura Keigo from forming a cabinet in 1914, and brought down cabinets in 1936 and 1940 to boot (Izu and Matsushita, 1938: 360–62; Matsushita, 1963b: 262). More often, politicians avoided collapse by deferring to the military in advance. Aware that the military could destroy their government if it wished, they gave it what it wanted at the outset (Shinmyō, 1961: 71–77).

5.2. The London Naval Treaty[25]

Although party politicians did not always lose, when they won they only beat the military by rare good fortune. Consider the London Naval Treaty of 1930. Although it took him six months, Minseitō Prime Minister Hamaguchi Osachi did clear the treaty with the Emperor, the Diet, and the Privy Council. All this he did in the face of opposition from the Navy general staff. The general staff opposed the treaty because it limited the Navy to less than 70 percent of U.S. tonnage. They further argued, how-

Table 7.1. *Turnover in the Japanese Army, 1924–1931*

Date	6/11/24 Katō Kenseikai	6/30/26 Wakatsuki Kenseikai	4/20/27 Tanaka Seiyūkai	7/2/29 Hamaguchi Minseitō	4/14/31 Wakatsuki Minseitō	12/13/31 Inukai Seiyūkai
Cabinet						
Party						
Administration						
Minister	—	—	x (1 day)	x (1 day)	x (1 day)	x (1 day)
Vice Minister	—	x (1 mo.)	—*	—	—	—
General Secretariat (I)	x (2 mos.)	—	—	—	—	—
General Secretariat (II)	—	—	—	—	—	—
Senior Adjutant	—	—	—	—	—	—
Chief Military Investigations	None	None	—	x (1 mo.)	—	—
Bureau chiefs						
Military Office	—	x (1 mo.)	—	—	—	—
Personnel Affairs	—	—	—	x (1 mo.)	—	—
Justice	—	—	—	—	—	—
Accounting	—	—	—	—	—	—
Medical Office	—	—	—	—	—	—
Munitions	—	—	—	x (1 mo.)	—	—
Strategic Equipment	—	—	—	x (1 mo.)	—	—

Command			
Chief of Staff	—	—	x (10 days)
Vice Chief of Staff	—	x (1 mo.)	—
Superintendent of Education	—	—	—
Grand Chamberlain	—	—	—
Chief Home Office	—	—	—
Chief Military Police	—	—	—

Notes: An X indicates that the cabinet made a new appointment. We indicate in parentheses the amount of time the cabinet waited before making the appointment. We do not record new appointments after lapses of more than two months following the formation of a new cabinet.

* A new person was appointed a week before the cabinet change.

Source: Compiled from data found in Nihon kindai shiryō kenkyū kai (ed.), *Nihon rikukaigun no seido, soshiki, jinji* [*The System, Organization, and Personnel of the Japanese Army and Navy*], (Tokyo: Tokyo daigaku shuppan kai, 1971).

Table 7.2. Turnover in the Japanese Navy, 1924–1931

	6/11/24 Katō Kenseikai	6/30/26 Wakatsuki Kenseikai	4/20/27 Tanaka Seiyūkai	7/2/29 Hamaguchi Minseitō	4/14/31 Wakatsuki Minseitō	12/13/31 Inukai Seiyūkai
Date / Cabinet / Party						
Administration						
Minister	x (1 day)	—	x (1 day)	x (1 day)	—	x (1 day)
Vice Minister	x (1 mo.)	—*	—	—	—	—*
General Secretariat (I)	—	—	—	—	—	—
General Secretariat (II)	—	—	—	—	—	—
Senior Adjutant	—	—	—	—	—	—
Bureau chiefs						
Military Office	—	—	—	—	—	x (1 day)
Personnel Affairs	—	—	—	—	—	—
Justice	—	—	—	—	—	—
Accounting	—	—	—*	—	—	—
Medical Office	—	—	—	—	—	—
Munitions	x (1 day)	—	—	—	—	—*
Command						
Chief Military Command	—	—	—	—	—	—
Vice Chief Military Command	—	x (1 mo.)	—	—	—	—
Fleet Commander	—	—	—	—	—	—*
Fleet Chief Staff	—	—	—	—	—	—*

Notes: An X indicates that the cabinet made a new appointment. We indicate in parentheses the amount of time the cabinet waited before making the appointment. We do not record new appointments after lapses of more than two months following the formation of a new cabinet. * A new person was appointed within a month before the cabinet change.

Source: Compiled from data found in Nihon kindai shiryō kenkyū kai (ed.), *Nihon rikukaigun no seido, soshiki, jinji [The System, Organization, and Personnel of the Japanese Army and Navy],* (Tokyo: Tokyo daigaku shuppan kai, 1971).

ever, that in negotiating matters that concerned military strength, Hamaguchi compromised the independence of military command. In fact, the idea that the Prime Minister could not negotiate treaties would have taken the notion of military independence to bizarre lengths. Nonetheless, the Seiyūkai wanted badly enough to replace the Minseitō cabinet that even it echoed the military's argument.

Hamaguchi prevailed only because of two facts: because he controlled a Diet majority and because – unusually – senior Navy officers disagreed on the issue. The Chief and Vice Chief of the General Staff opposed the treaty, while the Navy Minister, Vice Minister, and several influential Admirals sided with Hamaguchi. Only by exploiting that internal Navy dissension did Hamaguchi beat the Navy general staff.

It was all for naught, of course. That October the Navy replaced its minister with a more compliant man, and retired the earlier minister from active service. The next April a rightist activist shot Hamaguchi, precisely because he had outmaneuvered the General Staff. Although the Minseitō cabinet survived eight more months under Wakatsuki, it never again controlled the cabinet.

5.3. The Manchurian incident[26]

The Army acted even more boldly than the Navy. Beginning in 1928, it engineered a series of faits accomplis that eventually led the Japanese government into war with China. When the Army concluded that Manchurian warlord Chang Tso-lin would be more convenient dead, it blew up his train. In September 1931, when Army Minister Minami Jirō demanded reinforcements for Manchuria and the Wakatsuki cabinet hesitated, the garrison commander in Korea sent in two divisions on his own.[27] When the cabinet promised the United States that Japan would not attack Chinchow, the Army did so anyway.

By the time the Wakatsuki cabinet fell in December 1931, the military largely did as it pleased. Inukai Tsuyoshi headed a Seiyukai cabinet, but only for six months before a right-wing activist shot him too. His was the last party cabinet in pre-war Japan.

5.4. Ugaki Kazushige

Even military men who established personal ties to political parties did not usually consider the military accountable to the cabinet. Consider the career of Army officer Ugaki Kazushige. Ugaki proudly traced his lineage back to Yamagata: He was a protege of Tanaka Giichi, who in turn was a favorite of Katsura Tarō's protege, Terauchi Masatake (Osadake, 1938: 20–21; Yamamoto, 1985: 1). Katsura, as noted in more detail in Section

6, had been Yamagata's own heir apparent. Like Katsura (who had headed the Dōshikai party) and Tanaka (who headed the Seiyūkai), Ugaki befriended politicians to further his own ambitions. Forging ties with parties, each of these men seemed to reason, would let him influence civilian affairs without losing place in the Army.

Ugaki himself chose to use politicians in the Kenseikai and Minseitō. Although he became Army Minister in January 1924 in Kiyoura Keigo's non-partisan cabinet, he kept his position through the successive Kenseikai cabinets of Katō Takaaki and Wakatsuki Reijirō. But when Tanaka became Seiyūkai Prime Minister in April 1927 and invited Ugaki to stay, Ugaki refused.

Ugaki did not decline Tanaka's offer out of any Kenseikai loyalty. He was furious at Kenseikai leader Wakatsuki for disclosing that Tanaka had routed Army funds to the Seiyūkai. Where Wakatsuki was just discrediting a political enemy, to Ugaki he had publicly betrayed the Army (Inoue, 1975: 200–204).

Ugaki instead declined Tanaka's offer for simple ambition: He wanted more than Tanaka offered. Influential members of the Kenseikai/Minseitō had led him to believe that they would make him party president, and hence Prime Minister in their next cabinet. By contrast, Tanaka offered him only the Army Ministership. In fact, Ugaki miscalculated. Rather than Ugaki, Minseitō leaders tapped Hamaguchi and Wakatsuki for their next Prime Ministers.

Discouraged but still scheming, Ugaki now entertained a coup attempt by a few young Army officers. Through the coup, he planned to become Prime Minister after all. Their coup plans became public before the plotters could engineer it, however, and Ugaki's plans collapsed. Although he escaped prosecution by disavowing complicity (Inoue, 1975: 225–235), the Army officers (who also escaped punishment) never forgave him that combination of ambition and treachery. When in 1937 the last of the oligarchs, Saionji Kimmochi, asked Ugaki to form a cabinet, the Army blocked the appointment.[28]

5.5. Military coordination

Political activity did not disappear completely. The military did let the parties compete for Diet seats until 1937.[29] At least in the early years of the decade, senior Army officers had their own differences as well. Only after a group of young officers launched an abortive coup in 1936 were the senior officers able to consolidate the Army.[30] With the Army now under control, they began directing the government itself. Eventually, Army Minister Terauchi Juichi even picked the new cabinet.[31]

Just as the oligarchs found it hard to coordinate their differences, however, the Army and the Navy general staffs found themselves locked in their own rivalry. Without an overarching authority (the oligachs were dead, and the Shōwa Emperor involved himself in political quarrels only rarely), they had to resolve their differences on their own. Competition among the oligarchs had eventually dissolved their monopoly on power. Competition between the branches now threatened to do the same.

Unlike the oligarchs, the military leaders did solve their coordination problem. Rather than fight over the spoils of empire, they established geographical spheres of influence: The Army took north China, the Navy southeast Asia.[32] Domestically the solution worked. Internationally it was a disaster. Had Japan invaded either north China or southeast Asia, Western leaders probably (if reluctantly) would have tolerated it for a while. By doing both – by solving their domestic coordination problem through a logroll – they pushed their country into a disastrous war.

6. THE STRATEGIC GAMBLE

Consider again why Yamagata kept the Army institutionally independent. Precipitating as it did the Second World War, that independence did not serve the country well. Yet that it was bad for the country ex post need not imply that it was a bad gamble for Yamagata ex ante. Two points stand out. First, the gamble insulated the Army from the party politicians. Unless his oligarchic rivals could control the Emperor better than he, it insulated the military even from them.

Second, notwithstanding its institutional independence, Yamagata kept the Army personally loyal to himself. As a career Army officer, he had stacked it with his proteges. Through that personal loyalty, he could control it without institutionalized civilian controls. Probably, civilian controls would even have reduced his power – they would have increased the risk that his oligarchic rivals would usurp it. Rather than give them that chance, he fought all institutionalized civilian supervision.

By 1922, Yamagata was dead. With him, oligarchic control over the Army disappeared, for Yamagata had bequeathed his personalized loyalty to no one. Fully independent, the Army could now move unrestrained. Military independence had served Yamagata well while he lived. After his death, it served Japan disastrously.

The question is why Yamagata chose a strategy that brought Japan such catastrophic results. Frankly, we doubt that he did not care what happened after he died – much as we excluded such concerns from our rational-choice framework in Chapter 1. Even the most rational and self-centered leaders usually do care who follows them. Part of the reason

Yamagata's policies wreaked such havoc, we suggest, is that Yamagata had designed them for a world ruled by his successor – and then failed to choose one.[33]

As heir, Yamagata had initially groomed Katsura Tarō. To Katsura, he had planned to bequeath his control network within the Army – and thus ensure that the Army would stay under control. Like many heirs-apparent, however, Katsura was both disloyal and prematurely mortal. Before Yamagata died, Katsura had already broken with him and allied himself with the party politicians. Even if had stayed loyal to Yamagata, however, he would have made a poor heir – if only because he predeceased Yamagata. Yamagata had gambled on transferring his control over the Army to Katsura, in short, and lost. For reasons we do not understand, even though he lived another nine years, he apparently never seriously tried to find another heir.

That Yamagata lost his gamble need not mean he chose badly.[34] Gambles are not mistakes because they ultimately go wrong. Ten dollars for a one in ten chance of winning $1,000 is a gamble worth taking, even though nine times out of ten one will lose. Had Yamagata established a successor, he might have bequeathed his personalized control within the military, and his successor might have ensured that the Army stayed within reasonable bounds. Yamagata failed, and no successor emerged to keep the Army in check. Japan lost, but not necessarily because Yamagata chose foolishly. Sometimes when nature plays its randomized hand, even good bets go wrong.

7. CONCLUSION

The oligarchs who ran turn-of-the-century Japan acted as principals to three sets of agents: bureaucrats, judges, and military personnel. The first two sets they purported to keep independent from the cabinet, but did not. The third set they purported to keep independent, and did. When they wanted to create institutional independence, they knew how.

Although the oligarchs made the military formally independent, for most of the Imperial decades they did not make it substantively independent. Instead, at least the Army answered to Yamagata. For decades, Yamagata had assiduously stacked it with personal followers. He had done this because he could then use his influence to maintain his power within the ruling oligarchy. Where his rivals competed for political rents within the oligarchy by catering to the politically dispossessed, Yamagata competed by controlling the Army. So long as he lived, the Army stayed in bounds. Only when in 1922 he died without an heir was the Army finally on its own.

8

Financial politics

1. INTRODUCTION

Scholars of pre-war Japan routinely trumpet the bureaucrats' developmental, nation-building prowess. A close examination of pre-war policy, however, reveals a different picture. In Chapters 9 and 10 we examine government policy in the railroad and cotton textile industries. In this chapter, we consider financial policy. We find that at least in the 1920s when the political parties controlled the cabinets, financial policy took on a distinctively partisan quality.[1] Financial regulation was more a weapon in the electoral battle for a legislative majority than a means to achieve any economic supremacy.

That the two main parties had distinct constituencies, as we discussed in Chapter 4, shaped their financial policy choices. The Kenseikai and Minseitō favored big banks and international firms, whereas the Seiyūkai cultivated ties to farmers, small firms and small banks, and domestically oriented manufacturers. This chapter recounts the financial policy shifts that accompanied changes in cabinet control.

Section 2 provides a broad historical sketch of pre-war financial regulation, noting that the Meiji oligarchs never achieved bank consolidation. Section 3 focuses on the Banking Act of 1927. Once in control of the cabinet, the Kenseikai drafted banking regulations that favored the largest banks, undermining the Seiyūkai's support base among the small banks.

In banking regulation, as with any area of policy governed by statute, control of the cabinet alone was not enough. However loyal and clever the bureaucrats, an obstreperous Diet could thwart legislative plans. Lacking a Diet majority in 1927, the Kenseikai had to make concessions to the other parties to get its banking bill through the legislature. The Seiyūkai, also lacking a Diet majority, was unable to nullify the effects of the law when it took over the cabinet in 1927. By the time the Seiyūkai regained a

Diet majority in 1932, the military had already foreclosed the party's option of rerigging banking regulation toward the interests of Seiyūkai constituents.

Section 4 examines the banking panic of 1927, and its consequences for partisan politics. In Section 5 we review Japan's pre-war foreign exchange policies, and in particular its stance toward the gold standard. Because the government's foreign exchange policy did not require legislative backing, policies changed with every party cabinet. The Kenseikai and Minseitō cabinets consistently supported the gold standard, at the behest of the big banks and internationally competitive firms. The Seiyūkai, with its constituency base rooted in agriculture and domestically-oriented manufacturing firms, just as consistently opposed it.

2. EARLY BANKING REGULATION

Various people tried several times to consolidate the banking sector, but were thwarted every time by the Diet.[2] In 1892 Shibusawa Eiichi, banking committee chairman of the Tokyo Bankers' Association and founder of the Daiichi Bank, asked the Ministry of Finance (MOF) to impose minimum capital requirements on banks as a way of erecting barriers to entry and limiting competition in the banking industry.[3] In 1894 the MOF submitted a bill imposing such requirements on banks, but the Lower House refused to pass it out of concern for small banks.[4] In April 1896 the Diet passed the Bank Merger Act to facilitate bank mergers, but with only carrots – such as tax breaks – and no sticks.[5] It was still unwilling to impose capital requirements that would disqualify small banks from operating.

In 1902 and again in 1906, the MOF submitted bills that would have imposed a capital requirement, but each time the Lower House refused to pass the law. Even with the proviso that banks in rural areas could meet a separate, lower standard, it refused (Gotō, 1973: 37–82). Perhaps the oligarchs did not think banking consolidation important enough to warrant a deal with Lower House politicians. Perhaps the large banks had not yet learned how to work the legislature. Whatever the reason, the capital requirements did not pass.

Although the Lower House blocked the capital-requirement legislation that would have forced many small banks to close or merge, the number of banks fell anyway. The Lower House used its veto against onerous legislation, but it could not yet demand regulation that would actually help small banks. Government guarantees against bank failure, large-bank-subsidized deposit insurance, and rules against price competition were still institutions of the future. The number of banks fluctuated with the business cycle, but after 1902 gradually fell (see Tables 8.1 and 8.2).

Table 8.1. *Number of "regular" banks, 1898–1945*

	Number of banks	Bank closings	Mergers	New banks
1898	1,305	20	9	171
1899	1,485	19	6	184
1900	1,634	45	12	293
1901	1,854	45	7	94
1902	1,890	31	5	6
1903	1,857	26	5	5
1904	1,780	39	4	3
1905	1,730	31	3	9
1906	1,697	21	3	5
1907	1,670	24	8	27
1908	1,663	28	5	7
1909	1,635	28	3	14
1910	1,617	10	3	11
1911	1,618	7	1	10
1912	1,615	5	6	18
1913	1,621	18	2	21
1914	1,457	12	2	13
1915	1,445	4	2	4
1916	1,442	10	7	6
1917	1,427	19	16	15
1918	1,398	15	21	16
1919	1,378	20	31	29
1920	1,344	11	32	38
1921	1,326	15	31	25
1922	1,331	17	42	12
1923	1,799	16	85	2
1924	1,701	32	49	8
1925	1,629	37	69	14
1926	1,537	46	87	16
1927	1,429	58	90	11
1928	1,283	59	222	29
1929	1,031	54	110	14
1930	881	26	79	6
1931	782	52	56	9
1932	683	102	60	17
1933	538	13	11	2
1934	516	18	18	4
1935	484	7	13	2

(*continued*)

Table 8.1. (*Continued*)

	Number of banks	Bank closings	Mergers	New banks
1936	466	24	21	3
1937	424	12	39	4
1938	377	4	29	2
1939	346	5	25	2
1940	318	1	35	4
1941	286	3	108	11
1942	186	0	37	1
1943	148	0	52	7
1944	101	0	18	2
1945	86	0	24	5

Note: The sizeable jump in number of banks between 1922 and 1923 reflects the large number of savings banks that changed their status to regular banks that year (see Table 8.2). In 1921, the Savings Bank Act was revised (effective 1922), raising the capital requirement of savings banks to ¥500,000 and hence reducing the incentive of small banks to retain their savings bank license.

Sources: Bank of Japan, *Honpō keizai tōkei [Economic Statistics of Japan]* (Tokyo: Bank of Japan, 1935), pp. 6–39; Shin'ichi Gotō, *Honpō ginkō gōdōshi [History of Bank Mergers in Japan]* (Tokyo: Kin'yū zaisei jijō kenkyūkai, 1973), pp. 55, 93, 127, 211, 359, and 377.

By 1926 the number of banks had dropped from 1,857 in 1903 to 1,537 (Table 8.1).

3. THE BANKING ACT OF 1927

In July 1926, Wakatsuki Reijirō's Kenseikai Cabinet established a Preparatory Committee for a Financial System Research Council (*Kin'yū seido chōsakai jumbi iinkai*) to begin considering a new banking law. The committee consisted almost entirely of zaibatsu bankers: representatives from the Mitsubishi Bank, the Daiichi Bank, the Sumitomo Bank, the Mitsui Bank, and the Bank of Japan (Okano, 1927: 90–101).

The Kenseikai's reason for excluding representatives from the smaller banks is not hard to understand. Small banks, along with much of the small business sector, disproportionately supported the Seiyūkai. The Kenseikai, by contrast, had closer ties to big, internationally-oriented businesses, including the nation's largest banks. Even if it included on the committee a representative of its rival's largest banking patron, the Mitsui Bank, it excluded the many small patron banks. By shifting the weight of economic activity to big banks, it could benefit its own constituents at the

Table 8.2. *Number of savings banks*

	Number of banks	Transition to regular banks	Bank mergers	Bank closings	New banks
1904	696	12	4	11	14
1905	683	2	3	6	11
1906	683	3	0	8	15
1907	687	11	4	9	15
1908	278	2	1	13	7
1909	669	0	2	11	4
1910	660	6	0	11	3
1911	646	4	1	0	5
1912	646	8	7	2	11
1913	640	2	0	2	12
1914	648	5	3	3	21
1915	658	154	2	4	159
1916	657	6	2	9	24
1917	664	1	4	8	13
1918	664	3	4	6	10
1919	661	3	20	3	22
1920	657	4	20	3	31
1921	661	28	24	5	32
1922	670	515	10	7	8
1923	146	1	4	2	0
1924	139	1	1	2	1
1925	136	0	2	1	0
1926	133	0	6	3	0
1927	124	0	1	10	0
1928	113	0	11	2	0
1929	100	0	3	3	0
1930	95	0	3	2	0
1931	90	0	1	1	0
1932	88	0	1	0	0
1933	87	0	0	2	0
1934	85	0	5	1	2
1935	79	0	1	1	1
1936	79	0	2	1	0
1937	74	0	4	0	0
1938	72	0	2	1	0
1939	72	0	0	0	0
1940	71	0	0	0	0

(*continued*)

Table 8.2. (Continued)

	Number of banks	Transition to regular banks	Bank mergers	Bank closings	New banks
1941	71	0	0	0	1
1942	69	0	0	0	0
1943	69	0	29	0	0
1944	40	0	16	0	0
1945	24	0	21	0	1

Source: Shin'ichi Gotō, Honpō ginkō gōdōshi [History of Bank Mergers in Japan] (Tokyo: Kin'yū zaisei jijō kenkyūkai, 1973).

expense of the Seiyūkai's, and induce those constituents to contribute to its campaign coffers in time for the universal suffrage elections.

As one would expect given the committee's membership, the bill it drafted favored larger banks. It established stringent capital requirements. In the process, it potentially disqualified nearly half of the 1,400-odd banks (see Table 8.1).

The strategic considerations that drove the Kenseikai to adopt the Banking Act were less economic than political. Consider, for example, what economic advantage the large banks might have thought they would gain by closing small banks. They probably did not expect to establish a cartel to hold down deposit rates. If they had the political power to close down competitors, they would also have had the political power to establish deposit rate regulations. Given the large number of banks that survived the Banking Act, such regulations would have held down interest rates far more effectively than any price cartel. Notwithstanding, they chose not to demand maximum deposit rates.[6]

Perhaps, however, the large banks hoped that with fewer banks they could more effectively raise the rates they charged unaffiliated borrowers. Zaibatsu banks would not, of course, have earned their ultimate owners additional rents by charging their affiliated borrowers higher rates; the Mitsui Bank did not raise Mitsui family income by charging the Mitsui trading company a higher interest rate. Still, even the Mitsui Bank loaned money to non-Mitsui borrowers. Perhaps the large banks hoped to earn monopoly rents on these unaffiliated loans.

Yet a loan-rate cartel was even less likely than a deposit-rate cartel. A loan-rate cartel would have been a hard strategy to enforce. Enough banks survived the Banking Act to make any cartel precarious – but a loan-rate cartel would have been particularly precarious. At least deposit rates are usually standard, given deposits of a particular size and term.

108

Cartel members can thus relatively cheaply monitor each other. Industrial loans, by contrast, depend on idiosyncratic assessments of the borrower's risk. That in turn can be notoriously hard to police.

Even if the banks had successfully raised interest rates, their gains might have been minor. If they did raise rates, some of their best borrowers would have turned to the securities markets.[7] Borrowers may incur larger transactions costs in securities markets than at banks (particularly for small amounts), and small and untested borrowers may not be able to borrow in such markets at all. At least for the largest borrowers, however, the stock and bond markets in Osaka and Tokyo provided relatively cost-effective substitutes.

Apart from any advantages large banks earned through the Banking Act, the Act fit with the Kenseikai's political strategy. As noted earlier, the smallest local banks disproportionately supported the Seiyūkai.[8] In the new elections under universal suffrage, those banks could give the Seiyūkai invaluable help. Under the MMD-SNTV electoral rules (see Chapter 4), the parties had evenly and predictably to divide voters in each district. Under universal suffrage, that task was harder – and more important – than ever before. With their extensive ties to local firms and investors, politically loyal banks were ideal for the task.

For the Kenseikai, the attractions of the Banking Act lay in the way it summarily closed institutions that would otherwise have helped the Seiyūkai divide the vote. Those that it did not close, it could induce other local banks to acquire. Indeed, if it induced Minseitō-affiliated banks to buy the small firms, it thereby transformed a local institution that would have helped the Seiyūkai into one that would instead aid the Kenseikai.[9]

To reward its own banks for acquiring the small Seiyūkai-affiliated banks, the Kenseikai probably induced the MOF to auction the small banks at "fire-sale" prices. Had the larger banks freely competed for such banks, they would not have found bargain prices; absent financial detail on the purchases, we cannot be certain whether they did. Yet if the Kenseikai and larger banks could shut down the smaller banks, they could also stop efficient auctions. If they did, they thereby transferred wealth from shareholders in Seiyūkai-affiliated institutions to Kenseikai firms as well. To the Kenseikai, the scheme was a double winner: The party divided the vote, and its supporters earned a profit.

The government's bill included minor concessions to small banks. Basically, it gave banks five years to raise new capital or merge in order to meet the new standards.[10] Yet the concessions were minor, and Seiyūkai members as well as some backbenchers in the Kenseikai continued to fight the bill. After heated discussions on the floor, the Diet amended the bill to allow banks in rural areas with a population of less than 10,000 to operate with ¥500,000 in capital.[11] Most banks had to maintain ¥1 million in capital, and Tokyo and Osaka money-center banks were required to have ¥2 million.[12]

Finance Minister Kataoka Naoharu – himself the founder and former president of the giant Nippon Life Insurance Company – defended the legislation in the Diet. To critics who argued that cutting the number of banks would hurt local economies, he simply asserted that Japan had too many banks. To those who demanded assurances that banks would not be forced to merge against their will, he said only that best efforts would be made to satisfy all involved. And to legislators who wanted further concessions to the smallest banks, he insisted that the government would not let any bank operate with less than ¥500,000 in capital.[13]

Because the Kenseikai had only a plurality in the Lower House after the 1924 election, it forged a majority coalition with the Seiyūhontō.[14] The five-year delay and the lower capitalization requirements for the small-town banks were the price it paid to hold this coalition together. The bill passed without incident in February 1927, to take effect on January 1, 1928.[15] The Kenseikai and the larger banks had finally obtained the statute they more or less wanted.

4. THE FINANCIAL PANIC OF 1927

The political calm that had surrounded the passage of the new banking law ended when the Seiyūkai learned in March that the Kenseikai was negotiating a merger with the Seiyūhontō.[16] If the two parties merged, they would have an absolute majority, and the Seiyūkai would have no voice in the budget. Because budgetary allocations to electoral districts helped win elections, the Seiyūkai had reason for alarm.[17]

Just as the news of the planned two-party merger broke, the Kenseikai was attempting to pass a bill guaranteeing more generous government help to the Bank of Japan (BOJ) for losses it incurred in rediscounting "earthquake bonds."[18] Following the devastating Tokyo earthquake of 1923, the government had authorized the Bank of Japan to rediscount bonds held by private banks rather than to allow massive defaults.[19] Under the program, banks would be able to sell to the BOJ any bonds they held that were issued by firms that had suffered in the earthquake and might now default. By the spring of 1927, the banks demanded BOJ rediscounting on more generous terms. Because BOJ losses would require new budgetary allocations, Diet approval was necessary.[20]

Concerned about the Kenseikai's merger plans, the Seiyūkai was determined to bring the cabinet down. Toward that end, it charged that the Kenseikai's real goal was to save the Bank of Taiwan and its largest borrowers from bankruptcy. The Bank of Taiwan, a government-controlled financial institution based in Japan's colony Taiwan, had held a huge number of "earthquake bonds" issued by Suzuki Shōten. As a trading company, it had risen meteorically in the post-World War I boom, but had fallen equally quickly during the ensuing recession.[21] Although it never recovered, the Bank of Taiwan had continued to lend it huge sums. The Bank in turn had borrowed heavily from the interbank call market and from the BOJ.

The Seiyūkai argued that Suzuki Shōten had cultivated strong ties to the Kenseikai, and had obtained the funds from the government-controlled Bank of Taiwan through those ties.[22] Not that the Seiyūkai opposed such schemes in principle. When it was in the cabinet, it willingly exchanged favors for campaign contributions. But faced with the prospect of a solid Minseitō majority in the Diet, it was determined to bring down the cabinet. First, its leaders collected as much evidence as they could find on the Suzuki-Kenseikai link. They then passed that material to the House of Peers, the Privy Council, and the newspapers.[23] Second, the Seiyūkai asked the Mitsui Bank – the only large bank with which it had close ties – for help. Apparently, after consultation with the party leaders, the bank called in its outstanding loans to the Bank of Taiwan. In the process, it crippled the Bank of Taiwan and worsened the Kenseikai government's predicament (Oe, 1968: 89).

During the rancorous Diet Budget Committee deliberations over the BOJ rediscounting legislation, Kenseikai Finance Minister Kataoka tried to underscore the severity of the liquidity problem in the banking industry. He did so, though, by announcing that the large Tokyo Watanabe Bank was about to fail.[24] If Kataoka had intended to evoke multi-partisan cooperation, he could not have been more mistaken. The Seiyūkai relished his predicament.

As news of the imminent bankruptcy spread throughout the country, many depositors lost no time in withdrawing their funds from their own banks out of fear of a nationwide run.[25] Their prophecy fulfilled itself. On March 15, 1927, the Watanabe Bank closed its doors. Rather than help calm depositor fears, the Seiyūkai organized a rally at Shiba Park on the 18th to protest the Kenseikai's bill. A few weeks later, the Fifteenth Bank, a bank owned by peers and widely thought to be indestructible, also closed its doors.[26] The stock market fell, and other banks seemed about to fail as well.[27]

Wakatsuki allowed the Diet session to end in late March as scheduled without a bailout. Presumably, he had abandoned hopes of passing a statute in the face of the Seiyūkai's efforts to weaken the Kenseikai-Seiyūhontō coalition. Even if he could have forced the bill through the Lower House, he would not have obtained his statute. The House of Peers had publicly decried the Kenseikai's irresponsibility in channeling Bank of Taiwan money to Suzuki Shōten, and appeared resolutely to oppose any Suzuki Shōten bailout.[28]

Yet Wakatsuki had not abandoned hopes of rediscounting the earthquake bonds more generously – only of rediscounting them by statute. On April 14, his cabinet passed the BOJ rediscounting bill in the form of an emergency Imperial Order. Under Article 8 of the Meiji Constitution, it could do so, subject to the emperor's approval, whenever the Diet was not in session. The emperor's approval, however, meant the approval of the Privy Council, and the Council president Baron Kuratomi promptly appointed a special committee to study the question. After two days, the committee refused to approve the order. The plenary Council upheld its refusal, and Wakatsuki had lost the fight.

The Privy Council claimed to reject Wakatsuki's order on the ground that the cabinet should not have used an emergency order when it could have called a special session of the Diet. The argument directly contradicted Itō Hirobumi's commentaries on the Constitution (1889: 118). There, Itō had insisted that the question was whether the Diet was in session, not whether it could be.[29] Nonetheless, the Privy Council did win academic support for its position. Constitutional law scholars Sasaki Sōichi (1932, 610) and Ōtani Yoshitaka (1939: 338–39), for example, eventually took the Privy Council's side in the question.

The real reason for denying the cabinet's wish may not have involved the niceties of constitutional interpretation at all. Instead, the Privy Council's deliberations suggest that the reason probably lay in the formation of an anti-Kenseikai coalition within the Council. Former military officers on the Council resented the Kenseikai's "soft" foreign policy toward China. They apparently had joined forces with the former Seiyūkai-affiliated bureaucrats who believed they would have more influence on policy if the Seiyūkai returned to power.

Members of the Privy Council knew that Prime Minister Wakatsuki and his cabinet would have to resign if they could not forestall a wider banking panic. They knew too that they could count on the Seiyūkai to replace them. As soon as the Privy Council rejected the Imperial Order, Wakatsuki and his cabinet duly resigned. Seiyūkai president Tanaka Giichi became Prime Minister three days later on April 20.[30]

The Seiyūkai leaders did not oppose the rediscouting bill in principle – if, indeed, they were principled about anything besides winning elections. Aside from the rhetoric about a bailout for Suzuki Shōten, they knew that investors worried about bank runs. When the Tokyo Bankers' Association and the Tokyo Commercial Paper Exchange on April 21 urged them to act quickly, they immediately reconvened the Diet. Because they had to give Diet members two weeks to gather, they declared an immediate bank moratorium to stop bank runs in the meantime (Takahashi, 1955: 672–73).

On May 10, the Diet passed a law that closely resembled the one drafted by the Kenseikai cabinet. Because the House of Peers had added the proviso that the BOJ not save Suzuki Shōten, the BOJ let the firm go bankrupt unceremoniously. It did, however, salvage the Bank of Taiwan. In several respects, the Seiyūkai leaders had drafted a law that was more generous than what the Kenseikai had proposed. They did not want public blame for destroying the Japanese financial services industry. Accordingly, through the law they raised the government guarantees for BOJ losses to ¥500 million from the ¥200 million in the Kenseikai bill. They authorized the BOJ to lend the money over the course of a year, and to use 10-year notes at the low interest rate that applied to loans backed by government bonds. These were exactly the terms that the directors of the Tokyo Bankers' Association had requested in a private meeting with Prime Minister Tanaka and Finance Minister Takahashi Korekiyo.[31]

The rediscounting bill had mixed results. The large banks survived. But many small banks failed, as skittish depositors shifted accounts to those larger banks.[32] By May 1927 twenty-nine banks had failed. On October 5, 1927, the new Seiyūkai Finance Minister Mitsuchi Chūzō told the *Tokyo asahi shimbun* newspaper that small banks had lost about ¥830 million in deposits, mostly to large banks.

By January 1928, when the new Banking Act took effect, 790 of the 1,238 banks that survived the panic did not meet the new capital requirements (Sakairi, 1988: 212–17). Although the Seiyūkai controlled the cabinet, it lacked a legislative majority and thus could not repeal the Act.[33] Granted, the law did give banks five years to raise the extra capital. Many banks, however, still despaired of meeting the new requirements.[34]

The Seiyūkai cabinet did what it could to help the small banks. During its two-year tenure, it apparently bent some of the rules to help banks raise capital and qualify (Gotō, 1973: 271). It also helped banks merge rather than close, producing an upward blip in the number of mergers in those years (see Table 8.1).

Seiyūkai efforts notwithstanding, the number of banks dropped to 683 by 1932. As small banks began to disappear, the market share held by large banks grew. In 1931, the 13 largest banks held 58.9 percent of total deposits. Of that amount, the zaibatsu banks and Shibusawa's Daiichi Bank controlled 65 percent, or 38 percent of all deposits. Five years earlier, the 13 largest banks had held 40.8 percent and the big five only 24 percent (Sumitomo, ed., 1979: 250).

The Kenseikai had badly damaged the small bank sector on which its rival the Seiyūkai had relied. But the maneuver still did not guarantee it a bright political future. Its successor Minseitō did win a Diet majority by a wide margin in the January 1930 elections. Yet the victory gave it only two years' reprieve before the Seiyūkai would triumph in new elections. And in the heat of political competition, the Seiyūkai and the Minseitō were unable to combine their forces in dealing with their common opponent, the military.

By the time the Seiyūkai regained a Diet majority in February 1932, it could no longer rewrite the banking laws. The military had designs of its own for the financial system, and was increasingly vocal about its policy preferences for streamlined funding for the munitions industry. Three months later, when Seiyūkai Prime Minister Inukai was assassinated, the military simply took over the cabinet.

Under military government, the Ministry of Finance now shifted its goals from "maintaining the stability of the financial system" to "centralized control." One of its assigned tasks was to reduce the number of local banks to one per prefecture, and to ensure that local banks efficiently transferred their funds to production-center banks in the cities (Zenkoku, 1988: 54–55). Although the zaibatsu banks survived under military rule since their large size suited the military's goal of centralizing production and allocation, they lost profit-making opportunities and operating discretion (Tiedemann, 1971: 267–316). Their heyday had been the brief era of party cabinets, particularly under the Kenseikai – when party politicians had wanted to win elections badly enough that they would skew financial policy for electoral advantage.

5. THE GOLD STANDARD AS POLITICAL INSTRUMENT

Policy decisions concerning the gold standard mirrored the political interests of the ruling cabinet even more clearly than banking regulation. Under the Constitution (Articles 8, 9), once the Diet had legislated on a matter, the cabinet could not revise the law except through another statute (thus requiring a return to the Diet) or through an emergency order (which required submitting the matter to the next Diet). Because the banking industry had long been regulated by statute, changes in those regulations required a Diet majority. Absent a clear majority in the Diet, they necessitated compromises with the other side. By contrast, the Diet had never passed a statute on the issue of the gold standard. As a result, the cabinet would take the country on or off the gold standard with a simple cabinet order.

By the turn of the century, gold had increasingly become the unit of measure for national currencies. As early as 1893, a government commission of Finance Ministry bureaucrats, politicians, and academics had recommended that Japan adopt the gold standard to put Japan's trade on firm ground and to protect the domestic economy against inflation (Horie, 1927: 329). Prime Minister Matsukata took the commission's advice in 1896 and adopted the standard.

With the onset of World War I, Japan along with the rest of the industrialized world abandoned the gold standard. The United States led the world in returning to gold in 1919, and the United Kingdom followed in 1925. Beginning in 1924, Kenseikai cabinets adopted policies – imposing austerity measures and allowing substantial gold exports – that led observers to suspect that they would return Japan to the gold standard at the earlier par. This speculation had buoyed the value of the yen to $0.49 by the end of 1926. But the weakness of the economy following the Tokyo earthquake of 1923, and later the 1927 bank panic, delayed the move. Once the Kenseikai lost control of the cabinet in mid-1927, the yen fell once again to $0.45. The market knew, apparently, that the Seiyūkai was not enthusiastic about the gold standard and a strong currency.[35]

Internationally active banks and trading firms, and their party of choice, the Kenseikai/Minseitō, believed it was critical to be on gold if trading partners were. The discipline of the gold standard, they argued, would restore equilibrium in Japan's markets. Most importantly, gold prevented inflation for the following reason: higher domestic prices curtailed exports, which in turn led to outflows of gold. The outflows of gold translated directly into a shrunken domestic money supply, which would put downward pressure on domestic prices. The gold standard would function, in other words, as an external discipline on monetary policy. The resulting strong yen – and with it, the yen's desirability as a store of value – would give Japanese banks more business as international financial intermediaries.[36]

Firms in the more domestically oriented sectors of the economy (for example, agriculture and heavy industry) opposed the gold standard. They apparently feared that the standard would have disruptive deflationary effects. Through their spokesmen, the Seiyūkai politicians, they characterized the gold standard as a scheme to enrich the patrician few at the expense of the plebian many (Takahashi, 1932: 122–133; Hida, 1955: 282).

To anyone familiar with the gold issue, Prime Minister Hamaguchi's appointment of Inoue Junnosuke as Finance Minister in June 1929 signaled his intention to return Japan to the gold standard. Inoue, formerly the president of the Yokohama Specie Bank and then governor of the Bank of Japan, had been one of the most vocal and ardent proponents of the gold standard.[37] As observers expected, on November 21, 1929, the Hamaguchi cabinet finally lifted the gold embargo as of January 11, 1930. The MOF followed with a ministerial order effectively placing Japan back on the gold standard for the first time in thirteen years

115

(Kishimoto, 1990: 110). Although Hamaguchi might have hoped to add some permanence to the order by passing a statute to the effect, to do so he needed a Diet majority. That he did not have. Ten days later, however, he did dissolve the Diet and call new elections, precisely because he hoped to capture that majority.

The Minseitō campaigned on a platform of fiscal responsibility and rehabilitation, and the Seiyūkai countered with a platform of economic recovery and fiscal stimulus (Kishimoto, 1990: 111). Perhaps because its platform struck a resonant chord with the Japanese public,[38] perhaps because it cheated so effectively, the Minseitō won a comfortable Diet majority.

Unfortunately for the Minseitō, the timing of the return to gold had been bad. Just a few months earlier, the stock market in New York had crashed and the U.S. economy was in a tailspin. The end of American prosperity had a disastrous effect on Japan. In just one year, Japan's silk prices had fallen by half, and its export trade as a whole was down 27 percent from 1929 (Allen, 1981: 107–8). In returning Japan to the gold standard, the Minseitō had exacerbated these international effects by returning at the pre-World War I rate of $0.49 per yen – when by 1929 the yen had fallen to $0.44. Not only did this exchange rate choice raise the short-term price of Japanese products abroad; it also had predictable deflationary effects at home.

The Minseitō government lent huge sums to distressed producers, but persisted in its efforts to carry through its deflationary policies. Hamaguchi and his successor Wakatsuki were determined to reduce the government's budgetary deficit, primarily by cutting military expenditures.[39] But the Minseitō was stopped in its tracks when Britain abandoned the gold standard once more and devalued the pound on September 21, 1931. Until currency markets equilibrated, this move necessarily exposed Japanese producers to fiercer British trade competition. Calculating that their own government would retaliate by devaluing the yen, Japanese investors sold yen and bought gold.

In order to stanch the outflow of gold, the government raised the Bank of Japan's discount rate twice, once in October and once in November. Putting on a bold face in a dismal situation, the government reaffirmed its commitment to the gold standard. But the market overwhelmed the central bank's leaning against the foreign exchange winds. Between July 31, 1930 and the end of 1931, the Bank of Japan had sold ¥440 million's worth of gold, and used over half of its reserves (Hida, 1955: 277). By December, the Minseitō government had collapsed.[40]

One of the first acts of Inukai's Seiyūkai government in December 1931 was to take Japan back off the gold standard.[41] This was just part of the Seiyūkai government's reversal of the Minseitō's "small government" policies. His Finance Minister Takahashi Korekiyo, for example, is famous for being Japan's "first Keynesian Finance Minister," although to Takahashi's distaste, the military ensured that much of the spending came their way (Ōkurashō, ed., 1977: 167).

6. CONCLUSION

Neither bank consolidation nor Japan's foreign exchange policies were the result of a bureaucratic plan to achieve rapid economic development. Instead, the Kenseikai/Minseitō engineered the bank consolidation policy of 1927 as part of an electoral strategy to cripple its rival Seiyūkai by destroying the small bank community on which the Seiyūkai relied. Even clearer is the partisan flip-flopping on Japan's foreign exchange regime. By selling anti-inflation policies, the Kenseikai/Minseitō raised large campaign contributions with which they competed in elections.

Some scholars have lamented the fact that the major political parties were spending all their resources fighting each other when they had a common enemy that was far worse. While the parties were winning electoral battles against each other, they were losing the greater struggle for ultimate control against the military. As we argued in Chapter 4, however, stable collusion between the parties was not for them an individually optimal strategy. Given the institutional framework they had inherited from the oligarchs, the parties behaved exactly as one would expect.

9

Railroad politics

1. INTRODUCTION

Trains are different from other investments. Basic to our enterprise here, they differ in the significance historians attach to them. For decades, scholars routinely thought them *the* revolutionary technological change of the nineteenth century.

Trains also differ in their externalities. For decades, scholars routinely argued that they created a wide variety of beneficial spillovers. They generated larger labor markets, smoother national defense strategies, and broader trade patterns. Because railroad shareholders could not capture all these spillovers, scholars argued, left alone they invested suboptimally. Hence a role for government: Perhaps, if it subsidized the industry, it could induce more efficient investment patterns.

Trains differ too in the coordination problems they generate. Not only must firms match their competitors' track gauges and negotiate ways to handle shippers who send freight across more than one railroad. They must overcome special problems in buying the land they will use. Because they need contiguous parcels, sellers (if they know a railroad's plans) can hold up a firm for enormous prices. Hence the other role for government: Perhaps, by easing these hold-up problems, it could alleviate transactions costs too.

These claims are not specific to a particular country. Scholars do not just make them of the United States and Europe. They routinely make them of Japan as well. In his survey of the Japanese economy, Takatoshi Ito (1992: 20, 29) lists railroads prominently among Japan's infrastructural investments. He then finds in the way the government promoted them a "key to Japan's fast economic growth." Railroads figured crucially in the infrastructure, the infrastructure helped drive economic growth, and the government developed the infrastructure.[1]

None of this is proven, of course. Indeed, much of it may be false. Even

118

in the United States, it is far from clear that railroads played a critical role in economic development. By Robert Fogel's (1964: 47) classic calculations, in transporting farm products American railroads saved at most 0.6 percent of the national income in 1890.[2]

So too perhaps in Japan. It is far from clear that railroads played a critical role there either. Trains faced close substitutes on their principal routes. They carried the most freight and passengers on the lines connecting Tokyo with Osaka, Kyūshū, and Hokkaidō. Yet there, coastal shipping firms offered close competition – at least for the freight.[3] By the end of the Tokugawa period, their boats had already created national markets for a wide variety of products. To be sure, boats could not handle transportation to and from the hinterlands (though most economic activity was not in the hinterlands anyway). For most of the pre-war period, though, neither could trains. By the time railroad firms had finally laid tracks to the more remote villages, shippers could usually reach them by trucks and buses.[4]

Just as it is not clear how important railroads were to Japan, neither is it clear that the Japanese government did what it did in the railroad industry to promote national growth. Granted, it promoted railroads. It built some lines itself, subsidized others, and lent private firms the power of eminent domain. In the process, it may have promoted growth – although that depends on what taxpayers would otherwise have done with the money the government spent on the railroads. Yet any such promotion was at most a small part of the story, for railroads created enormous graft and routinely swayed elections. By 1980, the Japanese national railroad had graced newspapers around the world with tales of its waste. Indeed, Liberal Democratic Party kingpin Tanaka Kakuei had spent ¥480 billion to lay 300 km of wide gauge track and dig 100 km of tunnels, all to run the bullet train to his remote home district (Ramseyer and Rosenbluth, 1993: chap. 7). Only the scope of his pork, however, was new. Railroads had been a pork barrel from the beginning of this century.

In this chapter, we ascribe that pork-barrel political logic to the early Japanese railroad industry. We find that the politicians who nationalized the private lines in 1906 used a pricing formula that transferred enormous wealth to their patrons (Section 2). We discover that the politicians did not always subsidize rides (Section 3) but may have tried to buy equipment from their political allies (Section 4). And we show that those who drew support most heavily from rural voters tried (as Tanaka later did so spectacularly) to extend tracks into the countryside, while their competitors tried to enhance the commuter rail network in the cities (Section 5).

Like Washington, like Tokyo; like Tammany Hall, like Kasumigaseki. To anyone who reads a newspaper, the political logic in this chapter will seem tiresomely familiar and embarrassingly mundane. If so, they should rest assured that such *is* the point: In pre-war Japan, even apparently benign industrial policy incorporated a relentlessly electoral logic.

2. MEIJI RAILROADS

2.1. The national railroad[5]

Trains first crossed the American continent in 1869. By then, Americans were already in Japan, and with them they had brought the tales of these trains (even working models). An American entrepreneur convinced the shogunal government to let him run trains from Tokyo (then called Edo) to Yokohama. Within a year, renegade samurai had toppled the government. Lest foreign railroads make Japan the effective colony that China had become, the new leaders canceled the American's license at once.

These leaders of the new government hoped instead to build railroads themselves. Like the American, they began with the Tokyo-Yokohama line. From Yokohama, they planned to continue to Osaka and Kobe, nearly 400 miles away. The route had long been the central artery for Japanese merchants. It now seemed sure to remain that.

Railroads take money, however, and this the new government leaders did not have. Accordingly, they swallowed their fear of foreign power and turned to Britain for funds. The process was anything but smooth. The leaders first agreed to borrow one million pounds through one Englishman at 12 percent interest. When they soured on his plans, they changed their minds and paid him a cancelation penalty. From the British Oriental Bank, they borrowed the money at 9 percent instead.

Railroads also take technology, and that the government leaders did not have either. Once again, they turned to the British. By 1876, they employed 94 British technicians. By 1887, they had bought 95 of their 97 locomotives from British firms (Shima, 1950: 68, 71).

Workers began laying the track in 1870. Within two years, they had finished the 18 miles from Tokyo to Yokohama. Within two more years, they had finished the line from Osaka to Kobe, and the Tokyo-Yokohama line was carrying 1.6 million passengers a year. By 1882 they had laid 170 miles of track; by 1889 they had finished the entire line from Tokyo to Osaka (Table 9.1).[6]

2.2. The private railroads

Not until the early days of parliamentary politics in the 1890s did government leaders begin to encourage private railroads in earnest. Although the oligarchs used railroads to private ends, they did so less than the party

Table 9.1. *Track mileage*

Year	New track (miles)		Total track (miles)	
	National	Private	National	Private
1872	18.00	0	18.00	0
1873	0	0	18.00	0
1874	20.27	0	38.27	0
1875	0	0	38.27	0
1876	26.64	0	65.11	0
1877	0	0	65.11	0
1878	0	0	65.11	0
1879	8.11	0	73.22	0
1880	25.03	0	98.25	0
1881	24.01	0	122.26	0
1882	48.40	0	170.66	0
1883	10.68	63.00	181.54	63.00
1884	0	17.63	181.54	80.63
1885	42.11	53.73	223.65	134.56
1886	41.02	31.21	264.67	165.77
1887	35.56	127.27	300.43	293.24
1888	205.18	113.14	505.61	406.38
1889	105.30*	179.27	550.49	585.65
1890	0	262.60	550.49	848.45
1891	0	316.77	550.49	1165.42
1892	0	154.66	550.49	1320.28
1893	7.00	60.55	557.49	1381.03
1894	23.20	156.32	580.69	1537.35
1895	12.40*	159.66	593.22	1697.21
1896	38.40	176.48*	631.62	1875.29
1897	30.03	439.09	661.65	2287.05
1898	106.49*	364.22*	768.37	2652.13
1899	73.40*	153.70*	832.72	2806.00
1900	117.16*	100.18*	949.69	2905.16
1901	109.59	62.43*	1059.48	2966.48
1902	164.35*	43.37*	1226.56	3010.60
1903	118.14	138.51*	1344.70	3150.57
1904	116.52*	82.17*	1461.38	3232.08
1905	70.30*	19.56*	1531.58	3251.23
1906	16.73*	8.48	3116.22+	1691.57+

Notes: * Sums do not total because some mileage dropped from use that year.
+ The dramatic shift from private to public lines reflects the fact that some (but not all) of the private railroads nationalized were transferred in 1906.
Source: Teishin shō tetsudō kyoku (ed.), *Tetsudō kyoku nempō (1906) [1906 Annual Report for the Railroad Bureau]* (Tokyo: Teishin shō tetsudō kyoku), pp. 35–36.

politicians. For railroads fit the pork-barrel logic to electoral government as few other industries would ever fit it. When Japanese government leaders (whether politicians or oligarchs) decided to promote a rail line, they did so by giving investors advantageous "licenses." The first license the oligarchs apparently gave to a group of their own: to peers and former higher samurai. With ¥20 million of their own money and funds from their private bank (the Fifteenth National Bank), these aristocrats formed the Nippon tetsudō company.

The investors in Nippon tetsudō obtained the license for the route destined to become the most important line after the one to Osaka: the line from Tokyo toward Hokkaidō to the northeast. In addition to permission to run this line, they gained two other benefits.[7] First, the government promised to obtain for them the land they needed. If it already owned the land, it would give it to them. If others owned the land, it would buy it by eminent domain and resell it to them. Second, it guaranteed them an annual profit. Until the trains began running, it promised them an 8 percent return on their investment. Thereafter, it promised them 8 percent on various segments of their line for another 10 to 15 years.[8]

Nippon finished the first portion of its line by 1883 (see Table 9.1), and the entire route from Tokyo to Aomori by 1891.[9] When times were good, it earned large profits; when they were bad, it collected government subsidies. Other investors soon saw the logic to this game, and began to lobby for licenses of their own. By the early 1890s, some 50 groups had petitioned for railroad licenses, and the government had granted 15. These private firms grew quickly. From 1882 to 1892, the national railroad increased its tracks from 171 to 550 miles. Private firms increased their tracks from 0 to 1320 miles. In 1902, the national railroad owned 1227 miles of track. Private firms owned 3011 miles (Table 9.1).

Besides Nippon, three private firms held particularly important licenses. The first, San'yō tetsudō, ran trains from Kobe to the southwestern tip of Honshū island. The second, Kyūshū tetsudō, held the license for the major trunk lines within that southern island and controlled access to the large coal deposits there. The third, Hokkaidō tankō tetsudō, held the license for the major lines within the northern-most island. Like the Kyūshū, it too controlled the transportation to crucial mineral fields. To each of these three firms the government promised subsidies. To Hokkaidō tankō it guaranteed 5 percent profits. To the Kyūshū and San'yō railroads it promised ¥2000 per mile of track.[10]

Having offered these subsidies, the government incurred large expenses. From 1893 to 1905, it paid profit guarantees of ¥9,034,094 and ¥1,384,411 to Nippon and Hokkaidō tankō, respectively. To San'yō and Kyūshū it paid track-completion payments of ¥488,877 and ¥546,567.

In addition, to the smaller Hokkaidō tetsudō, it paid subsidies of ¥1,109,827. For three of the firms, these were major subsidies: To Nippon, Hokkaidō tankō, and Hokkaidō tetsudō, they represented 18.8, 17.5, and 12.9 percent of their paid-in capital.[11]

All this private development occurred over the complaints of the railroad bureaucracy. Headed by one Inoue Masaru for more than 20 years, the railroad bureau consistently advocated national development (Inoue, 1906). It both opposed railroad development by private firms and urged the nationalization of the private companies already operating. At least until 1906, it had little effect. When it opposed a license, investors simply turned to the oligarchs or politicians.

In 1886, for example, several investors petitioned for the route from Kobe to Himeji. Inoue Masaru fought their petition on the ground that the Kobe-Shimonoseki route (of which this was a part) was a major trunk line. It was bad economics, he argued, to license the heavily traveled routes and keep only the branch lines for the government; it was bad transportation to splinter the major lines into short segments. To meet the latter objection, the investors asked for the entire line to Shimonoseki. They then turned to Prime Minister Itō Hirobumi and Foreign Minister Inoue Kaoru, and obtained the license. Through it, they created the San'yō line (Kawakami, 1967: I-72).

2.3. Nationalization

A year after the Imperial Diet opened in 1890, the government introduced a bill to nationalize all railroads. Yet even if the bureaucrats in the Railroad Bureau had the clout to introduce such bills, they lacked the power to pass them. The bill went nowhere, and a similar bill failed again in 1892. By the end of the decade, the Diet was again studying the subject. Not until 1906, though, did it eventually pass such a bill.[12] As initially proposed, the bill would have nationalized 17 companies. Saionji's Seiyūkai party cabinet then raised that figure to 32. Eventually, the Upper House lowered it back to 17 and passed it (Table 9.2).[13] These 17 companies together constituted 45 percent of the private companies operating, and owned 87 percent of all private track (Tables 9.1 and 9.2).

In the end, the politicians passed the bill because it paid so high a price for the lines that most of the railroads did not mind. Under the law, the government paid the firms twenty times their annual profits. More specifically, it calculated their average annual accounting profits from the middle of 1902 through the middle of 1905 and paid twenty times that amount.[14] Superficially, it was a reasonable price: Current stocks of railroad firms not subject to nationalization did trade at about eighteen times annual accounting profits (Table 9.3).[15]

Table 9.2. *Railroad nationalization, 1906*

	Acquisition date	Track mileage	Purchase price (¥)
Bōsō	9/7	39.32	2,156,998
Hankaku	8/7	70.11	8,175,719
Hokkaidō	7/7	158.77	11,452,097
Hokkaidō tankō	10/6	207.51	30,997,088
Hokuetsu	8/7	85.65	7,776,887
Iwagoe	11/6	49.36	2,521,498
Kansai	10/7	280.72	36,129,873
Kōbu	10/6	27.65	14,599,547
Kyōto	8/7	22.16	3,341,040
Kyūshū	7/7	446.02	118,856,448
Nanao	9/7	34.27	1,491,355
Nippon	11/6	860.35	142,551,944
Nishinari	12/6	4.44	2,663,609
Sangū	10/7	26.10	5,728,901
San'yō	12/6	414.51	81,983,994
Sōbu	9/7	73.16	12,871,155
Tokushima	9/7	21.39	1,341,431
Total		2,823.09	484,639,584

Sources: Tetsudō shō (ed.), *Kokuyū jūnen: Hompō tetsudō kokuyūgo no shisetsu narabi seiseki [Ten Years of Nationalization: The Facilities and Performance of the Railroads of our Country After Nationalization]* (Tokyo: Tetsudō shō, 1920), p. 14; Teishin shō tetsudō kyoku (ed.), *Tetsudō kyoku nempō (1906) [1906 Annual Report for the Railroad Bureau]* (Tokyo: Teishin shō tetsudō kyoku, 1908), pp. 14–15.

In fact, the government paid much more. Actual government payments apparently did not work the way a superficial reading of the law would suggest. Where railroad stocks generally traded at eighteen times accounting profits, and the government purported to buy them at twenty times profits, it actually bought them at fifty times profits (Tables 9.3 and 9.4). The investors lost their railroads, to be sure. But they lost them for a handsome price. For just that reason, most did not mind.

Nonetheless, nationalization did not charm *all* investors. As implemented, the process represented a strategic victory of the Mitsui group over the Mitsubishi. The Mitsubishi group had fought the nationalization bill, even bribing Diet members to oppose it (Harada, 1984: 49–52). They did so for a good reason: Although superficially neutral, the bill penalized the Mitsubishi. The Mitsubishi group had made its largest investments in the Nippon, Kansai, Kyūshū, Sangū and San'yō railroads

Table 9.3. *Market-value earnings ratios for railroads not nationalized*

Railroad	Market value	Earnings	MV/E
Hakatawan	¥1,162,000	¥61,999	18.7
Kawagoe	384,000	34,739	11.1
Narita	1,084,945	146,494	7.4
Tōbu	1,932,910	109,790	17.6
Ueno	226,800	6,635	34.2
Mean			17.8

Notes: "Earnings" refers to operating profit less interest and unusual expenses for 1906. "Market value" refers to the number shares of stock outstanding, multiplied by the average stock price for 1906.
Sources: Calculated from data found in Tetsudō shō (ed.), *Kokuyū jūnen: Hompō tetsudō kokuyūgo no shisetsu narabi seiseki [Ten Years of Nationalization: The Facilities and Performance of the Railroads of our Country After Nationalization]* (Tokyo: Tetsudō shō, 1920), p. 14; Teishin shō tetsudō kyoku (ed.), *Tetsudō kyoku nempō (1906) [Annual Report for the Railroad Bureau]* (Tokyo: Teishin shō tetsudō kyoku, 1908), pp. 258–59; Tokyo kabushiki torihiki sho (ed.), *Tokyo kabushiki torihiki sho 50 nen shi [A 50-Year History of the Tokyo Stock Exchange]* (Tokyo: Tokyo kabushiki torihiki sho, 1928).

(Table 9.5).[16] As Table 9.4 shows, these 5 railroads sold for 26.2 times earnings. The other 11 relevant railroads sold for over double that multiple: 60.2 times earnings.

Even so, why the Mitsubishi fought the bill so hard remains a puzzle. Twenty-six times earnings may be less than 60, but it is a good price if the stock otherwise trades at 20.[17] Yet fight the Mitsubishi did. That fact alone suggests (it certainly does not prove) that their stock may have been worth more than the statutory price. When the bill finally passed, cabinet member Katō Takaaki promptly resigned. Tied by marriage to the Mitsubishi family, he had fought nationalization. Having lost, he took the blame and quit (Kawakami, 1968: I-95).

Effectively, the nationalization bill represented an early example of a tactic the zaibatsu firms would use throughout the early twentieth century: manipulate politicians for private gain. The Mitsui had cultivated the Seiyūkai party, the Mitsubishi its rival. Given Seiyūkai control over the cabinet in 1906, the Mitsubishi group had little chance.[18]

3. TRAVEL SUBSIDIES

Suppose the usual tales of Meiji Japan were true, and visions of efficient growth best explain government policy. If the government involved itself

Table 9.4. *Purchase-price earnings ratios for railroads nationalized*

Railroad	Purchase price (¥)	Earnings (¥)	PP/E
Bōsō	2,156,998	24,776	87.1
Hankakau	8,175,719	197,747	41.3
Hokkaidō	11,452,097	(82,669)	N.A.
Hokkaidō tankō	30,997,088	376,992	82.2
Hokuetsu	7,776,887	199,757	38.9
Iwagoe	2,521,498	53,758	46.9
Kansai	36,129,873	1,629,159	22.2
Kōbu	14,599,547	110,174	132.5
Kyōto	3,341,040	106,114	31.5
Kyūshū	118,856,448	5,224,002	22.8
Nanao	1,491,355	31,949	46.7
Nippon	142,551,944	6,553,097	21.8
Nishinari	2,663,609	44,281	60.2
Sangū	5,728,901	253,521	22.6
San'yō	81,983,994	1,961,422	41.8
Sōbu	12,871,155	526,105	24.5
Tokushima	1,341,431	19,149	70.1
Mean			49.6

Notes: "Earnings" refers to operating profit less interest and extraordinary expenses for 1906.

Sources: Calculated from data found in Tetsudō shō (ed.), *Kokuyū jūnen: Hompō tetsudō Kokuyūgo no shisetsu narabi seiseki [Ten Years of Nationalization: The Facilities and Performance of the Railroads of our Country After Nationalization]* (Tokyo: Tetsudō shō, 1920), p. 14; Teishin shō tetsudō kyoku (ed.), *Tetsudō kyoku nempō (1906) [1906 Annual Report for the Railroad Bureau]* (Tokyo: Teishin shō tetsudō kyoku, 1908), pp. 258–59.

in the railroad industry for those efficiency reasons, it should have subsidized railroad travel. After all, by hypothesis it invested in railroads because railroad travel created positive externalities. Because railroads generated benefits that the investors who created them could not fully capture, private entrepreneurs would necessarily develop railroads only at socially sub-optimal levels (by definition, they would invest at the optimal level only if there were no externalities). If so, then to encourage greater railroad use, the government had to create and operate railroads at fares private entrepreneurs would not have found profitable. Necessarily – if these tales of efficient government involvement are true – it should have subsidized travel.

Table 9.5. *Principal Mitsubishi railroad holdings*

Company	Mb s/h rank	Mb s/h %	Other s/h rank	Other s/h %
Chikuhō	1	59.5	2	4.5
Kansai	1	9.0	2	3.8
Kyūshū	1	24.5	2	13.8
Nippon	?	2.0	1	14.1
Sangū	6	2.6	1	6.3
San'yō	1	13.7	2	2.8

Notes: "Mb s/h rank" refers to the position of the Mitsubishi group relative to the other shareholders of the firm, with a 1 meaning that the Mitsubishi group held the largest block of shares.
"Mb s/h %" refers to the percentage of the firm's stock held by the Mitsubishi group.
"Other s/h rank" refers to the position of the single largest shareholder other than the Mitsubishi group. Where the Mitsubishi group is the largest shareholder, the "other shareholder" listed here will always have the rank of 2.
"Other s/h %" refers to the percentage of the firm's stock held by the largest shareholder other than the Mitsubishi group.
The figures are as of 1891 for Nippon and as of 1895 for the other firms. The Kyūshū railroad acquired the Chikuhō railroad in 1897.
Sources: Ken'ichi Nakanishi, *Nippon shiyō tetsudō shi kenkyū [A Study of the History of Private Japanese Railroads]* (Tokyo: Nippon hyōron sha, 1963), pp. I: 65–68; Tokyo kabushiki torihiki sho (ed.), *Tokyo kabushiki torihiki shō 50 nen shi [A 50-Year History of the Tokyo Stock Exchange]* (Tokyo: Tokyo kabushiki torihiki sho, 1928); Steven J. Ericson, "Railroads in Crisis: The Financing and Management of Japanese Railway Companies During the Panic of 1890," in William D. Wray, (ed.), *Managing Industrial Enterprise: Cases from Japan's Prewar Experience* (Cambridge: Harvard Council on East Asian Studies, 1989), pp. 121–82, at 136.

The late nineteenth century Japanese government did nothing of the sort. Instead, it generally charged *higher* fares on its national railroads (on a per-kilometer basis) than the private lines charged (Table 9.6A). Were it running lines that private firms would have found cost-*in*effective, its higher fares would not alone disprove the subsidization hypothesis. Yet in the late nineteenth century it did not run unprofitable lines. Rather, its trains both carried heavier traffic than the private firms and carried those passengers longer distances. Notwithstanding, it charged higher fares.

Matters did not change until the 1910s and 1920s. Then, national railroad fares did begin to fall below private line fares (Table 9.6B). In turn, however, this phenomenon is consistent with the hypothesis advanced elsewhere in this book (see Chapters 4 and 10): As the government expanded the suffrage and political power devolved to the popularly elected politicians, those politicians began to manipulate government in-

Table 9.6. *Railroad travel and fares*

	Mean fare		Mean ride		Traffic density	
	National	Private	National	Private	National	Private
A. Pre-nationalization						
1890	6.94	6.59	40.7	25.8	517	89
1892	6.93	6.84	37.4	29.3	543	215
1894	6.51	6.34	43.6	31.5	714	276
1896	6.94	7.10	37.9	23.5	863	338
1898	7.10	7.74	34.4	22.8	973	361
1900	9.07	8.42	36.1	23.4	881	409
1902	9.77	9.31	37.1	23.5	740	379
1904	8.96	8.33	46.2	28.6	689	414
B. Post-nationalization						
1910	8.6	12.9	35.3	11.9	624	374
1912	8.6	9.9	36.3	11.6	695	293
1914	8.6	8.6	35.1	11.3	637	230
1916	8.3	11.0	34.7	11.3	726	225
1918	9.9	13.1	36.7	11.0	1081	307
1920	13.4	18.0	33.2	10.6	1293	384
1922	12.7	18.6	30.6	9.8	1393	393
1924	12.2	17.7	28.4	9.5	1497	429
1926	11.9	17.8	26.1	8.8	1501	442
1928	11.5	17.5	25.5	8.1	1576	501
1930	11.2	16.4	24.1	8.5	1364	516

Notes: "Mean fare" is in thousandths of a yen, and is the mean cost of one passenger-kilometer of travel.

"Mean ride" is in kilometers, and represents total passenger-kilometers divided by the total number of passengers.

"Traffic density" is total thousand passenger-kilometers, divided by the kilometers of track in place.

Source: Calculated from data found in Tetsudō shō (ed.), *Tetsudō tōkei shiryō (1932)* *[Railroad Statistical Materials (1932)]* (Tokyo: Tetsudō shō, 1932), Appendices to vols. I & II.

stitutions to benefit their constituents.[19] If true, this suggests that the fare changes at the national railroads may primarily have reflected electoral concerns. If fare changes had reflected concern over railroad spillovers, the government would have charged less than private developers from the start. Instead, it lowered fares only as power began to shift away from the electorally unresponsive oligarchs toward the popularly chosen politicians.[20]

4. PROCUREMENT

If zaibatsu firms manipulated the government to their private advantage, they should have tried to manipulate railroad procurement policies. Some procurement patterns do suggest they may have done that. By law, though, the oligarchs in 1889 had mandated competitive bidding.[21] As a result, explicit evidence that the zaibatsu firms manipulated the process is hard to find.[22]

The zaibatsu firms may have tried to skew locomotive purchases. Consider two pieces of (admittedly inconclusive) evidence. First, the Kenseikai party favored the Mitsubishi shipbuilding firm. Although precise figures are unavailable, during the 1920s the government bought most of its engines from four Japanese firms: Kawasaki jūkō, Nippon sharyō, Kisha seizō, and Hitachi seisakusho (Sawai, 1992). Notwithstanding this pattern, while in control of the cabinet the Kenseikai instead routed substantial locomotive contracts to the Mitsubishi shipbuilding firm. The firm had almost no experience in the railroad industry, but did have long-time connections to the Kenseikai.[23]

Second, the Kenseikai also may have favored Kisha seizō. Of the four standard locomotive manufacturers, three had affiliated themselves with a major political party. As part of the Kawasaki combine, Kawasaki jūkō supported the Seiyūkai. So too did Nippon and Kisha, for by 1930 the Ōkura group owned both 7.4 percent of Nippon sharyō and 24.3 percent of Kisha seizō, and Ōkura itself had cultivated ties to the Seiyūkai.[24] Only Hitachi seems not to have invested in political support. Among the three Seiyūkai firms, therefore, the Kenseikai leaders might not have cared who won the government contracts.

Nonetheless, the political leaders did care, for the Mitsubishi group owned 11.0 percent of Kisha seizō. All else being equal, Kenseikai leaders would thus have preferred to route contracts to Kisha, even if Kisha also had ties to the Seiyūkai through the Ōkura group. At least very tentatively, some aspects of firm profits reflect these political ties. The data on Kawasaki jūkō and Hitachi do not help, since both firms primarily produced other products – ships in the case of Kawasaki, electrical equipment in the case of Hitachi. Because Nippon sharyō and Kisha seizō both specialized in railroad equipment, their profits do reflect government procurement contracts. As one would expect, Kisha flourished under the Kenseikai. When the Keiseikai took office in mid-1924, Nippon sharyō had the larger profits. Shortly after the Seiyūkai recaptured the cabinet in mid-1927, the two firms were tied.[25]

Firm profits (¥ million)	1924–25	1927–28
Nippon sharyō	2.82	2.52
Kisha seizō	1.70	2.53

5. TAISHŌ-SHŌWA RAILROADS

5.1. The national railroads

Not only did politics determine the mechanics of nationalization in 1906, it continued to shape railroad development into the 1930s. Throughout the first decades of the century, political leaders relentlessly intervened in the industry to reward their friends and punish their enemies.

For the leaders of the Seiyūkai, rewarding friends meant playing what would become the Tanaka Kakuei game: laying railroad lines deep into the countryside. For those in the Kenseikai, it meant repairing the heavily used lines in the cities. The logic behind that contrast appears in Table 9.7: Throughout the period, the Seiyūkai tended to rely on rural voters, while the Kenseikai tended to rely on those in the cities (even if the distinctions were far from absolute, as the table shows).[26] Driven by that

Table 9.7. *Urban and rural party support (percentage in parentheses)*

Election	Urban			Rural		
	Seiyūkai	Kenseikai	Total	Seiyūkai	Kenseikai	Total
1915	7,315	33,382	97,245	439,619	489,846	1,308,592
	(7.5)	(34.3)		(33.6)	(37.4)	
1917	12,265	26,749	82,914	492,455	442,494	1,210,788
	(14.8)	(32.3)		(40.6)	(36.5)	
1920	59,248	56,409	192,529	1,412,570	663,207	2,427,548
	(30.8)	(29.3)		(58.2)	(27.3)	
1924	24,236	85,098	242,022	635,830	787,435	2,709,168
	(10.0)	(35.2)		(23.5)	(29.1)	
1928	184,987	423,482	846,222	4,059,397	3,832,528	9,019,973
	(21.9)	(50.0)		(45.0)	(42.5)	
1930	189,848	500,995	926,838	3,754,645	4,968,119	9,520,357
	(20.5)	(54.1)		(39.4)	(52.2)	

Notes: "Kenseikai" includes all parties of that lineage (primarily the Minseitō). For the elections through 1924, "urban" includes the urban and suburban districts (shi, ku) of Tokyo, Kyōto, Osaka, Kanagawa, Hyōgo, Aichi, and Fukuoka. Because of the different electoral districts drawn up for the 1928 and 1930 elections, cities (shi) consolidated into rural (gun) electoral districts have been dropped, and only the urban (ku) areas of Tokyo and Osaka and the cities of Yokohama, Kobe and Nagoya are included.
Source: Calculated from data found in Yukio Itō, *Taishō demokurashii to seitō seiji [Taisho Democracy and Party Politics]* (Tokyo: Yamada shuppan sha, 1987), p. 208.

electoral logic, railroad policy during the years at stake alternated between new rural lines and urban repairs.

The contrast between Seiyūkai and Kenseikai policies appears most closely in railroad construction and maintenance outlays. The money the government railroad spent on "construction" primarily went toward new lines in rural areas. The money it spent on "repairs" went to enhance service in the heavily used urban areas (Itō, 1987: 180, 192).

As Prime Minister, Hara aggressively promoted the Seiyūkai's rural construction drive. In order to reward his constituents, he dramatically increased the railroad budget, and proposed 194 new lines.[27] For years, his 1919 plan remained the Seiyūkai master plan. During 1920 and 1921, the government spent at least as much on construction as he had planned in 1919. In 1922, the Seiyūkai lost control of the cabinet to unaffiliated politicians. Even they, however, continued to follow his plans (Table 9.8, col. D).

Things changed in 1924 when the Kenseikai leaders took office. These men scrapped Hara's plan, and by 1925 spent on construction only 70 percent of what he had earlier intended. By 1927 they spent only 66 percent. That year, though, they lost the cabinet to the Seiyūkai, and

Table 9.8. *Railroad expenditures*

	A Construction	B Repair	C A/B	D A/(1919 Plan)	E New track (km)
1920	59,027	108,167	54.6	100.0	308.1
1921	58,297	124,831	46.7	144.6	388.3
1922	68,044	138,513	49.1	144.6	434.5
1923	64,496	121,013	53.3	125.8	519.0
1924	57,291	132,641	43.2	99.6	334.0
1925	44,772	145,409	29.8	71.5	409.9
1926	47,950	153.274	30.8	71.1	262.8
1927	49,217	156,245	31.5	66.5	244.8
1928	51,824	139,635	37.1	86.0	300.8
1929	68,907	125,199	55.0	186.9	449.3

Note: Columns A and B are in ¥1000.
Sources: Railroad expenditures taken from Tetsudō shō (ed.), *Tetsudō tōkei shiryō (I)* [*Railroad Statistical Materials (I)*] (Tokyo: Tetsudō shō, 1933), p. App. 20; data on the 1919 planned budgets taken from Tetsudō shō (ed.), "Tetsudō kensetsu oyobi kairyō hi yosan nendo wari hyō [Chart Showing Annual Budgets for Railroad Construction and Repair Costs, by Year]," *Tetsudō kaigi giji sokki roku* [*Records of the Proceedings of the Railroad Meetings*] (Tokyo: Tetsudō shō, 1919).

construction budgets again began to climb. By 1929, the government spent almost double what Hara had planned a decade earlier (Table 9.8, col. D).

Similarly, compare the ratio of construction to repair expenditures (Table 9.8, col. C). During the early Seiyūkai years, the ratio hovered at about 0.5, and the ensuing non-party cabinets maintained that ratio. The 1924 Kenseikai cabinet both lowered construction expenses and raised repair expenditures. It did so again in 1925, and by then the ratio of construction to repair expenditures had fallen below 0.3. Upon taking office in April 1927, the Seiyūkai leaders reversed the trend. They increased construction expenses, and eventually cut the amount they spent on repairs. By 1929 they had once more pushed the ratio of construction to repair expenses above 0.5.

Last, take the new track mileage (Table 9.8, col. E). Under Hara's Seiyūkai cabinet and the non-party cabinets that followed, the government increased the new track it laid from 308 km/year to 519 km/year. During the Kenseikai years, it cut that mileage to 245 km/year. Under Seiyūkai leadership, it once again boosted that amount, and by 1929 laid 449 km/year.

5.2. The private railroads

The Seiyūkai and Kenseikai leaders waged a similar war over the private railroads: The Seiyūkai fought to subsidize spur lines into the countryside, and the Kenseikai opposed the practice. The battle mattered crucially, for by 1930 private railroads again constituted a major part of the industry. Where the government now ran 14,487 km of track, the 408 private railroad and tram firms operated 9,725 km.[28] Where the government railroad carried 824 million passengers a year, the private firms carried 1,252 million.[29]

The private railroads collected generous subsidies. Under the 1911 Light Railroad Subsidy Act, if they earned profits of less than 5 percent on their fixed investments, the government paid them the difference.[30] Under the 1921 revisions to the Act, the government paid them up to 7 percent.[31] Naturally, this gave them an incentive to lay tracks even where the traffic would not earn a private firm a market return on its investment.

The Seiyūkai leaders masterminded these subsidies to the private railroads in order to help their rural supporters. Granted, the large firms running the commuter trains in the metropolitan centers carried the most private-sector passengers.[32] In 1924, for example, 12 firms carried 72 percent of all passengers. These large urban firms did not, however, earn most of the subsidies. Instead, they ran highly profitable operations – and thus were ineligible for the subsidies. The 9 largest firms earned profits of 12.5 percent on their construction expenses, for example, while the 33 smallest ones earned profits of 6.2 percent. Because several of these smaller firms ran profitable freight railroads for local mining operations, most of the small firms earned profits of only 3–4 percent.[33]

As a result, the private-firm subsidies largely promoted rural travel. In the cities, the railroads earned a large return, and were well-enough organized to stop any new licenses that would lower their profits. In the countryside, many of the firms could not even earn a market return. Because a railroad nonetheless benefited the area, local people supported new licenses. In effect, most new railroad licenses created unprofitable railroads, unprofitable railroads collected money from the government, and the benefit of that money went to the people living in the rural areas. In effect, through the railroad licenses the government could transfer wealth from urban taxpayers to rural residents.

Table 9.9 illustrates the political dynamic: a policy seesaw that tracked the fortunes of the two principal parties. During the early Seiyūkai years, the government granted licenses generously and voided them sparingly.

Table 9.9. *Private railroad licenses*

| | Licenses | | Licenses | | |
	Granted	km track	Voided	km track	Total subsidies
1920	39	785	4	86	620,514
1921	34	594	5	60	914,066
1922	73	1,350	7	106	1,564,427
1923	52	955	9	112	2,218,875
1924	43	598	31	731	2,988,770
1925	32	421	18	260	4,152,609
1926	64	933	21	230	4,962,883
1927	106	1,683	20	322	5,295,405
1928	57	830	15	166	6,298,172
1929	34	776	32	340	6,968,545
1930	7	22	42	695	7,499,934

Notes: Includes local railroads (chihō tetsudō), and excludes tramways (kidō).
Sources: Tokyo shisei chōsa kai (ed.), *Hompō chihō tetsudō jigyō ni kansuru chōsa* [*A Survey of the Local Railroad Business in Our Country*] (Tokyo: Tokyo shisei chōsa kai, 1932); Tetsudō shō (ed.), *Tetsudō tōkei shiryō (I)* [*Railroad Statistical Materials (I)*] (Tokyo: Tetsudō shō, 1933).

Indeed, by 1922 it granted 73 and voided 7. When the Kenseikai captured the cabinet, it tightened licensing standards (Nihon kokuyū, 1971: x-156), and by 1925 had cut the number of new licenses to 32. Under Seiyūkai control in 1927, the cabinet once more reversed course and boosted the number of new licenses to 104. When the Minseitō (the former Kenseikai) retook the cabinet in 1929, it cut that number back to 34, and by 1930 to 7. Simultaneously, it increased the number of licenses voided to 42.

The Seiyūkai leaders did not license the private firms just to run tracks to their constituents. They also used the licensing process to earn the bribes they needed for the expensive elections. This too the Minseitō leaders attacked in 1929. Upon taking office that year, they promptly prosecuted the former Seiyūkai Railroad Minister.[34] The Minister had extracted side-payments, it seems, from the private railroad developers to whom he had granted the licenses. In doing so he broke the law, and the courts duly convicted him. Ultimately, the Supreme Court sentenced him to two years in prison and fined him ¥192,220.[35]

6. CONCLUSION

It is not a sordid tale. It is not even a very seamy tale. Instead, it is a mundane tale. It is a tale, told by budgets and election returns, full of nothing more than ordinary political sins, signifying only bribes and pork.

The mundaneness of the story is key, however, for the quotidian grime is the story. In the long run, national railroad policy may or may not have promoted efficient growth. We do not know, since historians and economists of Japan have generally missed Fogel's basic intuition, and largely ignored the way ships, trucks and buses could substitute for trains. In the short run, trains could promote the electoral odds of the politicians in power – and the short-run goes a long way toward explaining government policy.

Whether or not Japanese railroads promoted efficient growth, they are tied to pork-barrel politics. Railroads and pork go together, as St. Bernard of Clairvaux once almost put it: "Qui me amat, amat et canem meum." Take nationalization. Perhaps it served broad national goals, or perhaps it did not. Either way, it transferred enormous wealth to the cabinet's patrons. Procurement policies may have done the same. And when the cabinet had to decide whether to improve rural service or urban, the single most important determinant was electoral: how much the cabinet depended on either rural or urban voters. In the end, political strategy largely determined Japanese railroad policy.

10

Cotton politics

1. INTRODUCTION

It stands in the middle of the Kenyan desert, hundreds of miles from the sea. As befits a minor Kenyan military outpost, it is a modest cement brick affair. Inside, it contains a warped pool table. Outside is a swimming pool, empty of everything except a decade's worth of accumulated sand. There is little to distinguish it from any other Kenyan outpost. Indeed, there is little else to it at all, except the plaque on the side of the building. But it is a plaque with a difference: "The Wajir Royal Yacht Club."

It seems Prince Edward (later Edward VIII) is to blame. The building had once been a British army outpost, and the prince, in a pique of imperial zeal, had once promised to visit it. When the palace thought better of his royal enthusiasm, he prudently canceled the trip. The troops, however, missed neither the snub nor the chance for some cheap Edwardian revenge. If his majesty could not visit them, they asked, could he at least designate his scheduled stop a "royal yacht club"? The embarrassed palace only too eagerly obliged.

Some royal favors come dear, others come cheap. Some redistribute massive wealth to the favored few. In Chapter 8 we explored how the Imperial Japanese government may have transferred funds to the large banks from the small banks and the depositing public. In Chapter 9 we explored how it transferred funds to its patrons' railroads from the public treasury. For these lavish favors, government officials sometimes charged their beneficiaries high prices.

Other government largesse resembles the Wajir Royal Yacht Club. It bestows little, costs little. Superficially, at least, the regulation in the Japanese cotton industry seems a case in point. Although the oligarchs had intervened in the industry very little, the party politicians were not so deferential. By the early 1930s, firms in both the spinning and the weaving sectors worked within government enforced cartels. Notwithstanding, the firms in neither sector earned monopoly rents. Although the government helped the weaving industry cartelize in 1925, the industry contained over 50,000 independent firms. As a result, the firms could not have raised prices through the cartel, state sanction or no. The government helped the spinners cartelize in 1931, and they at least had fewer competitors. Nonetheless, they never limited total investments in productive capacity, and never, therefore, limited the quantity produced. Not only did they not earn monopoly rents, they let the government intervene to raise labor costs by banning women from working nights.

As a result, the pre-war cotton industry presents three principal puzzles. First, why did the politicians organize the weaving sector when the firms involved had no chance of earning monopoly rents? Did it merely designate them a royal yacht club, or did it accomplish something more? Second, why did the spinning firms – with a better chance of fixing prices – wait to obtain their cartel designation until 1931, and even then not limit production? Did they too see their cartel as a yacht club? Last, why did the spinning firms let the government raise their labor costs by prohibiting female night labor? Who – if anyone – gained from the ban?

In each case, we argue, the firms in the industry did not see the regulation merely as a yacht club designation. The key to what they did see lies in the institutional structure of electoral competition. In this chapter we outline that electoral logic. We first introduce the Japanese cotton textile industry (Section 2). In Section 3 we address the government-sponsored cartels in the weaving sector, in Section 4 we discuss the cartels in the spinning sector, and in Section 5 we explore the night work ban.

2. THE INDUSTRY[1]

2.1. Early growth

In the middle of the nineteenth century, Japanese farmers were growing 49 million pounds of cotton, and by 1887 were growing 67 million. They never, however, grew more. They had no comparative advantage in cotton production, and by 1887 Japanese cotton spinners were already importing almost 10 million pounds. Ten years later, nearly all the cotton farmers had switched to other crops.[2]

Even if Japanese farmers could not grow raw cotton competitively, Japanese industrialists soon learned to sell the yarn they spun and the fabric they wove. Entrepreneurs began to import modern cotton spinning machines into Japan in the nineteenth century. Until then, English textile firms had dominated the cotton spinning industry. By the 1920s, things had changed. Japanese firms had mastered the British technology. They now consumed more raw cotton than their British competitors, and spun more yarn. Domestically, they created enormous wealth. By 1930, textile firms in toto (not just cotton) produced over a quarter of all Japanese manufactured goods (Table 10.1) and employed over 40 percent of all factory workers.[3]

Notwithstanding the American accounts of Japanese government leadership, the firms that learned this cotton textile technology did so on their own. Not that government leaders did not try to promote the industry. They just did so badly. The first modern cotton spinning mill opened in 1867 when one local government leader (the Satsuma daimyo) imported several English steam-powered spinning machines. In 1878, the national Ministry of Home Affairs imported two more, and the next year imported another ten. None of these mills succeeded. At most, they showed entrepreneurs how to fail. In the end, the spinning firms that did well were the firms that private entrepreneurs built on their own.[4]

2.2. Economies of scale

The cotton textile industry contained several distinct sectors – most importantly, spinning and weaving. Large firms consistently dominated the former. Small firms dominated the latter at the end of the nineteenth century, but lost that status over time. Consider, first, the cost of spinning a bale of cotton yarn. Factories with fewer than 5,000 spindles incurred about 75 percent again as much in costs as factories with over 60,000 spindles (Table 10.2A). Consider, too, contemporary estimates of 1929–34 spinning firm profits. Where the largest firms earned returns averaging 11.51, 3.83, 8.12, 9.12, and 9.96 percent for each of these years, the smallest firms earned 3.23, -5.86, 4.06, 5.95 and 7.99 percent.[5] Given these apparent scale economies, during most of the pre-war period fewer than 100 companies spun cotton. Among these firms, the largest spun most of the yarn: The largest 10 percent of the firms produced over half (Table 10.2B).

Small firms competed more successfully in the weaving sector. Here too the biggest firms produced the most, and that domination did increase over time (Table 10.3). Yet most weaving firms were small. Most were so small and their status so precarious that few reliable statistics about their total numbers remain.

Take, for instance, just those cotton weaving firms that joined their local trade associations. As of the early 1930s, they numbered 8,300 (Isobe, 1936: 431–38). Or take factory size. During the same period, 440 cotton spinning factories employed five or more employees, but nearly 5,000 cotton weaving factories employed five or more. Even these comparisons mislead, for most weaving factories did not join the trade asso-

The politics of oligarchy

Table 10.1. *Industrial production (constant 1934–36 ¥1000)*

	Cotton weaving	Cotton spinning	All textiles	All manufacturing
1886	N.A.	N.A.	163,733	1,038,022
1888	N.A.	N.A.	225,027	1,184,377
1890	N.A.	N.A.	300,419	1,329,326
1892	N.A.	N.A.	402,335	1,529,484
1894	N.A.	60,375	468,878	1,734,633
1896	N.A.	85,674	539,823	1,896,616
1898	3,598	133,724	569,962	2,103,720
1900	4,839	138,518	508,749	2,100,985
1902	9,722	173,354	515,433	2,093,414
1904	11,430	155,754	469,038	2,094,648
1906	17,045	211,866	611,852	2,446,967
1908	18,483	200,737	642,078	2,624,880
1910	28,597	256,718	804,394	2,959,515
1912	43,187	313,794	942,136	3,357,739
1914	58,200	388,988	986,438	3,543,959
1916	71,214	451,958	1,324,487	4,714,574
1918	85,724	433,827	1,505,510	5,854,107
1920	100,583	440,165	1,498,966	5,688,986
1922	111,174	539,082	1,849,897	6,411,538
1924	133,139	523,847	1,907,455	6,661,359
1926	169,182	678,412	2,343,639	7,776,840
1928	190,320	618,972	2,588,210	8,491,713
1930	186,032	616,854	2,601,077	9,261,342
1932	204,641	687,641	3,317,806	10,154,418
1934	245,499	858,922	4,239,744	13,155,213
1936	246,584	904,439	4,455,271	16,036,095

Notes: Data on cotton weaving cover only those weaving operations integrated into cotton spinning firms. N.A.: data not available.
Source: Shōzaburō Fujino, Shino Fujino and Akira Ōno, *Chōki keizai tōkei: Sen'i kōgyō [Long-Term Economic Statistics: The Textile Industry]* (Tokyo: Tōyō keizai shimpō sha, 1979), pp. 244–45; Miyohei Shinohara, *Chōki keizai tōkei: kōkōgyō [Long-term Economic Statistics: Mining and Manufacturing]* (Tokyo: Tōyō keizai shimpō sha, 1972), pp. 140–45.

ciations, and most weaving factories did not employ five people. Instead, the total number of cotton weaving factories in the early 1930s was about 50,000. Most of these "factories" were simply a room with a loom. A family that wanted to weave would buy or lease a loom, and sell (or return on consignment) the fabric its members wove to a local wholesaler.

138

Table 10.2. *Apparent scale economies in cotton spinning*

A. *Relative processing costs*

Spindles/factory	Materials	Wages (labor)	Amenities (labor)	Operating costs	Total
5,000	21.77	104.14	16.92	22.37	165.20
10,000	21.77	73.59	11.95	19.34	126.65
20,000	21.77	57.66	9.35	18.84	107.64
30,000	21.77	51.53	8.37	18.33	100.00
40,000	21.77	49.25	8.00	18.09	97.11
50,000	21.77	47.97	7.79	17.93	95.46
60,000	21.77	47.14	7.66	17.83	94.40

B. *Firm size*

Number of spindles	Number of firms	(%)	Total spindles	(%)
under 10,000	10	(12.5)	51,268	(0.4)
10,000–49,999	25	(31.3)	614,820	(5.0)
50,000–99,999	14	(17.5)	932,828	(7.5)
100,000–299,999	20	(25.0)	3,040,996	(24.6)
300,000–499,999	3	(3.7)	1,050,604	(8.5)
500,000 and over	8	(10.0)	6,668,248	(54.0)

Notes: In A, costs are indexed by expenses for 30,000-spindle factories (given constant value of raw cotton used), and are for 20-count yarn. Total costs at 30,000-spindle factory are 100. In B, firm size is as of 1937.
Source: Keizō Seki, *Nihon mengyō ron* [A Theory of the Japanese Cotton Industry] (Tokyo: Tokyo daigaku shuppan kai, 1954), pp. 204, 473.

All told, the spinning firms during this period employed about 170,000 people; the weaving firms employed about 230,000.[6]

3. THE WEAVING CARTELS

3.1. The shape of the cartels

Although there were too many weaving firms to have cartelized themselves, in 1925 the government seemed to help. That year, it passed the weavers a cartel statute. Called the "Vital Export Products Industrial Associations Act,"[7] the statute let those firms designated by the Minister of Commerce & Industry as "manufacturers engaged in the production of vital export products" (§1) organize trade associations.

Once designated, the firms could adopt whatever restrictions necessary

The politics of oligarchy

Table 10.3. *Factory size in cotton weaving*

	fewer than 10 looms		10–49 looms		50 or more looms	
	No. of factories	No. of looms	No. of factories	No. of looms	No. of factories	No. of looms
1923	112,453	151,834	4,506	95,039	1,020	158,825
1924	102,137	139,127	4,091	88,570	1,015	159,695
1925	91,789	123,063	4,149	87,449	948	154,847
1926	71,140	105,063	4,051	89,969	1,057	170,938
1927	70,304	99,661	4,189	91,577	1,042	177,834
1928	68,121	99,708	4,055	88,077	1,039	182,162
1929	69,821	88,847	3,859	86,346	1,054	187,626
1930	61,628	79,090	3,814	82,282	1,049	187,531
1931	62,553	79,296	3,788	80,753	1,033	181,558
1932	56,884	72,276	3,710	80,731	1,089	199,290
1933	48,648	62,574	3,835	85,052	1,159	215,240
1934	45,897	59,644	4,024	83,361	1,218	233,699
1935	43,164	58,274	3,969	86,893	1,256	240,813
1936	41,623	54,979	4,003	87,844	1,289	250,118

Notes: The table divides cotton weaving firms into three groups – fewer than 10 looms in the factory, 10–49 looms, and 50 or more looms. Within each group, the first column gives the number of factories and the second column gives the number of machines at use in those factories.
Source: Shōkō daijin kanbō chōsaka(ed.), *Shōkō shō tōkei hyō [Statistical Tables for the Ministry of Commerce and Industry]* (Tokyo: Tokyo tōkei kyōkai, various years).

"to promote and improve the industry." They could agree to coordinate sales, for example, to cut production, or to fix prices (Act, §§1, 3). With no antitrust statute, that much they could have done on their own. Under the 1925 Act, they could now also invoke government sanctions on non-members who refused to comply with association rules.[8]

The cotton weaving industry was among the first designated under this statute.[9] The firms responded promptly. Within four months, they began to organize trade associations (Isobe, 1936: 431–32). They grouped themselves into regional associations, and consolidated those associations under umbrella national federations.

Of these associations and federations, the weaving firms formed all sorts. The Federation of Japanese Cotton Fabric Industrial Associations covered a broad scope and included 57 associations. The Federation of Japanese Towel Industrial Associations included only 8. By the mid-1930s, 53,000 firms in assorted industries had organized themselves into 37 federations and 600 associations. Within the cotton fabric industry, they formed 7 federations and 110 associations containing over 8,300 member firms.[10]

3.2. Money and elections

(a) The statute as a price-fixing scheme. Although the Act may have looked like a price-fixing statute, for weaving firms it was nothing of the sort. As of 1935, only one cotton trade association had even tried explicitly to fix prices.[11] With good reason: Government sanctions or no, price-fixing never had a chance. Most basically, given the huge number of cotton-weaving firms (over 50,000), their variety, their geographic dispersion, and the ease of entering the industry, association members had enormous incentives to cheat on any cartel. In their study of American price-fixing schemes, Hay and Kelley (1974) found an average cartel size of 7.25 firms.[12] With 50,000 firms, the Japanese cotton weaving industry was a beast of another species.

(b) The statute and vote division. The logic to these weaving cartels may lie not in a monopoly pricing scheme but in the electoral system. As with the railroad industry, the oligarchs had not involved themselves heavily in regulating the textile industry. The party politicians, however, did so with a vengeance. Yet the "cartels" they authorized were not cartels at all. Rather, they were organizations that the politicians had apparently designed to help them divide the vote in multi-member electoral districts. As explained in Chapter 4, a party determined to control the Diet in the late 1920s had to divide its supporters among multiple candidates in the same district. For that, it needed access to highly organized industries. Through such an industry's trade association, it could then assign its supporters to specific candidates (or at least prod them toward those candidates). By letting specific politicians patronize specific weaving groups, it could induce weavers in those groups to vote for that politician. In the process, it could reduce the randomness that would otherwise ensue.

Consider the problem that the politicians in the plurality Kenseikai party faced in the mid-1920s. They were about to run for office under universal male suffrage with multi-member districts and a simple non-transferrable vote (Chapter 4). If they could but use their control over the cabinet to dispense pork to their supporters through candidate-specific support groups, they could use the government to their private electoral advantage – to attract supporters, to divide them, and thereby to solidify their control over the Diet. Yet personal support groups did not come cheap. Creating them itself cost money that the party could ill-afford to spend.

If the Kenseikai politicians could use industry trade associations, however, they could route pork to their supporters more cheaply. For this purpose, the cotton weaving industry seemed ideal. It employed large numbers of workers, and after 1925 these workers came from households with a vote. Unfortunately, in 1925 it was still unorganized. If the Kenseikai politicians could only organize the firms in the industry into trade associations, they would have groups they could use for electoral ends.

In this context, recall the timing of the Industrial Associations Act – passed in 1925. Before 1919, vote division had mattered, but the electorate had been small and rich. Workers in the cotton weaving firms had come from households that did not vote. The 1919 Act expanded the suffrage a bit, but simultaneously eliminated multi-member districts. Vote division no longer mattered. The 1925 Act now did two things: It extended the vote to all families, and reinstituted multi-member districts. In this new world, politicians needed both to attract and to divide the poor. In this world, for Kenseikai politicians weaving trade associations were ideal.

(c) Subsidies. As much as the Kenseikai politicians wanted cotton weaving firms to form trade associations, they could not convince the firms to organize just by asking them. Then as now most firms did not stay in business through political charity. Neither could they convince the firms to organize by telling them they could cut production and fix prices. Weaving firms knew both that price-fixing in a 50,000-firm industry was not likely to work, and that even if it did, most tactics were already legal. To convince the weavers to organize, the politicians apparently routed them government funds instead.

Politicians dispensed these subsidies to the new trade associations in two ways. First, they gave direct cash subsidies. Already in 1927, they paid a total of ¥299,500 to 15 associations (in a variety of industries). By 1935, they had paid ¥1,974,145 to 125 associations. Of this amount, they had paid the cotton weavers nearly half – ¥882,100 (Kōgyō, 1936: 21–22, 47–48).

Second, the politicians routed the associations low-interest loans. In 1928, they began the program by loaning 16 associations a total of ¥1,356,800. By 1934, they had loaned ¥5,506,800. All this occurred at a time when bank loans averaged 8 to 10 percent interest and many small firms probably could not obtain bank loans at any price. By contrast, through this program the weaving associations could borrow at 3.9 percent through September 1932, and at 4.8 percent thereafter.[13]

(d) Kenseikai success. Just as the Kenseikai politicians hoped, these associations may have given (the evidence is only suggestive) their party a modest advantage. As of 1925, the Kenseikai had a plurality in the Lower

142

House with 151 seats, and control of the Prime Ministership. The Seiyūhontō had 116 seats and the Seiyūkai 101. When the Diet passed the 1925 Industrial Associations Act, the largest number of weaving workers were in the Osaka and Aichi prefectures (Shōkō shō, 1925: 9). These two areas were also well-organized: Of the 112 cotton weaving associations in place by late 1935, 27 were in Osaka and 13 in Aichi (Kōgyō, 1936: 30).

The Kenseikai did unusually well in these weaving districts. In the next general election, in 1928, the party (now renamed the Minseitō) lost power to the Seiyūkai, 217 to 216. Nonetheless, in the weaving districts in Osaka and Aichi it elected 14 Minseitō candidates to the Seiyūkai's 5. It won these 14 seats, moreover, with only 56 percent of the vote. In proportional allocation, it would have won 12, the Seiyūkai 6, and the other parties 3. By playing the vote division game better than its competitors, it won 14 seats, and held the Seiyūkai to 5 and the other parties to 2.[14]

Nor did the Minseitō party do well among the weavers simply because of its traditional urban bias. As noted in Chapter 9, it did cater to urban voters while the Seiyūkai courted the rural. Yet it did not always find this strategy a success. In 1928, it won 43 percent of the popular vote nationally and 46 percent of the seats. In the large urban centers it won only 34 percent of the vote. Although it won 51 percent of the seats there, it won them only through apportionment and vote division games.[15] By contrast, in the weaving districts it won both votes and seats: 56 percent of the popular vote and 67 percent of the seats (Seisen, 1930: app.; Fujisawa, 1928: 221).

4. THE SPINNING CARTEL

4.1. The cartel

Unlike the weaving firms, the cotton spinning firms had already organized themselves into a cartel by 1882. They called themselves the "Great Japan Spinning Federation" (the Dai-Nippon *Bōseki Rengō* Kai, abbreviated "Bōren"). The conventional story is simple enough. Initially, they used the Bōren to gain monopsonistic power in the labor market: to lower wages by not bidding for each others' workers (Hashimoto, 1935: 26). Soon, they used it to gain monopolistic power in the product market: to raise profits by enforcing quantity restraints. Workers and consumers suffered, but with no anti-trust statute it was all legal.

In fact, as a price-fixing strategy the cartel was a long shot at best. It included 30 to 70 firms — fewer than the weavers' 50,000, but far more than most successful price-fixing conspiracies. It never explicitly set prices, even though it could have tried if it had wanted to do so. It never included all members (much less all potential members) of the industry.

The politics of oligarchy

Most basically, the Bōren never cut quantity. Periodically, it ordered cuts in operating hours or days or in the percentage of spindles in use (Ramseyer, 1993). Yet it never tried to limit the total number of spindles. To earn its members monopoly rents, it needed to cut the quantity produced. To do that, it could not just cut hours or furlough existing machines. It needed also to prevent firms from buying new machines. That it never did. By allowing firms to buy new machines but prohibiting them from using them fully, it merely ensured that its members invested inefficiently.

Even as the Bōren mandated cuts in hours and the percent of spindles operated, firms continued to invest in new equipment (Table 10.4).[16]

Table 10.4. *Spinning cartel cheating*

	A Mandated reductions (%)	B Spinning factories	C Spindles (x 1000)
1920	31.5%	(40)	355
1921	47.0	89	299
1922	0	(159)	394
1923	0	(1)	284
1924	0	20	(91)
1925	0	(8)	451
1926	0	37	293
1927	28.9	(22)	263
1928	47.2	6	531
1929	23.6	38	233
1930	21.8	18	595
1931	25.3	15	221
Mean new spindles while restrictions in place			328,000
Mean new spindles while no restrictions in place			266,000
Mean new spinning factories while restrictions in place			14.8
Mean new spinning factories while no restrictions in place			−22.2

Notes: A. Cartel-mandated reductions in the Bōren. B. Net increase (or decrease) in number of spinning factories with five or more employees. C. Net increase (or decrease) in number of operating spindles.

Sources: Calculated from data found in J. Mark Ramseyer, "Credibly Committing to Efficiency Wages: Cotton Spinning Cartels in Imperial Japan," *University of Chicago Law School Roundtable*, 1993: 153 (1993); Shōkō daijin kanbō tōkei ka (ed.), *Kōjō tōkei hyō [Census of Manufactures]* (Tokyo: Tokyo tōkei kyōkai, various years); Tsūshō sangyō daijin kanbō chōsa tōkei kyoku (ed.), *Kōgyō tōkei 50 nenshi [A Fifty Year History of the Manufactures Census]* (Tokyo: Ōkura shō insatsu kyoku, 1961); Keizō Seki, *Nihon mengyō ron [A Theory of the Japanese Cotton Industry]* (Tokyo: Tokyo daigaku shuppan kai, 1954), p. 446.

Despite the Bōren's restraints, they aggressively built new factories and installed new spindles. Indeed, they built more factories and installed more spindles while the restraints were in place than while they were not. If this were a production-restriction cartel, it was one that failed. As the leading American authority on the Japanese spinning industry put it, the Bōren firms earned no monopsony rents in the labor market, and did not "restrict industry output, even on a cyclical basis."[17]

4.2. Political quiescence among the spinning firms

The Bōren firms might have done more. Having organized a trade association and coordinated spindle furloughs, they might have installed a scheme that would actually earn them some monopoly returns. At the very least, they might have limited the number of spinning machines they each could buy. They might then have used the government to enforce those limits. With the right legislation, they might even have imposed the limits on the non-Bōren firms.

The spinning firms did not do so – and the reason probably lies in the political power of the Mitsui zaibatsu.[18] During most of the years at issue, the major zaibatsu conglomerates maintained enormous leverage over the elected politicians. They gave heavily to the mainstream political parties and, having given, demanded the statutes they wanted. Often, they succeeded.

The Mitsui zaibatsu had economic preferences that consistently ran counter to those of the Bōren. It had invested very little in the spinning firms themselves (Table 10.5). All told, it owned stock in seven spinning firms, and that combined investment gave it a 3.25 percent stake in the industry. The other three major zaibatsu groups had a total stake of less than 1 percent. As a result, any advantage that the Mitsui or any other zaibatsu earned from a successful price-fixing cartel in the spinning industry was minimal.

At the same time, the Mitsui group maintained large stakes in two industries directly threatened by any effective spinning cartel. First, it dominated the cotton trade. Through a vast network of overseas offices, the Mitsui trading firms acted both as sales agent (often exclusive) for cotton yarn and fabric, and as buying agent (again, often exclusive) for raw cotton.[19]

Second, the Mitsui sold spinning machines. For decades, it served as exclusive selling agent for the English Platt Brothers firm. There were alternatives, but as of 1909, 87 percent of the spindles in Japan were Mitsui-imported Platt spindles (Saxonhouse, 1991). When one Toyoda Sakichi – his family would eventually build the Toyota Motor firm – began a textile machinery company, the Mitsui invested in it. When it

Table 10.5. *Zaibatsu investments in the cotton spinning industry*

A. *Zaibatsu holdings in spinning firms*

| | Mitsui Zaibatsu | | |
Textile firm	Mitsui shareholdings	Firm spindles	Mitsui share of spindles
Kanebō	6.71%	615,192	41,279
Kinka bōseki	41.36	144,624	59,816
Toyoda bōshoku	5.97	79,824	4,765
Tenma bōshoku	48.58	65,792	31,962
Utsumi bōshoku	48.97	72,500	35,503
Tokyo mosurin	48.52	79,128	38,393
Kikui bōshoku	1.43	62,428	768

| | Mitsubishi Zaibatsu | | |
Textile firm	Mitsubishi shareholdings	Firm spindles	Mitsubishi share of spindles
Nagasaki bōshoku	2.79	98,656	2,753
Fuji gasu bōseki	1.43	502,104	7,180

| | Sumitomo Zaibatsu | | |
Textile firm	Sumitomo shareholdings	Firm spindles	Sumitomo share of spindles
Osaka gōdō bōseki	0.67	427,524	2,864

| | Yasuda Zaibatsu | | |
Textile firm	Yasuda shareholdings	Firm spindles	Yasuda share of spindles
Osaka gōdō bōseki	0.86	427,524	3,677

B. *Zaibatsu share of total industry spindles (6,529,394)*

	Spindles	Percentage
Mitsui	212,486	3.25
Mitsubishi	9,933	0.15
Sumitomo	2,864	0.04
Yasuda	3,677	0.06
Total	228,960	3.50

Notes: Figures are from Takahashi (1930) where available, and from stockholder lists in company semi-annual reports where not. Mitsui ownership in Kinka and Tokyo mosurin are Takahashi's estimates. Stock classes are combined on an equal (one-share-to-one-share) basis. Figures are as of about 1928.

Sources: Kamekichi Takahashi, *Nippon zaibatsu no kaibō [An Analysis of the Japanese Zaibatsu]* (Tokyo: Chūō kōron sha, 1930); semi-annual company reports for Kikui bōshoku, Tenma bōshoku, and Osaka gōdō.

developed its own spinning machine, the Mitsui sold that machine as well.[20]

Mitsui records illustrate how heavily the group depended on the cotton trade (though dividend and internal company data pose obvious problems).[21] The Mitsui holding company (a partnership known as Mitsui gōmei) owned 100 percent of the stock in Mitsui bussan (the conglomerate's trading company). For the first half of 1928, Bussan paid dividends of ¥5.97 million on profits of ¥8.98 million. To the holding company, those dividends constituted 44.9 percent of its dividend income and 37.0 percent of its total income. Of its profits, Bussan earned a relatively small amount (¥147,000, or 1.64 percent) from textile machinery sales. It earned a much larger sum by handling raw cotton and cotton products. Exactly how much it earned from this cotton trade is less clear, but at least several years earlier it had handled the following accounts[22]:

Raw cotton
¥43 million: 15.36 percent of all Bussan trades and 24 percent of all raw cotton imports.
Cotton yarn
¥23 million: 8.18 percent of all Bussan trades and 32 percent of all cotton yarn exports.
Cotton fabric
¥16 million: 5.62 percent of all Bussan trades and 51 percent of all cotton fabric exports.

To the Mitsui zaibatsu, all this gave it financial interests that directly clashed with those of the spinners. The Mitsui depended on Bussan. To Bussan, raw cotton sales were the single largest item on its books, and the cotton industry was over a quarter of its business. If the Bōren cut raw cotton imports, the Mitsui lost import fees. If the Bōren cut yarn and fabric exports, it lost export fees. And if the Bōren bought fewer spinning machines, it lost machine profits. True, if the Bōren raised prices, it did earn monopoly rents in the spinning industry – but only 3.25 percent of those rents.[23]

4.3. The 1931 Control Act

In 1931, the Diet finally passed the Bōren cartel statute. Called the "Major Industry Control Act,"[24] the statute let cartels in designated industries use the government to enforce their terms. More specifically, if two-thirds of the firms in a cartel petitioned the Minister overseeing their industry, the Minister could force members and non-members alike to comply with the cartel.[25] To do so, the Act required him first to consult a "Control Association." By the end of the year, the government had both

147

specified the details of the Association (up to eighteen people named by the Cabinet)[26] and designated the cotton spinning industry as an industry covered by the Act.[27]

The Act's passage and the spinning industry's designation under it raise two puzzles relevant here. First, no obvious institutional or economic changes explain their occurrence in 1931. If the spinners needed government help to enforce a cartel in 1931, they needed it decades earlier. If the Mitsui group opposed effective quantity restraints decades earlier, it would have opposed them in 1931.

Second, the spinning firms seem not to have used the statute. Although they now had the right to invoke the government, they apparently never did. On the one hand, they continued to mandate percentage reductions in spindles used; on the other, they continued to invest in new capacity. From 1932 to 1934, the number of operating spindles increased 16.3 percent, and from 1934 to 1936 another 20.8 percent (Seki, 1954: 446). Notwithstanding the mandated percentage reductions in spindles used, this new investment increased production: From 1932 to 1934, production increased 24.9 percent, and from 1934 to 1936 another 5.3 percent (Table 10.1).

These two puzzles are probably related, and the answer to both may lie not in 1931 but in 1932. That year, the Japanese military effectively ended democratic government (see Chapter 4). Signs of a forthcoming coup had been clear for years. Overseas, Army officers blew up a train carrying the leading north China warlord in 1928. By doing so, they hoped to incite the riots that would give them an excuse to overrun Manchuria. The Tokyo politicians they notified later. Domestically, officers and rightist collaborators had planned coups and assassinated business and political leaders at an increasingly frenetic pace. They shot Prime Minister Hamaguchi Osachi in 1930, plotted an unsuccessful coup in 1931, overran Manchuria later that year, and killed Mitsui CEO Dan Takuma and Prime Minister Inukai Tsuyoshi in 1932. By then, democratic government was over.

As rational agents, the bureaucrats behind the Control Act seem to have shifted loyalties in anticipation: Fundamentally, in 1931 they drafted a statute the military wanted. Only incidentally did their statute serve spinning interests.[28] Although the bureaucrats were still nominally under political control, by 1931 they knew they would likely soon answer to the military leaders. They anticipated that change, calculated that their new principals would place the economy on a planned basis, and prepared what they thought their new principals would want. The bureaucrats themselves – men who have since gone on to claim credit for post-war Japanese economic growth through the Ministry of International Trade and Industry – have long protested that such was not their intent (Johnson, 1982: 109). But they do protest too much.

The fate of the Control Act itself suggests its militaristic origins. Although the firms themselves never used the statute to limit capacity, the military used it as the basis for its command economy during the next decade and a half. By its own terms the Act was a temporary statute that expired in five years (Act, Appendix). Yet in 1936 the military leaders re-enacted it with few major changes.[29] Soon, they had the bureaucrats develop elaborate quantity and price controls and regiment the entire economy (Okazaki, 1987). In doing so, they both retained the 1931 concept of a Control Association and drew on the vast array of data that the 1931 Act had begun requiring businesses to submit.[30]

These developments did not serve the spinning firms well. To the contrary, by the late 1930s the government was prosecuting cotton yarn sellers for charging too high a price.[31] By 1941 it was melting down spinning machines. And by 1943 it was ordering the spinning firms to make airplanes (Nisshin, 1969: 542–62). As one spinning executive recalled:

It was all control, control. We had our hands in fetters, feet in chains. We'd read in the bureaucratic circulars that the transaction we'd done the day before was now illegal – and the economic police would have us. It was tough surviving the bureaucratic bullying, because the bureaucrats did have power – even if they didn't have much else. Certainly, when it came to national industrial policy, they had no views, no knowledge, no experience (Nisshin, 1969: 481).

5. THE FACTORY ACT

5.1. Introduction

Potentially related to the spinning cartel but equally problematic was the 1929 ban on night work by women. The ban began as part of the 1911 Factory Act.[32] That Act, which covered all factories with fifteen or more workers (Act,§1), closely resembled Western "protective" statutes of the same vintage. It outlawed child labor (workers under age twelve, §2); the use of adolescents (under age fifteen) or women for more than twelve hours a day (§3); and the use of adolescents or women for any night work (10 p.m. to 4 a.m.). Apparently because of industry opposition to the ban, the ban on night work at factories with two shifts (like cotton spinning mills) only took effect fifteen years from the statute's effective date (§§4, 6). Because the men surrounding the Emperor did not issue an Imperial Order making the Act effective until 1916,[33] the ban was not scheduled to take effect until 1931.

In 1923, the Diet amended the Factory Act.[34] As revised, it now applied to all factories with ten or more workers, revoked the ban on child labor, changed the limits on long shifts by adolescents to an eleven-hour maximum for workers under sixteen, and changed the definition of night work to 10 p.m.-5 a.m. For factories using two shifts, this revised night ban took effect three years after the implementation of the statute. Because the Emperor made the statute effective in 1926,[35] the night work ban took effect in 1929.

The spinning firms could have responded to the ban in one of three ways: switching to an all-male labor force, switching to two eight-hour female day shifts and one male night shift, or switching to two short female day shifts and closing down for the night. They chose the last. Even though they could have used an all or partially male work force, they did not (Fujino et al., 1979: 255).

For the spinning firms, women came cheaper than men. The Japanese firms had installed "ring-spindle" machines that were easy to operate. Like the New England spinners, they used adolescent girls on these machines and housed them in carefully supervised dormitories. Although they kept some experienced workers (generally women) as group leaders, in general they needed people with minimal strength or experience, few marketable skills, and little interest in building marketable skills. The young peasant girls they hired fit this bill. They came with little or no factory experience and only modest schooling, quit after a few years, and went home to marry (Saxonhouse and Wright, 1984a: 4–6; 1984b: 274).

Even so, one might have thought the firms would add a male night shift. Their investment in the machines, after all, was sunk. Even if they generally paid men 40 percent more than they paid women (Shindō, 1958: 358), they might have found it cost-effective to use them on an extra shift at night.

Notwithstanding, the firms did not hire men. The reasons are unclear. Perhaps running mixed-sex spinning mills added significant costs. Perhaps, for example, a firm would have had to modify the machines if it planned to have both men and women operate them. Perhaps, given the hothouse nature of any adolescent workplace, it would have incurred higher monitoring costs. Alternatively, perhaps the market wages for men simply priced them out of the spinning industry. Even with their investments sunk, perhaps the firms simply could not afford to pay them the going rate.[36]

5.2. The statute as cartel

In the end, the biggest puzzle may be discovering who – if anyone – gained from the night work ban.[37] Given the earlier discussion of the spinning cartel, consider first the chance that it enforced an otherwise unsuccessful Bōren price-fixing cartel. Unable to raise prices on their own, the spinning firms invoked (or bought) the power of the government to cut production by cutting hours worked.[38]

For the reasons discussed, this explanation does not work. As a price-fixing cartel, the Bōren's scheme contained a basic problem: Even during cutbacks, firms could freely expand productive capacity, and thereby freely expand the quantity they produced. The Factory Act did nothing to solve this dilemma. Instead, it simply reduced the efficiency with which they could use any capacity they installed. If a firm wanted to increase production, the Act did not stop it from doubling the number of its machines. What it did instead was prevent all firms, no matter how many machines they installed, from using women to operate them for more than seventeen hours a day.

5.3. The statute as intra-industry strategy

In explaining the passage of the 1833 British Factory Act, Howard Marvel (1977) advances a more complex strategic explanation.[39] Much like the later Japanese Act, the 1833 British Act limited work hours and imposed a variety of "protective" conditions. According to Marvel, these provisions affected different firms within the British textile industry differently. Specifically, they raised the costs at the smaller water-powered cotton spinning firms more than they raised the costs at the larger steam-powered firms. In the process, they raised profits at the latter.

However well it fit Britain, Marvel's logic does not apply to Japan. Table 10.6 shows the operating hours at the different sized firms, and the degree to which the different-sized firms relied on female workers.[40] Two points stand out. First, smaller firms did not rely more heavily than larger firms on night work. Whether large or small, firms in 1905 worked about 22.6 hours a day and firms in 1925 worked about 20.1 hours. As their incomes rose over the decades, workers negotiated shorter hours. Yet they negotiated them at large and small firms alike.

Second, the smaller firms were not consistently more labor-intensive than the larger firms. The very smallest did generally use more workers per spindle than the other firms. Whether the point applies to any firms other than the smallest quintile, however, is unclear. In 1925, it did not even apply there.

Even if the smaller firms had used labor more intensively than the larger firms, the Act's implications would be ambiguous. Fundamentally, the Act prevented firms from using their machines for more than seventeen hours a day. In the process, it reduced the returns to capital – and thereby decreased the incentives to invest in new machinery. As explained below, however, it also raised the costs of labor – and thereby increased

Table 10.6. *Hours and worker sex, by firm size*

Quintile	Mean factory hours				Female workers/male workers				Female workers/working spindles			
	1905	1915	1925	1930	1905	1915	1925	1930	1905	1915	1925	1930
First	22.7	22.3	19.7	N.A.	4.46	4.18	3.52	3.51	3.87	3.74	3.05	1.83
Second	21.7	21.9	21.1	N.A.	4.14	4.22	3.77	3.89	4.14	3.50	3.20	1.83
Third	23.3	23.0	19.6	N.A.	4.58	4.99	3.28	3.71	4.33	3.46	2.38	1.54
Fourth	22.8	23.1	19.9	N.A.	4.43	4.58	3.34	3.59	4.28	3.29	2.60	1.97
Fifth	22.4	22.8	20.2	N.A.	3.86	4.34	2.67	3.46	4.89	4.79	2.99	2.58

Notes: The firms are divided into quintiles on the basis of the number of spindles in each firm. The second set of columns gives the ratio of female workers to male workers at spinning firms. The third set of columns gives the ratio of female workers at spinning firms to the number of 100 operating spindles. The data are for the months of July for each year. The year of 1930 is substituted for 1935 because of data availability. Firm-level data on factory hours are not available for 1930.

Sources: Calculated from data provided in Dai-Nippon bōseki rengō kai (ed.), *Dai-Nippon bōseki rengō kai geppō [Great Japan Spinning Federation Monthly]* (Osaka: Dai-Nippon bōseki rengō kai, various months).

the incentive to automate production. The net effect thus remains unclear.[41]

5.4. The statute as animus

Elisabeth M. Landes (1980) suggests that legislators enacted the analogous American "protective" statutes out of an anti-immigrant bias. She argues that the statute primarily reduced the job opportunities of immigrant women. In Japan, one would be hard put to find any equivalent bias. Japanese employers did not use many immigrants in 1911 or even in 1923. Neither did they use many members of ethnic minorities in any industries heavily affected by the Act. Although the textile workers came from poor families, they came from the same ethnic group as the rich. Moreover, because the women involved generally sent a large portion of their savings to their families (Ramseyer, 1993), it is hard to see in the statute even any misogynistic bias. Ultimately, by cutting the work for young women, the legislators potentially cut the incomes on which their constituents relied.

5.5. The statute as electoral strategy

(a) The hypothesis. Ingenuously enough – and as contrary to modern political theory as the possibility may seem – the Japanese Factory Act may have benefited exactly the people contemporary observers thought it benefited: the women currently working in the textile factories. Assume Japanese workers, like workers in most societies, maximized a combination of leisure and money. Had they wanted to work fewer hours, they could have negotiated jobs with fewer hours. American workers did the same over the late nineteenth and early twentieth centuries (Atack and Bateman, 1992; Whaples, 1990). By 1925, even Japanese workers had negotiated a 14 percent shorter work day than they had worked in 1915 (Fujino et al., 1979: 27).

Alas for the workers, however, if they negotiated shorter hours in competitive labor markets, they had to *pay* for the hours. All else being equal, if they cut their work from ten hours to eight, they cut their productivity – and therefore their pay – by 20 percent. If in cutting hours they also cut operating efficiency, they sacrificed even more.

By manipulating the political market instead, the workers may have reduced the price of their extra leisure. Take the economics of a law that shortens the work day from ten hours to eight.[42] Most basically, the law potentially cuts a factory's output by 20 percent. Effectively, it requires employers to offer their workers sixteen daily hours of leisure instead of fourteen. Inevitably, it also lowers the equilibrium daily wage.

Under certain plausible conditions, however, workers may bear only part of the incidence of the pay cut that the statute causes. With an eight-hour maximum work day, the equilibrium daily wage will fall to a level where the value of the total compensation package (in pay and leisure) induces the marginal worker to take the job.[43] Although all workers will receive the same wage schedule, all workers will not value leisure equally. Yet the firm generally will need both (1) to offer a pay-plus-leisure package that attracts the marginal worker, and (2) to pay all workers the same wage. As a result, workers who value leisure more highly than the marginal worker may now receive a windfall: They may receive total compensation packages that they value more highly than the pay they received before (the competitive market equilibrium package, based on a ten-hour day). Because the firm must attract workers who do not value leisure highly, in short, the firm may not be able to cut wages by a full 20 percent. And if it cannot cut wages 20 percent, it will both (1) cut the quantity of person-hours it uses and (2) raise the hourly wage it pays.

Figure 10.1 illustrates this logic. On the horizontal axis, we plot the number Q of workers in the industry, and on the vertical axis the daily wage W. D_{10} gives the ten-hour-per-day industry demand curve for labor, and D_8 the eight-hour demand curve. For the sake of simplicity, we assume that ten-hour days generate no efficiencies. Hence, for any given Q, D_8 will give a W that is 8/10 the W on D_{10}. S_{10} gives the ten-hour-per-day industry supply curve for labor, and S_8 the eight-hour supply curve.

Note that S_8 rises more steeply than S_{10}. This follows from two assumptions. First (uncontroversially), we assume that some workers value the extra two hours of leisure more highly than others. Those who value it more highly will take an eight-hour per day job at a more heavily discounted wage than those who value it less. Second (perhaps more controversially), we assume that the workers otherwise most likely to quit (those with the highest reservation wage) are those who value leisure the least.[44] Conversely, those who value leisure most highly are the workers most satisfied with the new eight-hour job, and the workers least likely to quit. Graphically, the difference between S_8 and S_{10} gives the value of the utility each worker obtains from the extra two hours of leisure.

The potential gains to the workers from the night work ban appear on Figure 10.1 as worker producer surplus. Under a ten-hour day, they earn a producer surplus equal to area DEF. Under an eight-hour day, they earn the surplus of ABC. Given the assumptions behind Figure 10.1, ABC exceeds DEF – and workers have higher welfare after the statute. The point is not that a statutory night-work ban inevitably increases worker welfare. Most obviously, the relative sizes of ABC and DEF depend on the demand elasticity in the industry and the relative slopes of S_8 and S_{10}.[45]

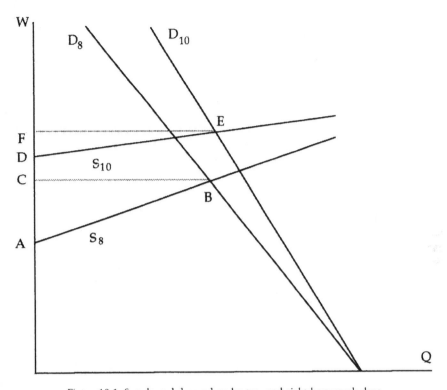

Figure 10.1. Supply and demand under ten- and eight-hour work days.

The point is simply that – under relatively plausible assumptions – the night work ban can increase worker welfare.

(b) The evidence. Data from the Japanese cotton spinning industry are consistent with this argument. The ban on night work took effect in 1929. In 1928, spinning firms had operated a mean 19.31 hours a day, and employees had worked a mean 9.66 hours. By 1930, those figures had fallen to 15.90 hours and 7.95 hours, respectively, and from 1930 to 1937, the mean employee work day never exceeded 8.2 hours. Effectively, the Act cut working hours by about 18 percent.

Daily wages fell too, but not by that full 18 percent. According to Table 10.7, in constant 1934–36 yen, daily female spinning firm wages fell 2 percent from 1928 to 1930 – from ¥1.13 per day to ¥1.11. Not until 1932 did they hit 18 percent below 1928 levels. Restated in hourly terms, from 1928 to 1930 cotton spinning wages rose 19 percent. Not until

Table 10.7. *Mean work hours, wages (constant 1934–1936 yen),
and work days under the Factory Act*

| | Cotton Spinning Industry | | | | |
	Work hours	Daily wage (¥)	Hourly wage (¥)	Work days	Agriculture daily wage (¥)
1926	9.68	1.04	.107	320	.43
1927	9.63	1.08	.112	315	.45
1928	9.66	1.13	.117	312	.39
1929	8.90	1.11	.125	326	.45
1930	7.95	1.11	.140	314	.42
1931	7.99	1.07	.134	312	.34
1932	8.15	.91	.112	308	.34
1933	8.20	.82	.100	314	.34
1934	8.20	.79	.096	319	.32
1935	8.19	.74	.090	314	.31

Sources: Calculated on the basis of data from Shōzaburō Fujino, Shino Fujino and Akira Ōno, *Chōki keizai tōkei: Sen'i kōgyō [Long-Term Economic Statistics: The Textile Industry]* (Tokyo: Tōyō keizai shimpō sha, 1979), pp. 27, 273–77; Kazushi Ohkawa, Tsutomu Noda, Nobuyuki Takamatsu, Saburō Yamada, Minoru Kumazaki, Yōichi Shinoya, and Ryōshin Minami, *Chōki keizai tōkei: Bukka [Long-Term Economic Statistics: Prices]* (Tokyo: Tōyō keizai shimpō sha, 1967), pp. 134–36; Takejirō Shindō, *Mengyō rōdō sankō tōkei [Reference Statistics Regarding Labor in the Cotton Industry]* (Tokyo: University of Tokyo Press, 1958), pp. 356–59; Mataji Umemura, Saburō Yamada, Yūjirō Hayami, Nobuhiko Takamatsu, Minoru Kumazaki, *Chōki keizai tokei: Nōringyō [Long-Term Economic Statistics: Agriculture and Forestry]* (Tokyo: Tōyō keizai shimpō sha, 1966), p. 221.

1932 did they return to their 1928 levels. Compared with other places a worker could have worked, textile firms were particularly attractive. The final column gives the daily agricultural wage for women under annual contracts – and illustrates the dramatic effect of the international depression. Most textile workers had come from the farm. In 1926, the average female spinning mill worker earned in one year 2.41 times what she could expect on the farm. By 1932 that multiple had increased to 2.67 times the farm wage.

Parenthetically, consider two further possibilities. First, some observers argued that spinning firms would respond to the shorter work day by lowering daily wages by the same proportion, and then increasing the number of days worked (Ō, 1930: 14; Pearse, 1929: 14). This strategy would have been effective of course only if workers were indifferent between free weekends and free evenings. In fact, they generally are not –

and in any case Japanese firms did not adopt this strategy on a long-term basis (Table 10.7).

Second, other observers argued that the firms would respond to the ban on night work by increasing the amount of work they expected women to perform per hour (Kitaoka, 1929: 344–45; Shakai, 1931: 16; Takamura, 1989). Although per hour productivity did rise, the increase was part of a larger secular increase caused by relatively steady improvements in spinning technology. Per-work-hour productivity increased during 1922–24 by 36 percent; 1924–26, 2 percent; 1926–28, 22 percent; 1928–30, 32 percent; and 1930–32, 28 percent (Shindō, 1958: 356–59).

(c) The politics. If the night work ban apparently redistributed wealth from textile firms to current textile workers, consider the electoral politics involved. By 1923, politicians knew (1) that universal suffrage would soon be the law, (2) that potential textile workers were not a coherent political force under any regime, and (3) that under universal suffrage, raising the welfare of current textile workers (who often pooled their incomes within households where at least one member had the vote) would be good politics.[46] Given the electoral returns to redistributive politics under universal suffrage, politicians who might earlier have opposed the night work ban now had an incentive to reconsider their position.

Nonetheless, under the Meiji Constitution laws took effect only upon the promulgation of an Imperial Order implementing the law. By the terms of the 1923 Factory Act, the ban on night work applied three years after the Act itself took effect. As a result, textile firms that lost in the Diet could still lobby the (unelected) men who controlled access to the Emperor.

This the spinning firms did, for they adamantly opposed the ban (Hunter, 1989). Notwithstanding the Act's passage in 1923, the Emperor did not implement it until 1926. By then, even the proletarian households had the vote. Diet members now directly answered to the poor. Because even the non-elected officials had to cut deals with those Diet members to govern, they too balked at the spinning firms' pleas. In effect, the political leaders showed varying – but perfectly predictable – responsiveness to the poor: the directly elected leaders responded earlier than the unelected leaders, but both groups grew more responsive over time.

6. CONCLUSION

During the first few decades of the twentieth century, the cotton firms endured a curious regulatory strategy. First, although there were 50,000 cotton weaving firms, the government gave them the right to organize themselves into a statutory cartel. Second, although the spinners maintained no restrictions on productive capacity in the industry, it gave them a cartel statute too. Third, although spinning firms wanted to operate their equipment around the clock, and although some poor women wanted to trade night work for money, it banned willing firms from hiring willing women for the night shift.

The reasons for these curiosities do not lie in the technology of the industry or the economics of cartelization. Instead, they lie in the structure of the political process – in the dynamics of regime change first set in place by the oligarchs in the late nineteenth century. First, the politicians in the incumbent Kenseikai party organized the weaving sector in order to obtain organizations they could use to divide their supporters among multiple candidates in the same district. The Kenseikai could control the Diet only if it could elect several candidates each from most of the districts. To do so, it needed a way to divide its supporters within each district. Trade associations served that purpose.

As a result, the Kenseikai did indeed encourage weaving firms to form trading associations, but not to route them monopoly returns (50,000-firm industries did not earn monopoly returns, government help or no). Instead, the Kenseikai used the associations to dispense pork (subsidies and loans) to the firms, through the resulting loyalty created personalized support groups for its candidates, manipulated the support groups to divide its vote, and by all this may have increased its electoral success.

Second, in 1931 the government did give spinning firms a statutory cartel, but primarily to please the military leaders who would soon run the country. For most of the pre-war years, the Mitsui and Mitsubishi zaibatsu had cultivated ties to the two leading parties. The Mitsui would have suffered large losses had the spinners cut production and earned monopoly returns. Perhaps because of that political power, during the 1920s the spinning firms did not even try to earn monopoly rents.

By 1931, many observers suspected that the military would soon take control of government. Accordingly, when the bureaucrats drafted a cartel for the spinning industry in 1931, they did not draft a statute the industry requested. They did not even draft a statute the industry would use. Instead, they drafted the statute that the military wanted. During the 1930s, the military would increasingly regiment the economy, and the 1931 cartel statute formed one basis for that militarization.

The 1929 ban on night work reflects the 1925 expansion in the suffrage. Unlike the 1833 British Factory Act, the Japanese ban did not transfer wealth from large spinning firms to small. Unlike the turn-of-the-century American protective statutes, it did not transfer wealth away from

158

newly arrived immigrants. Instead, it apparently raised the welfare of current textile workers.

By banning night work, the Act forced employers to cut hours by about 20 percent. In the process, it gave employees an extra two hours of leisure each day. To attract workers with infra-marginal tastes for leisure, however, owners could not cut wages by the full 20 percent. And because they did not, infra-marginal workers apparently received the extra two hours of leisure at a lower price (in foregone daily wages) than they otherwise would have paid. In the process, they received higher real hourly wages. In the process also, the political parties apparently increased the welfare of the newly enfranchised households.

11

Conclusion: Institutions and political control

1. INTRODUCTION

Power-seeking entrepreneurs cooperated with one another long enough to overthrow the Tokugawa regime and to install themselves in its place. But as they jockeyed for position in the new government, they eventually forfeited power to party politicians. All too soon, however, events turned as sour for Japan's budding democracy as they had for oligarchy. The military took over; not, we argue, because politicians were inept or because the Japanese public was unready for democracy. Instead, we blame the oligarchs for establishing an institutional structure – including, in particular, the independence of the military – that was designed to protect at least some of the oligarchs themselves. While it may have done that, it ultimately destroyed Japan's first experiment with electoral government.

In the course of this book, we make two principal claims. First, we argue that institutions in pre-war Japan became dysfunctional to all but the military, even though the military was not the group the institutions were designed ultimately to protect. The oligarchs fashioned the institutions as tools for their own purposes. Once established, however, they constrained the behavior of the oligarchs themselves, as well as the choices of successive groups of political party leaders. Institutions may be, as they were in pre-war Japan, costly to change. In Japan's case, the Meiji Constitution and its attending process of decision-making launched a chain of events that was nothing short of catastrophic for the Japanese public.

This first claim of dysfunctional institutions is missing from Japanese history textbooks not because historians find it objectionable; most of them take it for granted. Our quarrel here is instead with (admittedly, the few) social scientists who assume that political markets – even in non-electoral systems – are efficient.[1] In the extreme version of this argument, institutions are sufficiently malleable that political entrepreneurs will take

160

advantage of any possible mismatch between societal demand and institutional supply. Incumbent leaders are forced to meet the demand, or lose to these challengers who will. We find instead that institutions can impede competition and skew political behavior. Because institutions can create collective action problems as assuredly as they can solve others, they may poorly serve not only the interests of the public at large, but those of the incumbents and entrepreneurs as well.

Our second major claim is that – and here we tread with some trepidation on Japanological holy ground – pre-war civil servants were less autonomous and less influential than is routinely assumed. Japan, if we are right, was not a "strong state" in the conventional sense of the term.[2] We go on, therefore, to question the range of stylized facts that depend on this strong-state assumption, including the notion of Japan as a "late-developer."

In this final chapter, we summarize the book by addressing these two claims in greater depth. In Section 2 we examine pre-war Japanese politics in light of different theories of institutional change. We recapitulate our argument for why the oligarchs chose the institutions they did in the first place, and why those institutions outlasted their usefulness even to the oligarchs. Institutional inertia, we conclude, provides the key to understanding Japan's otherwise confounding militaristic misadventures.

In Section 3 we explore the argument for bureaucratic dominance, and our counterclaim of bureaucratic subservience, in the context of principal-agent theory. We then compare the independence of bureaucrats with that of judges and of military officers, and explain the differences. Finally, we consider the implications of bureaucratic subservience for the relationship between politics and economic development.

2. THE MYTH OF EFFICIENT INSTITUTIONS

In the first few chapters of this book, we recounted the strategic interaction among the oligarchs that led them ultimately to draft the Meiji Constitution. The Constitution was hardly a liberal document: While it permitted electoral competition, it sharply limited participation and political accountability. On the other hand, it conceded more power to non-oligarchs than the oligarchs – had they been better able to cooperate – would have wanted to concede. Given their disparate endowments and mutual suspicion, the structure of government it laid out may have been the best they could devise. They fell far short, however, of preserving their collective monopoly of power.

For the oligarchs, insuring the independence of the military was at most a second-best solution to their problem of mutual cheating. Knowing that the more charismatic oligarchs would continue to fight for position by appealing to the masses, other oligarchs – Yamagata in particular – cordoned off the military from accountability to those masses. It was this internecine stalemate, enshrined in legal codes and Imperial Orders, that paved the way for the eventual military coup.

One can imagine better solutions to the oligarchs' rivalries. They could have, for example, agreed to a repressive strategy of political control, by collectively manipulating the military. They might have combined repression with calculated concessions to the masses to reduce the costs of repression. In the process, they could have carefully calibrated the trade-offs in their use of the carrot and stick to protect their tenure as cheaply as possible. But as we have pointed out, some oligarchs were more influential in the military than others. These oligarchs foreclosed the more cooperative option because they were unable to convince their colleagues that they would not abuse this influence. Instead, the oligarchs made bigger concessions both to the military and to the public than they collectively wanted.

In effect, the oligarchs institutionalized their embattled relations in the Meiji Constitution. They empowered several groups, including the Privy Council, the House of Peers, the House of Representatives, and the military services, to stymie the decision-making capacity of the others. Judging from the political turmoil and oligarchic battles that persisted, this multiplicity of decision-making centers was not an efficient solution for the oligarchs. Even less, judging from the eventual military coup, did it serve the interests of the Japanese public at large.

2.1. Where do institutions come from?

One explanation for why institutions emerge and how they evolve is that society needs them to solve certain coordination or collective action problems. The most benign version of this view is that institutions mirror the preferences of society as a whole. According to sociologist Arthur Stinchcombe, for example,

a more nuanced and rational way of maximizing the long run welfare of [say] minor children or of scientific creativity will tend to win out. It will win out because the principles of reason are institutionalized over a long period of time, and people keep on applying their rational faculties to improving the rationality of that fictional child or improving the fictional utility function of the advance of science.[3]

A second, also benign, variant on the institutions-as-mirrors-of-societal-preferences argument comes from economics. Beginning perhaps with Coase (1937, 1960), a steady stream of economists have studied how organizational arrangements – principally within and among firms – deal with the costs of negotiating and enforcing contracts. Given uncertainty and opportunism in the marketplace, patterns of ownership such as vertical integration can allow all parties involved in the exchange to achieve greater returns. The most efficient forms of corporate organization tend to emerge and survive, because these are the forms most likely to survive market competition.

In recent years, this work in transaction-cost economics has spawned a parallel literature on the economics of political institutions. Some scholars working in this field argue that the political marketplace tends to produce efficient political institutions – that is, institutions that make everyone better off. To be sure, competitive electoral systems can give political entrepreneurs strong incentives to create precisely those institutions. Yoram Barzel, however, makes the case for efficient political institutions even when politicians face only anemic competition. According to Barzel, even a self-interested dictator should be motivated to devolve substantial power to a legislature. Only in doing so can he make credible his promise to investors that he will not confiscate their investments. He thereby improves his own lot, for in increasing the incentives of private entrepreneurs to create more wealth, he expands his revenue base.[4]

Note, however, that the Japanese oligarchs did not create a system of genuine checks and balances. Rather, their Meiji Constitution left the contours of ultimate authority as vague as it left the issue of who controlled the emperor. As a result, pre-war Japanese institutions were efficient neither from the standpoint of tenure- or wealth-maximizing leaders, nor from the perspective of the public that wanted political accountability and freedom from arbitrary confiscation.

An important caveat to the efficiency arguments is that coercive power may give political leaders wealth and security in office long before those leaders concede much to the public at large.[5] This should be true particularly when governments face only modest competition for survival from foreign would-be aggressors – which for most countries is most of the time. Douglass North, for example, points out that self-interested rulers can and do perpetuate inefficient property rights for long periods of time (1990: 7).

The pre-war Japanese case takes us one step farther in understanding institutions: Under certain circumstances, the leaders themselves may fail to collude effectively against the public. Drawing on cartel theory, we concluded that the Meiji leaders' heterogeneous talents (some had Army connections, others charmed the public) were a collective liability. Their divergent talents gave them different preferences for how to maximize their security in office – and therefore gave them strong incentives to cheat on each other. Just as crucially, their different areas of expertise and fields of activity also made it easier for them to cheat undetected.[6]

Unfortunately for the Japanese public, discord among the leaders did not shift power to the legislature. In adopting their second-best strategy of insulating the Army, the oligarchs "hard-wired" the system against popular control. Despite the signs that politics were evolving in the direction of greater public accountability by the 1920s, the military never relinquished its latent power. Once the military had a veto over its own future, only a countercoup could have toppled the military from its privileged position. And no countercoup, given the military's ability to deal with its internal dissension, ever succeeded.

Each of the political institutions that the Meiji oligarchs adopted can be understood as part of a second-best strategy. The oligarchs made the military independent, as we have said, to block further inroads by their own colleagues with popular appeal. Ideally, even the oligarchs would have wanted to keep the military subservient. That they could not do so suggests how severe their rivalries were.

The oligarchs established the Privy Council to keep one institutional check for themselves and their closest proteges. But reflecting their ambivalent feelings about one another, they left the Privy Council's powers only vaguely specified. The Councillors were effective, in retrospect, only when they were sufficiently unified to give the emperor coherent advice.

A popularly elected Lower House, it would seem, was the institution most at odds with the oligarchs' designs to control government. Clearly, no oligarchy would have wished a trouble-making rabble on itself. With some oligarchs already organizing political parties, however, their less charismatic colleagues made this concession to keep the power they still had. Better to give the trouble-makers an institutionally constrained role, they reasoned, than to let the entrepreneurship get out of hand altogether.

The House of Peers the oligarchs intended to be a conservative ballast against the anti-status-quo proclivities of the Lower House. Yet in the course of making appointments, the oligarchs managed to reduce even the Peers to groups of competing factions aligned with one or another group of oligarchs.

Of all the Meiji institutions, the oligarchs should have been most proud of the electoral system. While the oligarchs were unable to act as a unit, at least they could try to divide their opposition. This they managed to do in spades. By giving voters a single, non-transferable vote (SNTV) in multi-member districts in the 1900 Elections Act, the oligarchs forced members of political parties to compete against their fellow party members. As a result, for most (not all) of the pre-war period, party leaders were hard-pressed to impose party discipline; they had an even harder time devising distinguishable party platforms.

Instead, as we discussed in Chapter 4, politicians had to compete for Diet seats with promises of private goods for well-defined, organized groups of voters. As a result of the local, pork-barrel orientation of the political parties, voters eventually became disillusioned by the circus they called elections. If the oligarchs had wanted to distract political entrepreneurs from national politics, it is hard to imagine a better plan for doing so.

2.2. When do institutions matter?

Our discussion so far has assumed institutional inertia. But some will say that begs the more interesting question of the conditions under which institutions persist. When, by contrast, should we expect someone or some group to change those institutions?[7]

Our research on pre-war Japanese institutions corroborates the view that institutions can long outlive their usefulness to the coalition that established them – or for that matter, their usefulness to just about anyone else. Changing the Meiji Constitution required leaping over procedural hurdles that prior to 1945 no single group was able to do. This was the case even though the Japanese public had an interest in doing so.

The oligarchs had designed an institutional apparatus in which the military ultimately had the strongest position. The rules of the game, as enshrined in the Meiji Constitution, had established which resources mattered. The military had the most important asset, dual access to the emperor; charisma mattered only secondarily, and the Constitution circumscribed its value along with the Diet's powers.

That constitutions are usually hard to change is well known: Amendment procedures typically involve, as did the Meiji Constitution, super majorities and a variety of other checks. We noted, however, that the pre-war political parties were hard pressed to change even the electoral rules, which were mere statutory law. Perhaps the oligarchs had originally wanted to retain flexibility in the choice of electoral rules, not being sure of the results. Nonetheless, once the parties gained control of the legislative process, why did they not change the electoral rules to a system that would foster greater party cohesion and policy orientation?

Just as the oligarchs found it hard to collude, so too did the parties, once they were organized under the oligarchs' chosen rules. Each party's members, after all, were incumbents under the SNTV system; there was no guarantee that they had the requisite talents to compete as successfully under other rules. Any given electoral apparatus can generate powerful support for the status quo, however unfortuitous it might be for the party movement as a whole. As we described in Chapter 4, the parties themselves opted for an SNTV, multi-member district system in 1925, several years after Yamagata had died. This was a classic example of structure-induced equilibrium: The existing rules shaped the preference functions of the very Diet members choosing the new rules.

2.3. Which institutions, when?

In political development, several institutional equilibria are hypothetically possible. First, one can imagine political entrepreneurs establishing institutions that come close to reflecting the interests of society as a whole. But this requires that political markets be competitive in the first place. Pre-existing institutions must guarantee competition, or at a minimum, insurmountable institutions must not impede that competition. Pre-war Japan, sadly, was not blessed with such circumstances.

A second possible outcome is a set of institutions that is inefficient for society but that works well for keeping a small group in power. If members of this small group have similar political endowments, they are likely to have similar plans for staying in power. They are also likely to find it relatively easy to monitor each other, since their interests and activities overlap. This scenario may characterize some juntas – including Japan's military government, once it installed itself – but it does not describe the Meiji oligarchs.

Pre-war Japan's situation is a third scenario: The institutional equilibrium was inefficient for all, except, as we suggested, for the military. Unable to solve their conflict, the oligarchs instead made concessions to both the Diet and to the military. The oligarchs conceded more to the military, presumably because Yamagata was in a stronger bargaining position than Ōkuma and Itagaki. This in turn set the course of Japanese history for the next half century.

3. THE MYTH OF BUREAUCRATIC AUTONOMY

Our most controversial claim in this book may be an empirical one: Pre-war bureaucrats were never autonomous. They suffered in fact from a multiplicity of overseers, and were unable to play off those overseers against one another. The conventional wisdom – that bureaucrats made the important policy decisions because politicians could not easily fire them and because they drafted most of the laws – is based, we argue, on the wrong kinds of evidence.

3.1. Bureaucratic subservience

We rely on principal-agent theory to distinguish good evidence from bad for gauging bureaucratic influence. That literature alerts us to possible incentive schemes and monitoring devices that principals may use to guide the actions of their agents. Actions of loyal bureaucrats may be observationally equivalent to those of shirking ones in many circumstances. Only when we recognize that can we distinguish delegation (in which the agents reliably serve the principals' interests) from agency slack (in which they do not).

No one claims that the bureaucrats could or tried to defy the wishes of the oligarchs. Before writing the Meiji Constitution, the oligarchs retained nearly complete and arbitrary power over the civil service – not to mention the military and the rudimentary court system as well. Rather, it is the party politicians – even during their heyday in the 1920s – who are said to have been the bureaucrats' stooges.

To be sure, the oligarchs issued Imperial Orders that prevented politicians from firing bureaucrats on whim. A powerful motivating device those orders did not preclude, however, was the cabinet's power to promote bureaucrats selectively. This, the party politicians could and did, as we recounted in Chapter 5. Knowing this, many ambitious bureaucrats aligned themselves with one or the other of the most powerful parties. Not to do so was to forfeit the chance to rise to higher bureaucratic ranks.

Our case-study chapters provide further evidence, from policy decisions, that the bureaucrats did in fact implement policies that the politicians wanted. The potential problem with this kind of evidence, of course, is that the bureaucrats may independently have wanted the same policy outcomes. When we notice, however, how dramatically policies changed with changes in parties' majority status and their attending control of the cabinet, we realize that this possibility is slim indeed.

Financial politics. Either Ministry of Finance (MOF) bureaucrats changed their minds frequently, or they changed policies to reflect the interests of the alternating parties in power. If the former, it is uncanny how closely bureaucratic mind-changing corresponded to changes in the cabinet. A simpler explanation, we argue in Chapter 6, is that principals – the parties – were able to get their bureaucratic agents to implement their partisan policies.

Under the control of the oligarchs, the MOF had not pushed for consolidation of the banking market. It was the Kenseikai cabinet and Kenseikai-controlled Diet that passed legislation in 1927, drafted with the help of MOF bureaucrats, that would squeeze hundreds of Seiyūkai-supporting small banks out of business. The Seiyūkai, in turn, exposed the chummy ties among Suzuki Shōten, the Bank of Taiwan, and the Kenseikai, even though this risked triggering a nationwide financial panic.

The parties also made a football of exchange rate policy, contrary to the claim of some scholars that the issue was too arcane for partisan politics. Reflecting the interests of their respective business constituents, the Seiyūkai abandoned the gold standard, the Kenseikai restored it, and the Seiyūkai revoked it again. Different business interests wanted different policies, and their respective political patrons were willing and able to oblige them.

As we discussed in Chapter 4, the parties competed in an electoral system that required any party wishing a Diet majority to divide the vote among multiple candidates. The resulting expense of electoral campaigns gave the parties a seemingly insatiable appetite for campaign contributions. These they raised from organized groups in exchange for policy favors. Financial regulation was merely one case in point.

Cotton politics. Textile industry regulation, as we saw in Chapter 10, tells essentially the same story. The Kenseikai organized the weaving sector into trade organizations in the 1920s, it would appear, to create receptacles for government subsidies. In exchange for Kenseikai-directed government largesse, Kenseikai politicians may have received campaign contributions and a tidy vote-dividing apparatus in many districts. Judging from the Kenseikai's electoral performance in these districts, the plan worked.

Unlike the politically motivated organization of the weaving sector, neither party cartelized the spinning industry. Both parties, after all, cultivated close ties to zaibatsu firms, and those firms shipped raw cotton and cotton yarn – and thus wanted to keep industry production high. The spinning industry therefore remained competitive until 1931, when the parties lost their grip on policymaking. The military, by then increasingly in control, was more interested in streamlining industry for military purposes than in coddling the industries themselves.

In a third example of textile industry regulation, the Kenseikai cabinet banned night work in 1929. Following the universal suffrage bill of 1925, the parties competed for the votes of workers. The Kenseikai, which was particularly dependent on the urban vote, began producing a spate of relatively pro-labor regulations such as this measure. Bureaucratic rhetoric about the "welfare of the national family" notwithstanding, the Kenseikai's electoral motivation is all too clear.

Railroad politics. Nowhere is the partisan nature of pre-war policymaking more clear than in railroad politics. The Kenseikai routinely allocated budgetary resources toward refurbishing old railroad infrastructure – hardly surprising, given that existing track tended to be in urban areas where the Kenseikai had strong support. Seiyūkai cabinets, by contrast, consistently allocated more resources to laying new lines. Again, this is precisely what one would expect. In doing so, they serviced the rural districts where their constituents disproportionately lived.

Similarly, successive cabinets' railroad policies reflected the parties' respective ties to Mitsui and Mitsubishi. A Seiyūkai cabinet bought out

Mitsui-based lines at hugely inflated prices, and paid the Mitsubishi meagerly. When the Kenseikai got their chance to skew railroad procurement, they may have favored producers supporting them at the expense of Seiyūkai supporters. In allocating licenses for private railroad lines, the parties again favored the firms running lines to their supporters.

In all three industries – banking, textiles, and railroads – the policy shifts have partisan links that are too obvious to ignore. All three cases corroborate the evidence from Chapter 5 of political tampering with the administrative branch of government. Had the politicians no means of influencing bureaucratic behavior, economic policy should have been far more consistent over time than it was. It should also have been far less skewed toward the constituents of whichever party happened to be in power.

3.2. Judicial subservience

Judges, we found in Chapter 6, never became as partisan as the bureaucrats. The oligarchs clearly controlled them, and decades later Inukai's Seiyūkai government stacked the courts with judges of its choice. Yet the party governments in the intervening years seemed less inclined to control the personnel decisions of the judiciary than of the bureaucracy.

After considering several possible explanations for that puzzle, we concluded from the evidence that the political parties may have implicitly cut a deal with each other in those years not to intervene. The Seiyūkai may have broken that deal only when it found itself in an end-game. The remaining question, however, is why the parties interfered in the judiciary later than in the bureaucracy.

The answer, we suggest, is that politicians had less incentive to cheat on this deal than on any vows to respect bureaucratic independence. It seems they were following a sensible cost-benefit logic. First was the issue of potential benefit from control. Even within the ministries, as the aggregate data from Chapter 5 implied, politicians cared most about controlling bureaucratic positions with a clear electoral connection. Incoming cabinets most often turned over prefectural governors, public prosecutors, and police, for example, presumably because of their role in monitoring and prosecuting electoral fraud. They also appointed sympathetic bureaucrats to budget-related and regulatory bureaus that oversaw policy favors to loyal constituents. The safety and health bureaucrats, however, the politicians left largely alone.

So it may have been, it seems, with judges. Politicians could keep most politically sensitive matters out of the courts by statutorily manipulating access to the courts. Controlling the bureaucrats to whom the judges deferred in administrative matters was therefore more important. Politicians apparently saw less need to control what the judges might say in the remaining – and to them, less important – cases.

In addition to the weak benefits from judicial control, politicians also had to consider the costs of intervention. The oligarchs had made it marginally harder to interfere with the careers of judges than with those of bureaucrats. Politicians expended, then, their selection and oversight resources where the payoff was greatest.

3.3. Military independence

The military, we showed in Chapter 7, managed to avoid even the relatively modest personnel incursions that the judges suffered. The oligarchs gave the military three powers they gave neither to the bureaucracy nor to the judiciary: the ability to write military ordinances in the name of the Emperor, unaccountability of military strategy to the cabinet, and the requirement that military ministers be military men. These powers assured that the military services' general staffs were independent of cabinet oversight in a way that bureaucrats and judges could never hope to be.

Yamagata's reasoning in giving the military so much is not hard to fathom. Once forced to concede representative institutions to maverick oligarchs, he wanted to wall off from popular control the one institution over which he had the greatest personal influence. Both of these features of the Meiji system – an elected House of Representatives and military independence – followed from the demise of oligarchical cooperation. Once Yamagata died in 1922, the military was essentially accountable to no one but to the figurehead-emperor.

It was not that the politicians did not try to establish civilian control. In 1913, Yamamoto Gonnohyōe managed to downgrade the criterion for military minister from active duty to reserve duty status. The General Staff of each service, however, with its responsibility for strategic decisions, remained independent of even the Minister. The military services simply responded to this challenge by requiring, internally, that the Chief of Staff agree to any ministerial choice (Inoue, 1975: 95).

Cabinet governments were not free to refuse this arrangement. Either the Army or the Navy could bring down the cabinet at any time, by having their Minister resign and then by refusing to supply a replacement. With this power, the military had cabinets over the barrel from the day Yamagata died.

A potential weak link in the military's independence was dissension within its own ranks. Upgrading the personnel power of the General Staff was one way of preventing politicians from using a divide-and-conquer strategy to control the respective services.[8] Similarly, the two services bound themselves together in the face of civilian unfriendliness by settling on a strategic logroll – whereby the Army got China and the Navy got Southeast Asia. Able to check internal conflict in a way unmatched either by the oligarchy or by the politicians, the military sealed its dominance.

3.4. Questioning the late-development hypothesis

Having disputed that pre-war Japan was a "strong state," we also question the rest of the conventional wisdom that follows from that characterization. Pre-war Japan, it would appear, was not guided by national-interest-oriented bureaucrats who promoted and consolidated strategic industries to compete better in foreign markets. Indeed, it was not guided by bureaucrats at all.

Several decades have passed since Alexander Gerschenkron (1962: 354) first published the hypothesis that "late developers" tend to have more centralized, activist governments:

The more backward a country's economy, the greater was the part played by special institutional factors designed to increase the supply of capital to the nascent industries and, in addition, to provide them with less decentralized and better informed entrepreneurial guidance; the more backward the country, the more pronounced was the coerciveness and comprehensiveness of those factors.

Japan-related scholars continue to rely on Gerschenkron's ideas.[9] Even as late as 1989, Beasley (1989: 620) in the *Cambridge History* could proclaim: "Japan, like Germany, as a 'late developer' in the catching-up phase, found authoritarian government a more effective framework for modernization than democracy was."

To Gershenkron's credit, in 1962 the argument did seem to fit several prominent data points such as Germany and the USSR. Unfortunately, the case of Japan never really fit. Government policy may indeed have encouraged economic concentration, as Gerschenkron predicted. But we found, contrary to the late-development model, that economic concentration followed a domestic political rather than a strategic pattern. First, the timing is all wrong for the late-developer idea. A Gershenkronian would expect the Meiji oligarchs to have promoted key industries on a grand scale as part of state-building and international competition. In fact, they did no such thing. It was not until the 1920s, under party cabinets, that government policy encouraged firms to merge and form cartels.

Second, these cabinet governments helped or ignored industries and firms, on the basis not of their perceived contribution to Japan's economy but of their perceived contribution to party coffers. The Kenseikai nurtured the large, urban banks; the Seiyūkai fostered ties with smaller, rural banks. The Kenseikai organized the weaving industry; the Seiyūkai did not. The Kenseikai favored urban railroad development; the Seiyūkai busied itself laying track to its rural districts. The Kenseikai coddled Mitsubishi; the Seiyūkai, Mitsui. The logic of regulation, in short, was the same for both parties: to channel government resources to allied firms in exchange for votes and campaign contributions. The parties consolidated industries, in some cases, as a way of doing this.

It was the military, beginning in the 1930s, that formed cartels and consolidated the economy in earnest. The military established these cartels, however, for strictly military purposes – not for either general economic development or for the benefit of private firms. It channeled resources into munitions manufacturing at the expense of other sectors, and by the end of the war had driven Japan's economy into the ground. This, needless to say, is not generally what scholars mean by a late-development strategy.

4. CONCLUSION

Our goal has been to make sense of the otherwise puzzling flow of pre-war Japanese history. Why did the oligarchs simultaneously establish a representative assembly and insulate the military from civilian control? Why were pre-war political parties so corrupt? Why was Japan's experiment with democracy so brief? Why did the military slip into power unchallenged? These questions we address, with the aid of a rational-choice approach.

Armed with simple assumptions about self-serving behavior and simple theories of how institutions constrain action, we explored the choices successive generations of political leaders made between 1868 and 1932. The oligarchs, we suggested, collectively wanted neither to concede popular representation, nor to grant military independence; their internal strife left them no better option. They did manage, however, to keep politicians divided – and parties corrupt – by choosing electoral rules that pitted politicians of the same party against one another in their electoral districts. Yet scandalous politics or not, Japan's democracy operated on borrowed time. Given the military's independence, the coup was merely a matter of time, not of bad luck.

Finally, we used Japanese history to reflect back on the theoretical literatures. Institutions, we found, may long outlive their framers. These framers, moreover, may not select an institutional arrangement that maximizes their collective interests. Even political leaders with sufficient resources to rig the rules of the game may be unable to do so effectively – because they fail to collude. For all the weight of Japan's so-called "consensus-building" culture, the oligarchs just could not figure out how to get along. And that, we argued, turned out to be of no small consequence.

172

Notes

1. INTRODUCTION

1 Largely for reasons of length, we deal in this book primarily with the period 1868 to 1932. With few exceptions, we address neither the Meiji Restoration nor the Second World War.

2 By "oligarchs" we refer to the men who dominated government during the several decades between 1868 and the time power devolved to elected politicians. Although this definition is vague, it is vague for a reason – the group that wielded this power was itself a fluid group. Some men, like Saigō Takamori, could claim at the outset to wield power, but soon died. Others, like Ōkuma Shigenobu, found themselves excluded when their rivals consolidated new coalitions. We focus during much of the book, however, on precisely this shifting group of men. This group of oligarchs overlaps imperfectly with the *genrō*, the quasi-official imperial advisors: Kuroda Kiyotaka, Itō Hirobumi, Yamagata Aritomo, Matsukata Masayoshi, Inoue Kaoru, Saigō Tsugumichi, Ōyama Iwao, Katsura Tarō, and Saionji Kinmochi. This is because the *genrō* were self-appointed – and their membership thus reflected the most powerful coalitions among the oligarchs at the time of appointment. Ōkuma, for example, was powerful but not a *genrō* precisely because his rival oligarchs excluded him from their coalition. On the significance of the term *genrō*, see generally Momose (1990: 11–14).

3 We do not cite the *Cambridge History* because of any particular faults in the series. Indeed, we find the essays in the series among the best restatements of current scholarship available. We cite it precisely because it restates so carefully the approach that many of the leading scholars in the field take.

4 (1993: 222). See also Silberman (1982: 231): "The bureaucracy continued to enjoy the highest status and the most powerful place in the formation of public policy."

5 In 1878, oligarch Yamagata Aritomo collected a monthly salary of ¥500 as state councilor (*sangi*), ¥500 as Army minister (*rikugun kyō*), ¥400 as Army lieutenant general (*chūjō*), and ¥300 as councilor (*giteikan*) (Matsushita, 1963b: 315–16). All told, he collected ¥1700 per month from the government, where a typical carpenter earned ¥6.81 per month and a farmer ¥4.53 (mean 30-day wages for 1885, the first year for which the time-series has data; see Nihon tōkei [1988: tab. 16–1]).

6 See Cowhey and McCubbins (1994); Ramseyer and Rosenbluth (1993). For the conventional argument to the contrary, see Johnson (1982).

7 Though journalists and academics untrained in economics routinely make exactly that point.

8 See, for example, Friedman (1986: 190–96). In other words, any outcome proposed by one group of oligarchs can be blocked successfully by another group of oligarchs.

9 Silberman (1993: 188) argues that the oligarchs did not pick a single leader because "this would provoke charges of *lese majeste.*" Given that the To-kugawa government survived for two and a half centuries with a single shogun at a time, we find this implausible. We suggest a simpler reason: The oligarchs could not agree who the single leader would be.

10 For example, Barzel (1992); De Long and Shleifer (1993); North and Weingast (1989); Scully (1992).

11 Two obvious caveats may be in order. First, that the politicians rationally expected a military government does not mean they had complete foresight – only that they could see that the odds of a military government had increased steadily. Second, the differences between the politicians and the military lead-ers were never categorical. Some military leaders formed alliances with politi-cians (see Chapter 7); many politicians sympathized with many of the military leaders' aims (though we doubt many politicians wanted to relinquish their own power to a military junta).

12 Were one trying to find heirs, one might arguably consider Saionji to be Itō's protege and Hara to be Saionji's protege. Aside from whether the individuals involved saw any such relationship, note that Hara was only seven years younger than Saionji, and Saionji only eight years younger than Itō.

2. THE COLLAPSE OF OLIGARCHY

1 On our use of the term "oligarchs," see note 2, Chapter 1.

2 For an excellent study of the bureaucracy surrounding the Emperor, see Titus (1974).

3 According to F.C. Jones (1931), foreign powers exercised jurisdiction in all cases, civil or criminal, in which a citizen of a foreign treaty power was defendant. However, the treaties were of little use to a foreigner who wished to bring an action in Japan in a commercial dispute against a Japanese defendant. Had the extra-territorial jurisdiction extended to plaintiffs as well as defen-dants, foreign entrepreneurs might have been willing to lend money to Japan at lower interest rates despite Japan's still-weak domestic institutions. For the full text of the 1858 U.S.-Japan Treaty of Amity and Commerce, see Appendix A of Jones (1931).

4 This was the same Inoue who, only months before, had conspired to assassi-nate foreign representatives in Japan and had participated in an attack on a British legation in Tokyo (Hani, 1956: 311).

5 Relations between Japan and Britain – or for that matter between Japan and any Western power – had been less than cordial ever since these Western countries had begun to pry open Japan's closed ports. In September 1862, some anti-foreign samurai killed British diplomat Richardson, prompting Britain to demand financial compensation as well as access to Yokohama Harbor. On June 24, 1863, the shogunate paid the British 440,000 taels of silver, but ordered all foreigners out of the country. The British, Americans, French, and Dutch all refused to leave Japan, and the next day the Western ships exchanged gunfire with Chōshū soldiers in the southern port of Shim-

onoseki. Eventually, the Japanese recognized the futility of fighting the stronger Western navies. See Gaimushō, ed. (1965: 34–39) and Mōri (1982: 240–245).

6 Tagawa (1910); Tokufuku (1937); Hani (1956). Hani also cynically points out that despite Yamagata's rhetoric about the military coexisting harmoniously with the peasants, the relations between his own army and the peasants of his domain were anything but amicable. When Yamagata was leading the charge of Chōshū soldiers against the Tokugawa forces at Ogura in 1866, Chōshū peasants made off with the soldiers' rations, forcing Yamagata to retreat (Hani, 1956: 312).

7 Akita (1967: 22–26); Iwata (1964). Angry samurai assassinated Ōkubo because of his opposition to their plan to attack Korea. On Ōkuma, see also Watanabe (1958); Miyake (1911).

8 See, for exmaple, Katō (1978); Niwa (1978); Terao (1975); Ōkubo (1986).

9 Some of the feudal leaders brought into the ruling circle in this way were Saigō Takamori, Kido Takayoshi, Itagaki Taisuke, and Shimazu Hisamitsu.

10 *Chōhei rei* [*Conscription Regulation*], unnumbered, Dojōkan fukoku of Jan. 10, 1873. See also Umetani (1984); Ōishi (1989).

11 Jansen (1971: 185). The divisions within the oligarchy were certainly not ethnic, for such differences did not exist. By all accounts, they were not even ideological. Initially, they were largely geographical. As in any group, monitoring and cooperation came more easily among old friends than in the plenary group of oligarchs. For the particularly strong bonds among the Satsuma oligarchs, for example, see Itō (1981: 152–3).

12 Mason (1969: 4–5). Note, however, that Itō and Yamagata, both from Chōshū, came to be staunch rivals.

13 Tōyama and Adachi (1961: 22). It is interesting to note that Itō Hirobumi, Inoue Kaoru, and Kido Takayoshi placed themselves in the foreign affairs department; Saigō Takamori was in military affairs. Being in charge of policy implementation seems to be how these leaders came to be called "bureaucrats" in much of the literature, though there is very little that is bureaucratic about their positions. Another curiosity: Yamagata Aritomo is nowhere to be found on the first roster.

14 Osadake (1930: 121); Tōyama and Adachi (1961: 1–2); Ōkuboke (1928: 347ff.).

15 Osadake (1930: 94–95). The terminology of the Councils of the Right, Left, and Center dates back at least to the eleventh century.

16 Tōyama and Adachi (1961: 2). This is a French-based word, sometimes translated as "Council of Cassation." Because that makes no sense to English-language readers, we use Supreme Court.

17 The Rikken kaishintō platform included: 1) upholding the dignity and glory of the Imperial Household; 2) developing and strengthening the nation; 3) eradicating the intrigue of central interference; 4) keeping abreast of social progress and universalizing suffrage; 5) promoting trade relations with the outside world; and 6) establishing a monetary system on the basis of hard currency. To demonstrate that their party was not only for the intellectual and financial elite of Japan, several members of the Kaishintō spent several weeks in Tosa in 1880 pulling rickshaws (Ike, 1950: 107).

18 *Shō choku* [*Imperial Edict*] of Oct. 12, 1881.

19 Green and Porter (1984) present evidence of cycles of collusion and punishment in the U.S. railroad industry. They note that even if prices are unobserv-

able, members of a cartel can infer the prices other members are charging by observing the fluctuations in their own demand. Every time the demand falls below a certain level, members of the cartel will be motivated to punish the unknown offender by lowering their prices for a time. There is always the danger that punishment will be for naught, in the case that low demand was exogenous to the cartel. But such a collective commitment to punishment is required to preserve the collusion over the long run.

3. CONCESSION OR FACADE

1 Indeed, the Army and Navy supported each other in their respective areas of dominance. As David Titus points out, "[t]he 1937 China Incident, for example, expanded out of control when the *navy* sent troops into Shanghai. And the army desperately wanted a move into Southeast Asia to close supply routes to China." (personal communication, May 12, 1994).

2 *Hoan jōrei [Peace Preservation Order]*, Chokurei No. 67 of Dec. 26, 1887.

3 Itō was accompanied by Yamazaki Naotane of the Dajōkan, Itō Miyoji of the Sanji in, Kawashima Jun and Hirata Tōsuke of the Finance Ministry, Yoshida Masaharu of the Foreign Ministry, Miyoshi Taizō of the Justice Ministry, and Saionji Kimmochi, Iwakura Tomosada, Hirohashi Takamitsu, and Sagara Yoriaki of the Imperial Household Agency. Together, they visited Germany, France, Belgium, England, Russia, and Italy (Fujii, 1965: 160–164).

4 Osadake (1938) recounts the arguments of some oligarchs who were opposed to the adoption of a constitution altogether. Others felt that far-reaching institutional reform was the only means to survival. Itō Hirobumi held the coalition together by brokering the demands of both sides.

5 *Kazoku rei [Peerage Order]*, unnumbered Kunaishō tatsu of July 7, 1884.

6 Tsuji (1944: 115). The title of prince (*kō shaku*) would go to those who were related to the Emperor, members of the Tokugawa family, and those who had contributed importantly to the nation. Eligible for the title of marquis (*kō [sōrō] shaku*) would be the three feudal families most closely related to the Tokugawa family, feudal lords from largest domains, Okinawan royalty, and those who had contributed to the nation. Counts (*haku shaku*) would be appointed from among vassal lords of the Tokugawa, lords of middle-sized domains, and others who had contributed to the nation. Eligible to be selected as viscounts (*shi shaku*) were lords of the smaller domains, and other subjects who had contributed to the nation. Barons (*dan shaku*) were to be chosen from the ranks of lesser samurai and people who contributed to the nation.

7 Momose (1990: 242). In a 1907 revision to the Imperial Order on Peerage (*Kazoku rei [Peerage Order]*, Kōshitsu rei No. 2 of May 7, 1907, §§10, 12), a child of a deceased peer was required to register with the Imperial Household Agency within six months of the death of his father in order to inherit the title. Failure to do so meant forfeiture of the title (Momose, 1990: 243).

8 Of the ten members of the first cabinet, four each were of the Satsuma and Chōshū clans (Fujii, 1965: 186).

9 Kaneko Kentarō (1937: 116), one of Itō's subordinates, states that another of Itō's concerns was to lessen the Imperial Household Agency's involvement in government. The Imperial Household Agency was denied cabinet status under the new rules. See also Tsuji (1944: 115–125).

10 *Bunkan shiken shishin oyobi minarai kisoku [Regulation on Civil Service Examination and Apprenticeship]*, Chokurei No. 37 of July 23, 1887.

11 See *Sūmitsuin kansei [Privy Council Order]*, Chokurei No. 22 of April 28, 1888.

12 See, for example, Baba (1930); and Maeda (1934).

13 Itō (1889: 99).

14 *Kōshitsu tempan [Imperial Regulations]*, unnumbered, February 11, 1889.

15 *Dai-Nippon teikoku kempō [The Constitution of the Great Empire of Japan]*, promulgated Feb. 11, 1889. The quotations in this chapter are taken from the official translation.

16 Itō (1889: 62); Colegrove (1933: 890). Itō's interpretation of the power of the legislature was no doubt what most oligarchs intended, and was echoed by the more conservative constitutional theorists of the day: for example, Hozumi Yatsuka (1910) and Uesugi Shinkichi (1927). But other maverick legal scholars, notably Minobe Tatsukichi, disagreed. Minobe was harrassed into resigning from the House of Peers in 1935 for his views (Miller, 1965: 252; Titus, 1974: 130–31).

17 *Kizoku in rei [House of Peers Order]*, Chokurei No. 11 of Feb. 11, 1889.

18 In practice, most joined the Navy or Army and did not attend Diet sessions (Momose, 1990: 37).

19 By the 1920s, most princes and marquis, who were children and grand-children of feudal lords or of Imperial Household members, had dropped out of active political life (Momose, 1990: 38).

20 The House of Peers had eighteen slots for counts, and sixty-six slots each for viscounts and barons. Representatives were elected by other males of their own rank over twenty years of age See *Kizokuin hakushidan shaku giin senkyo kisoku [Regulations for the Election of Counts, Viscounts, and Barons to the House of Peers]*, Chokurei No. 78 of 1889.

21 By 1945, the Peers were dominated by former bureaucrats (39 percent), businessmen (25 percent), and former cabinet ministers (16 percent). (*Nihon kingendai shi [Contemporary and Modern Japanese History]*, 1978.)

22 *Kizoku in tagaku nōzeisha giin gosen kisoku [Regulations for the Election of High Taxpayers to the House of Peers]*, Chokurei No. 79 of June 4, 1889 and *Kizoku in rei [House of Peers Ordinance]*, Chokurei No. 11 of Feb. 11, 1889. Momose (1990: 242) states that in practice, 6,600 taxpayers, divided into prefectural districts, elected 66 Peers. Most prefectures had between 100 and 200 "big tax payers" who were eligible to vote and run for these 66 seats. In 1932, the highest and lowest amounts in taxes paid by eligible voters were, for example, ¥110,000 and ¥4,329, respectively, for Tokyo, and ¥2,856 and ¥420 for Yamanashi. Okinawa's taxpayers had the lowest hurdle to qualify, at ¥99 ("Tagaku nōzeisha meibō [Roster of High-end Tax Payers]" in *Nihon shinshi roku furoku [A Record of Japan's Gentlemen]* (1933); see also *Taishō Shōwa Nihon zenkoku shisanka jinushi shiryō shūsei [Collected Data on Capitalists and Landlords in the Taisho and Showa Periods]*).

23 *Shūgiin giin senkyo hō [Law for the Election of the Members of the House of Representatives]*, Law No. 3 of 1889; and *Giin hō [Diet Act]*, Law No. 37 of 1889. For a detailed discussion of the drafting process of the Diet Act, see Ōishi (1990).

24 Itō (1889: 134–5).

25 See, for example, Fujii (1940: 242). Itō (1889: 92–93), in his *Commentaries*, says "[w]hen a Minister of State errs in the discharge of his functions, the power of deciding upon his responsibility belongs to the Sovereign of the State: He alone can dismiss a Minister, who has appointed him. . . . The appointment and dismissal of them . . . is withheld from the Diet."

26 *Naikaku kansei [Cabinet Regulations]*, Chokurei 135 of Dec. 24, 1889.
27 See *Kōbunshiki*, Chokurei No. 1 of Feb. 24, 1886, which was superseded by *Kōshiki rei*, Chokurei No. 6 of Jan. 31, 1907.
28 See generally Ichiki (1892: 31–33, 141). In his *Commentaries*, Itō (1889: 69) wrote that "[i]t is futile to attempt, as is shown by constitutional experience as well as by scientific researches, to lay down distinctions between law and ordinance by reference to the nature of the subject matter."
29 Note that the Imperial Diet Act of 1890 was a statute, meaning that the House of Representatives could block proposed changes in its organization and function. Note also that the House of Representatives was precluded from reducing the powers of either the Privy Council or the House of Peers since each of these bodies had vetoes over their own fates. Short of such sweeping reforms, the House of Representatives probably could never have obtained the reins of government.
30 For two reasons, this probably was not a substantive requirement. First, it was not clear precisely who was required to sign the bill, whether it was the Prime Minister, the minister in charge, or all ministers. The Constitution itself specified only that it be a "national minister." For various perspectives on the issue, see Minobe (1926: 413), Uesugi (1935: 153) and Kaji (1926: 128). For only moderately helpful detail, see *Kōshiki rei*, Chokurei No. 6 of Jan. 31, 1907, §6, and *Naikaku kanrei*, Chokurei No. 135 of Dec. 24, 1889, §4. Second, the minister (whichever one it was) may not have had a veto power anyway. Minobe (1926: 428) and Fukushima (1926) both treat ministerial approval as a formality. Ichimura (1927: 269), Kanamori (1927: 243–44), Ōtani (1939: 332–34), Satō (1936: 213) and Uesugi (1935: 152) argued that the minister had no right to refuse to countersign the bill. Kaji (1936: 116–17) argued that a minister had the duty to refuse to countersign an improper bill.
31 Article 64 of the Constitution provided that "The expenditure and revenue of the state require the consent of the Imperial Diet by means of an annual budget. Any expenditures surpassing the appropriations set forth in the budget shall subsequently require the approval of the Diet." Further, in Article 65, "The budget shall be first brought before the House of Representatives."
32 Colegrove (1931: 602).
33 This principle was imported from Germany where the budget was only a *Verordnung* or ordinance for the year, rather than a *Gesetz*. See Colegrove (1934: 26); Hozumi (1910: 502–09); Uesugi (1927: 537–41).
34 The famous "Matsukata Deflation" of 1884–1885 can be viewed as one of the first attempts to extend the government's spending power in the face of revenue constraints. See Muroyama, ed. (1984: 63–66) and Horie (1927).
35 Const., Art. 5. *Sūmitsuin kansei [Privy Council Order]*, Chokurei No. 22 of April 28, 1888, as amended by Chokurei No. 216 of Oct. 7, 1890.
36 In general, the Privy Council was required to comment on: (1) certain Imperial Household regulations; (2) situations involving either (a) disputes over the Constitution or statutes or orders "relating to" the Constitution, or (b) proposed statutes or orders "relating to" the Constitution; (3) declarations of martial law under Art. 14 of the Constitution, emergency Imperial Orders under Art. 8, emergency budgetary orders under Art. 70, and Imperial Orders with penal provisions; (4) treaties; (5) Privy Council matters; and (6) when otherwise asked. See amendments to *Sūmitsuin kansei*, Chokurei No. 216 of Oct. 7, 1890, §6.
37 An order issued under the Emperor's general police power (Art. 9) could not

contravene an existing statute. The Emperor could issue an order at odds with
a statute only if the Diet were not in session and he submitted the order to the
Diet at its next session (Art. 8).

38 See note 30 for a discussion of counter-signature.

39 Asahi shimbun seiji keizaibu, ed. (1930: 43–45); Momose (1990: 63); Colegrove (1931: 599; 1933: 892).

40 The Constitution could be amended only upon the initiation of an Imperial
Order (Art. 73). Privy Council matters were reserved to the Emperor by Art.
56, and House of Peers matters were reserved to him by Art. 34.

41 See, for example, Murobushi (1988).

4. ELECTORAL RULES AND PARTY COMPETITION

1 *Shūgiin giin senkyo hō [Act for the Election of Representatives to the House of
Representatives]*, Law No. 3 of Feb. 11, 1889.

2 Section 6. In 1889, about two-thirds of the direct national taxes consisted of
land taxes, and a great majority of the voters were land-owning farmers.

3 Shimane 6th district had only 52 voters, Kagoshima 7th had 53, and Nagasaki
6th had 55. Meanwhile, Fukushima 5th had 4,295, Shiga 2nd had 4,379, and
Mie 3rd had 4,568 (Uyehara, 1910: 171).

4 Municipalities (except the cities of Tokyo, Kyōto, and Osaka, which were
treated as prefectures) had no separate electoral districts. Urban voters were
typically overwhelmed by the rural voters in the same district. According to
Chief Secretary of the House Hayashida in 1900, only 17 out of the 300
members of the House in that year represented the interests of the urban
business population (Uyehara, 1910: 172).

5 Masuda (1954: 471); Hani (1956: 315); Tomita (1986: 75).

6 See Toriumi (1967: 87), Akita (1967: 79, 107, 118), and Mason (1969: 173)
on the deals the government had to cut with members of the legislature to pass
government budgets in those early years.

7 Yamagata was so alarmed by the formation of this new gigantic political party
under the leadership of two wayward oligarchs that he urged the Privy Council
to suspend the Constitution to ban this party's activities. Yamagata's fellow
oligarchs rejected such a panicked response (Uyehara, 1910: 176).

8 Ōkuma's party also took the cabinet posts of Education, Justice, and Agriculture, while Itagaki's party got Foreign Affairs, Finance, and Commerce
(Nomura, 1931: 189).

9 Meanwhile, Yamagata Aritomo tried to induce the parties to destroy each
other. He and his men supplied damaging information about each party to the
other parties and to journalists (Fujimura, 1961).

10 Hani (1956: 316). Several years later, Ōkuma would write somewhat wist-
fully, "Although there are many things to be regretted, such as the ineffective-
ness of political parties, the imperfection of the Diet, the disorganized condition of public affairs, the backward tendency of the conservative elements, we
must wait, practice patience, and not expect too much in our passionate zeal"
(Ōkuma, ed., 1909: 191).

11 Chokurei No. 193 of May 19, 1900, and Chokurei No. 194 of May 19, 1900.
Ministers had to be selected from among generals or admirals (*daichūshō*).

12 For a detailed account of Seiyūkai president Hara's negotiations with Prime
Minister Terauchi, for example, see Tamai (1989).

13 *Shūgiin giin senkyo hō [Act for the Election of Representatives to the House of Representatives]*, Law No. 73 of Mar. 28, 1900, §§36, 45. Secret ballots were also introduced for the first time, perhaps because open ballots were more rankling than they were intimidating (§36). Alternatively, note that open ballots lower the transaction costs of bribery. Perhaps the oligarchs noticed that the political parties were able to bribe voters at least as effectively as the government was.

14 Forty-seven rural districts, coinciding with the prefectural administrative districts *(fu* or *ken)*, were alloted 4 to 12 seats according to population. Sixty-one urban electoral districts were each accorded 1 or 2 seats. The exceptions were the districts of Tokyo, Osaka, and Kyōto, which were treated as prefectures and therefore given 11, 6, and 3 seats, respectively (Act, Appendix). The total number of seats was increased to 369 in 1900, and to 381 in 1902 (Kobayakawa, 1940: 572).

15 The Elections Act of 1900 also eliminated the requirement of the 1890 Act that voters be registered (Act, §8). See also Uchida, Kanehara, and Furuya (1991: 244—47); Kamijō (1988: 4).

16 Yamagata is reported to have been ambivalent about expanding the electorate, even though it eased the revenue-raising problem. He was concerned that more voters would strengthen the parties, but he was overridden by the other oligarchs on this point. Itō Hirobumi wanted to lower the tax requirement even further. See Uchida, Kanehara, and Furuya (1991: 247—263). But the government had failed to get the elections bill passed by the same Diet in 1899. With no intervening elections to change the composition of the House, what had changed? The Kenseikai leaders had become convinced that they would do relatively better than the Jiyūtō with more urban voters (Matsuo, 1989: 26—27).

17 The logic of single-member districts has, as Duverger noted, both "mechanical" and "psychological" components. The mechanical effect is simply that a single candidate can win all representation of a district with a plurality of votes, though often less than a majority of the votes. The psychological effect is that voters will be reluctant to "throw away" their vote to a candidate who has no chance of winning under these rules. Candidates are similarly affected: Competent politicians will be discouraged from joining small parties in single-member district systems because their chances of winning are so slim. See Duverger (1955).

18 Closed lists, which give voters a choice only among party lists and not a say in the ordering of the lists, strengthen party leaders' control over backbenchers.

19 Itō (1983: 560—562); Tomita (1987: 74—81). See Hara's diary as early as December 16, 1911, for Hara's notes about his discussions with Yamagata over single-member districts.

20 Masumi (1986: 334). *Shūgiin giin senkyo hō kaisei hō [Act to Amend the Act for the Election of Representatives to the House of Representatives]*, Law No. 60 of May 22, 1919, App. As under the 1900 Act, voters used an unsigned ballot and had an SNTV.

21 More precisely, males 25 years or older could vote if they had resided in one district for six consecutive months and if they had paid ¥3 in the form of any national tax (whether land, income, or other) for one year (1919 Act, §8).

22 The rice riots in the summer of 1918, which began as protests against the high price of rice, turned into a nationwide protest against the existing form of government. The sheer scale of these protests, involving nearly three-quarters

of a million people around the country, forced the nation's leaders to consider universal suffrage seriously.

23 The Seiyūkai's logic was that the Privy Council would be alarmed and might hold the Kenseikai cabinet responsible for the entire universal suffrage issue. See Matsuo (1989: 305–311); Duus (1968: 158–200).

24 *Chian iji hō [The Peace Preservation Act]*, Law No. 46 of April 21, 1925, forbade the existence of any association whose object was to "change the fundamental nature of the state or to threaten private property." For an introduction to the act, see *Asahi nenkan [Asahi Yearbook]* (1926: 336–338).

25 Whatever their real reasons for going along with universal suffrage, the Peers dressed them up in high-minded rhetoric. Prince Konoe Fumimaro and others argued that because the suffrage bill governed the elections of only the House of Representatives, the Peers should defer to that House in the drafting of the law. See Kawabe (1941).

26 Of the 390 Peers, nearly half were members of a group, the *Kenkyūkai* [Research Group], with special ties to oligarch Yamagata Aritomo. Seiyūkai supporters outnumbered Kenseikai supporters 10 to 1 at this time in the House of Peers (Sasahiro, 1932: 344; Matsuo, 1989: 321–2).

27 *Shūgiin giin senkyo hō [Act for the Election of Representatives to the House of Representatives]*, Law No. 47 of May 5, 1925.

28 *Shūgiin giin senkyo hō [Act for the Election of Representatives to the House of Representatives]*, Law No. 47 of May 5, 1925.

29 This logic is discussed at greater length in McCubbins and Rosenbluth (1995) and Ramseyer and Rosenbluth (1993).

30 We are indebted to David Laitin for this suggestion.

31 That lack of identification, as we and others have argued elsewhere (McCubbins and Rosenbluth, 1995; Ramseyer and Rosenbluth, 1993), is due precisely to the electoral rules. When each candidate has an incentive to expand his own support base at the expense of his fellow-party-member in his district, the party label suffers.

32 Gary Cox pointed out to us these problems with ideologically based intra-party competition.

33 Sasahiro Yū, an outspoken critic in his day, claimed that the widespread use of election bribery was an open secret (Sasahiro, 1932: 42). See also Furushima (1951: 165–168).

34 The expenses were not to exceed 40 sen per voter. Actual campaign estimates are recounted in Sasahiro (1932: 216–231) and Hazama (1982: 635–636). One candidate, Uchida Nobuya, was charged in the *Chūō kōron* with spending ¥500,000 in the 1924 election, purchasing votes at the price of ¥100 to ¥150 each. This far exceeded the average "price" of votes, which was said to be one to ¥5 in rural areas, and ¥5 to ¥10 in urban districts (Colegrove, 1929: 334). In 1926, the mean annual income of factory workers was ¥312 (Ramseyer, 1991: 95).

35 The 1925 Elections Act lifted the ceiling on campaign expenditures to ¥12,000, a sum still far below the average actual expenditure. See, for example, Sasahiro (1932: 117).

36 Sasahiro (1932: 201–37); Hazama (1982: 625). Not surprisingly, given its support from electric power companies, a plank in the Minseitō platform was the regulation of public utilities (Colegrove, 1928: 402).

37 Unaffiliated firms formed the Jitsugyō dōshikai (Businessmen's Society) in time

to field candidates for the 1928 election. But they succeeded in getting only four representatives elected, and soon folded into the Minseitō.

38 Nowhere did the Meiji Constitution give the Diet the power to bring down a cabinet with a vote of no confidence. But they used no-confidence votes as signals that they would not cooperate with the cabinet unless they received concessions. This was a dangerous game of brinkmanship, because the cabinet could always dissolve the Diet, thereby imposing huge election costs on the legislators. The Seiyūkai and the Seiyūhontō did pass a no-confidence measure against the Kenseikai cabinet in January 1927. However, Prime Minister Wakatsuki prorogued the Diet for three days with an imperial rescript to give himself time to strike deals with his rivals. The newspapers speculated that Wakatsuki pledged to step down shortly in exchange for cooperation for a bit longer. By the time the Diet reconvened, the Seiyūkai and the Seiyūhontō were willing to withdraw their motion of no confidence. See *Kampō [Imperial Gazette]* Jan. 21, 1927: 419 and Jan. 25, 1927: 503. All of this prompted a newspaper to announce that "common sense forbids us to believe in any shred of sincerity in the party leaders of this country." Quoted in Colegrove (1927: 837).

39 Wakatsuki had already promised the other parties he would step down and would have faced stonewalling from the Diet if he did not. Meanwhile, Wakatsuki may have gained political capital with the public for appearing to act noble in the face of Privy Council bullying.

40 House-to-house canvassing and telephone campaigns were prohibited, as was dinner or other entertainment for voters or transportation to the polls.

41 In February 1928, the government raided the Minseitō headquarters in Tokyo and seized 2,000 campaign leaflets that accused Prime Minister Tanaka Giichi of embezzling funds when he commanded the Siberian Army in 1919.

42 *Jiji shimpō* January 26, 1928, p. 2; *Tōkyō asahi shimbun,* January 25, 1928, p. 2; *Tōkyō hōchi shimbun,* January 26, 1928, p. 2 (cited in Colegrove, 1928: 405); Shinmyō (1961: 209–210). On the political accountability of prosecutors, see Chapter 6.

43 Police repeatedly broke up campaign meetings of the leftist parties and arrested scores of election workers. Colegrove (1929: 335).

44 But the Seiyūkai's Home Affairs Minister was forced to resign after the election due to public outrage at his all-too-blatant tactics (see Chapter 5).

45 The Seiyūkai's 217 seats swelled to 234 when some opportunistic independents joined after the election. The Minseitō won 214. Apparently, the private-goods strategy of the two largest parties counteracted the expected proliferation of parties in multi-member district sytems (Cox, 1990).

46 What had formerly been the Kenseikai, now bereft of its coalition partner, kept the name Minseitō.

47 Sakai (1989) describes how, in the 1930 election, the Minseitō used its cabinet status and control of policy favors to shore up its electoral prospects.

5. THE BUREAUCRACY

1 McCubbins and Schwartz (1984) call this "fire alarm" monitoring, in contrast with more expensive "police patrols."

2 The oligarchs had had credibility problems too, of course, since they could renege on their own promises. Their longer expected tenure (at least during the nineteenth century), however, gave them expected future rents that enabled

them to make credible promises that politicians elected for short-term posts could not make. See Klein and Leffler (1981).

3 Essentially, each party played an indefinitely repeated prisoners' dilemma. In such games, cooperation is one possible equilibrium, but not necessarily the most likely. We explore this issue more fully in the context of judicial independence, at Chapter 6.

4 *Bunkan shiken shishin oyobi minarai kisoku* [*Regulation on Civil Service Examination and Apprenticeship*], Chokurei No. 37 of July 23, 1887.

5 *Bunkan nin'yō rei* [*Imperial Order Governing Civil Service Hiring*], Chokurei No. 183 of Oct. 31, 1893.

6 *Bunkan nin'yōrei o zenbun kaisei* [*An Amendment of the Entire Imperial Order Governing Civil Service Hiring*], Chokurei No. 61 of Mar. 28, 1899.

7 In 1869, bureaucrats were divided into eighteen ranks, the highest four of which were *chokuninkan*. The next two were *sōninkan,* and the rest were *hanninkan* (*Shokuin rei* [*Employee Ordinance*] of July 1869). In 1871, the system was revised into fifteen ranks with the highest three being *chokuninkan*. Seven and higher were *sōninkan,* and the rest were *hanninkan*. In 1872, commoners were appointed as high-level bureaucrats (*sōninkan* or higher) and were given aristocratic titles for themselves and their children [Dajōkan Order No. 335]. When the cabinet system was established in March 1886, Ministers were given the highest rank of *shinninkan*. Vice Ministers and secretary generals were given the rank of *chokuninkan*. Section chiefs and six ranks below them were labeled *sōninkan*. The hiring and firing of *chokuninkan* required a cabinet order; that of *sōninkan* required the approval of the Prime Minister or cabinet Minister and the cabinet's stamp of approval. The hiring and firing of *hanninkan* required the permission only of a cabinet Minister. In 1887, an additional bureaucratic rank was added, raising the total number to sixteen; other than minor tinkering of this sort, the ranking system basically remained the same until 1945.

Yamagata's ordinance of 1900 (Chokurei No. 61) required that *chokuninkan* bureaucrats be selected from among higher *sōninkan* or other *chokuninkan* bureaucrats. See Senzenki kanryōsei kenkyūkai (1981: 663–64) and Asahi shimbun seiji keizai bu (1930).

8 *Bunkan bungen rei* [*Civil Servant Separation Order*], Chokurei No. 62 of Mar. 28, 1899; *Bunkan chōkai rei* [*Civil Servant Disciplinary Order*], Chokurei No. 63 of Mar. 28, 1899.

9 For many bureaucrats, it seems, life was almost as risk-laden as it was for politicians. It is no wonder so many bureaucrats ran for office themselves in the 1920s. So long as they were going to bear the risks of electoral turnover anyway, they might as well be in a policymaking position themselves.

10 Hata (1981: 327–354). See also Itō (1984) and Tsutsui (1988) for accounts of how cabinet politics had permeated into local government by the 1920s.

11 Hata (1981: 355–359). See also Ikeda (1984) for how the tax policies of the cabinets differed.

12 For a full sketch of Yamaoka's life, see Hosojima (1964).

13 Sakai (1992: 270–3) describes the Minseitō's use of both the Police Agency and the Internal Affairs Bureau for electoral purposes. For more on the history of the Police Agency, see Takahashi (1976).

14 Hosojima (1964: 95). According to MOF bureaucrat Aoki Tokuzō (whose own case we discuss later), it was not uncommon for cabinets to select to the House of Peers a few loyal top bureaucrats just before being replaced by a

cabinet of another party (Ōkurashō ed., 1977: 250). The promise of long-term job security was a key device in the political competition for the loyalty of bureaucrats.

15 The position gave Yamaoka job security in the face of alternating party cabinets. It also boosted his name-recognition, probably helping him win the chairmanship of the Tokyo Bar Association in April 1931. But another career opportunity came in September 1931, when the Seiyūkai once again controlled the cabinet. The Prime Minister appointed Yamaoka director general of the Kwantung territory in China (*Kantō chōkan*), which position he held until the military took over the following year (Hosojima, 1964: 102–137).

16 Aoki (1958: 232) recounts that he was assigned to that desirable position on the recommendations of both Hamaguchi and Wakatsuki. Although the Minister's secretary was an official position, Aoki accompanied Wakatsuki on a three-week campaign tour around the country on behalf of Dōshikai candidates prior to the 1915 election. That is where Aoki first met Kataoka Naohara, later to be Aoki's boss as Minister of Finance (Ōkurashō ed., 1977: 253).

17 When the Seiyūkai replaced the Ōkuma cabinet, Aoki was assigned to the lower-profile position of bank examiner (Ōkurashō 1977: 233).

18 Both Wakatsuki and Hamaguchi themselves had been MOF bureaucrats before they switched to political careers. Aoki recounts the intra-ministerial rivalry between Hamaguchi, who had early in his bureaucratic career identified himself with the Dōshikai/Kenseikai/Minseitō, and Katsuda Shukei, who had close ties to the military. Finance Minister Wakatsuki was forced to promote Katsuda to Vice Minister over Hamaguchi in 1911, at the insistence of Prime Minister (and general) Katsura Tarō. In an unusual move, Hamaguchi became Vice Minister of Communications (*teishin jikan*) instead. Apparently there were no hard feelings, for both Wakatsuki and Hamaguchi joined Katsura's Rikken Dōshikai that year (Ōkurashō ed., 1977: 231–249).

19 This was a job Ministers often shared with Vice Ministers. In 1914, for example, Vice Minister Hamaguchi promoted one of his proteges from a lowly post in the Monopoly Bureau to what was considered the best section chief in the entire Ministry, that of the Budget Decision Section (*yosan kessanka*) (Ōkurashō ed., 1977: 251).

6. THE COURTS

1 A few scholars are less ambivalent. John Haley (1991: 80) leans toward complete independence: in the pre-World War II years, "the judiciary could claim full autonomy from all direct outside interference." So does Mitchell (1992). Percy Luney (1990: 137) leans the other direction: "The Meiji Constitution of 1889 did not provide for judicial independence."

2 Barzel (1991, 1992); North and Weingast (1989). Note that the Japanese government apparently had little trouble borrowing at advantageous terms. In 1870 – with no functioning courts at all – it borrowed abroad at 9 percent annual interest. By 1873 it had cut that rate to 7 percent. And by 1899 it was issuing 10-year pound sterling bonds at 4 percent (Ōkura shō, 1906: 32–47).

3 *Saiban sho kansei [Court Organization]*, Chokurei No. 40 of May 4, 1886, at §12.

4 In the language of modern political science, the revocable order may have created a structure-induced equilibrium. See Shepsle (1981); Krehbiel (1992: chapter 2).

5 Art. 58 (b); see Art. 57 (b). Further details they left to statute. On the significance of the requirement that a rule be specified by statute, see Chapter 3,
Section 4. Article 58 of the Constitution also provided that the qualifications
for judges and the details of disciplinary proceedings be specified by statute;
Article 59 provided that most trial proceedings be public; Article 60 provided
that special courts could be organized by statute; and Article 61 provided for
administrative courts.

6 On the procedures for amending the Constitution, see Art. 73 (Imperial Order
and a two-thirds vote of both houses of the Diet).

7 *Saibansho kōsei hō [Judicial Organization Act]*, Law No. 6 of Feb. 10, 1890.
Further details on the status of the judges were determined by the *Hanji kenji
kan nado hōkyūrei [Order Regarding the Compensation of Judges and Prosecutors, Etc.]*, Chokurei No. 17 of Feb. 14, 1894.

8 *Saibansho kōsei hō*, supra note 7, at §135. Under the post-war Constitution,
the courts would instead be under a nominally independent Supreme Court.
See *Kempō [Constitution]*, Arts. 76–77. On the unimportance of this change,
see Ramseyer and Rosenbluth (1993: chaps. 8–9).

9 *Hanji chōkai hō [Judicial Disciplinary Act]*, Law No. 68 of Aug. 20, 1890, at
§§2 through 9.

10 Mandatory retirement was introduced with Law No. 101 of May 17, 1921.

11 On the protections enjoyed by other bureaucrats, see *Bunkan bungen rei
[Order on Status of Civil Employees]*, Chokurei No. 62 of Mar. 27, 1899.

12 See *Kanshi onkyū hō [Government Employee Pension Act]*, Law No. 43 of
June 21, 1890; *Hanji chōkai hō*, supra note 9, at §7.

13 This account is based on Ramseyer and Rosenbluth (1993: chap. 8).

14 *Keihō [Criminal Code]*, Dajōkan fukoku No. 36 of July 17, 1880, §§116,
292–298.

15 *Keihō*, supra note 14, at §261.

16 *Kanpō [Government Gazette]*, No. 2748, Aug. 24, 1885, effective Aug. 23,
1885.

17 For detailed discussions of the incident, see Kusunoki 1989: ch. 2); "Ukō sen
Tokyo Bengoshi Kai chō Miyoshi Taizō kun yukeri [Sadly, Former Chairman
Miyoshi Taizō of the Tokyo Bar Association Passes]," *Hōritsu shimbun*, 517: 1
(1908).

18 *Kanpō [Government Gazette]*, No. 3162, Jan. 16, 1894, effective Jan. 15,
1894. It may not have been a total surprise. In February 1893, Chiya had been
docked a tenth of his pay by the disciplinary board of the Supreme Court for
negligence in his duties prior to becoming a Supreme Court justice. See
Kusunoki (1989: 82–83) (discipinary opinion reproduced).

19 *Kanpō [Government Gazette]*, No. 3159, Jan. 12, 1894, effective Jan. 11,
1894.

20 *Kanpō [Government Gazette]*, No. 3225, Apr. 4, 1894, effective Apr. 2, 1894.
The record does not indicate how they managed to convince the judge to
retire, since they appear not to have submitted the matter to a Supreme Court
vote as required by the *Saibansho kōsei hō*, supra note 7, at §74. On the
various inducements available, see Sec. 3.5, infra.

21 This account is taken from Kusunoki (1989: chapter 3); "Ukō sen Tokyo
bengoshi kai chō Miyoshi Taizō kun yukeri [Sadly, Former Chairman Miyoshi
Taizō of the Tokyo Bar Association Passes]," *Hōritsu shimbun*, 517: 1 (1908).

22 Reproduced in Kusunoki (1989: 103).

23 The capacity of the courts at the time was about 1200 judges. See Chokurei

No. 17 of February 14, 1894 (1220 judges); Chokurei No. 122 of June 20, 1898 (1195 judges).

24 The oligarchs had created a national court system by 1872. See *Shihō shokumu teisei [Rules Regarding Judicial Functions]*, Dajōkan unnumbered tatsu of Aug. 3, 1872. The Supreme Court (Daishin'in) was created by the *Daishin'in sho saibansho shokusei shotei [Rules and Duties of the Supreme Court and Other Courts]*, Dajōkan fukoku No. 91 of May 24, 1875.

25 The first government-sponsored legal training was offered in 1872, but the number of graduates in the early years was small. The first private law school began operation in 1880. See generally Kusunoki (1989: 297–99).

26 On the later educational requirements in the judiciary, see *Hanji tōyō kisoku [Judicial Appointment Rules]*, Dajōkan tatsu No. 102 of December 26, 1887.

27 See *Mimpō [Civil Code]*, Law No. 89 of Apr. 27, 1896 and Law No. 9 of June 21, 1898; *Shōhō [Commercial Code]*, Law No. 48 of Mar. 9, 1898; *Minji soshō hō [Code of Civil Procedure]*, Law No. 29 of April 21, 1890; *Keiji soshō hō [Code of Criminal Procedure]*, Law No. 131 of July 10, 1890.

28 See *Kanshi onkyū hō*, supra note 12, at §5.

29 Kusunoki (1989: 282–93) (Supreme Court tenure). For the size of the Supreme Court, see *Hanji kenji kan nado hōkyūrei*, supra note 7, at §2.

30 *Saibansho kōsei hō*, supra note 7, at §74.

31 *Hanji chōkai hō*, supra note 9, at §1. Of course, they could also try to induce him to quit by transferring him to a job he did not want. If they did, and he refused, they were then back at an impeachment hearing.

32 Chokurei No. 122 of June 20, 1898, canceled the court size specifications of *Hanji kenji kan nado hōkyūrei*, supra note 7. Having signalled what they *could* do if necessary, they then respecified court sizes with Chokurei No. 324 of Ocober. 22, 1898.

33 He could legally name lawyers to judicial and prosecutorial posts under §65 of the *Saibansho kōsei hō*, supra note 7.

34 On the disciplinary proceedings of prosecutors, see *Saibansho kōsei hō*, supra note 7, §80; Dajōkan tatsu No. 34 of April 14, 1876.

35 Ienaga's (1962: 10–11) claim that Ōkuma halted the forced resignations is incorrect.

36 These tables consider only the four months after taking office. The two phenomena are in fact more closely linked than one might suppose. Many judges about to be fired were first promoted to the Supreme Court for a few days as a face-saving and pension-boosting bribe.

37 August 2, 1925, is the date Katō reconfigured his cabinet. Note that this is also the date when he appointed the Minister of Justice who removed Yamaoka (see infra).

38 Alternatively, it is possible that it simply took time for the politicians to learn how to manipulate the various sectors of government. As Chapter 5 shows, they began manipulating the politically most important ministries first – most particularly the Ministry of Home Affairs. The data following may show that they turned to the Ministry of Justice only after they had learned how to control the more critical ministries.

39 Law No. 6 of April 5, 1913; Law No. 7 of April 5, 1913. Law No. 6 in fact provided that the transfer provision applied "when necessary for trial business." Because the Judicial Organization Act already allowed the Minister of Justice to transfer judges when it was necessary to fill a vacancy (Act, §73

proviso), usual canons of statutory interpretation would indicate this was a significantly looser requirement.

40 Law No. 101 of May 17, 1921.

41 "Yamaoka keiji kyoku chō kyūshoku ni kanshite [Regarding the Inactive status of Criminal Bureau Chief Yamaoka]," *Hōritsu shimbun,* 2438: 20 (1925); "Shihō shō keiji kyoku chō kyūshoku mondai [The Problem of the Inactive Status for the Bureau Chief of the Ministry of Justice Criminal Bureau]," *Hōritsu shimbun,* 2438: 19 (1925).

42 For other aspects of Yamaoka's career, see Chapter 5.

43 See generally Hosojima (1964: 45–95); "Shihō shō," supra note 41.

44 "Shihō shō," supra note 41.

45 Mitani's (1980: 18–19) claim that the judiciary remained independent from the political parties is simply false.

46 "Shihō kōkan idō hyō [An Evaluation of the Transfers of High Judicial Officers]," *Hōritsu shimbun,* 3352: 17 (1931). Ōhara defended his record at *Hōritsu shimbun,* 3355: 4 (1931).

47 Alternatively, if the Seiyūkai dominated the courts earlier, why did the Kenseikai/Minseitō not challenge that domination while it controlled the cabinet?

48 Why the oligarchs made this institutional choice we do not address – though we suspect it may have to do with convincing Western governments to abandon consular jurisdiction.

7. THE MILITARY

1 See generally Kyūsanbō (1966); Vlastos (1989: 382–402); Yoshino (1928: 295–300).

2 See Matsushita (1963a: 56–58); Matsushita (1966a: 48–50). Frequently, Yamagata's faction is discussed in the literature as the "Chōshū faction," after the province from which he came. The Saigō-Yamamoto clique is discussed as the Satsuma clique, after the province from which they came. Geography does not assure loyalty, of course, especially when several of Yamagata's competing oligarchs also came from Chōshū. Nonetheless, within the Army, the "Chōshū faction" did generally constitute the Yamagata faction. "Genealogies" of the various military factions can be found in the standard historical dictionaries. For a typical example, see Kyoto (1958: 724–26); see also, for example, Hackett (1971: 145); Matsushita (1967: I-74–75, 96–103); Murakami (1973: 210).

3 See Nihon kindai (1971: 126–28). He was not Army Minister continuously, however, since others did occasionally serve as Army Minister as well.

4 See Nihon kindai (1971: 128–30). On factional membership, see note 2, supra.

5 By an unnumbered tatsu of Dec. 5, 1878, the old command bureau (*sanbō kyoku*) was abolished. By another unnumbered tatsu of Dec. 5, 1878, the *Sanbō honbu jōrei,* the new, independent command was established.

6 *Sanbō honbu jōrei,* supra note 5, §2; see generally Izu and Matsushita (1938: 157–60); Murakami (1973: 203); Nakano (1936: 321).

7 Katsura had twice gone to Europe (in 1870 and 1875) to study the military organization. Sent to study the French Army, he arrived to find the Prussians occupying Paris. Rather than studying losers, he decided to study the Prussian Army. He did, and upon returning to Japan in 1878 began to remake the Japanese Army on the Prussian model. Being highly independent, the Prussian

Army suited Yamagata's purposes well. See Iwai (1976: 190–91); Koyama (1944: 216–17); Matsushita (1966b: 291–93).

8 *Kangun honbu jōrei*, unnumbered tatsu of Dec. 13, 1878. For detailed rules of jurisdiction, see *Rikugun shokusei* of Oct. 10, 1879; *Kakushō kansei*, Chokurei No. 2 of Feb. 26, 1886.

9 See Nakano (1936: 364 n.7). In fact, however, some observers considered direct appeals by the Navy and Army Ministers possible as well, on the theory that their work involved some command matters. See Momose (1990: 251 & n.1).

10 Dajōkan Tatsu No. 69 of Dec. 22, 1885; *Kakushō kansei*, Chokurei No. 2 of Feb. 26, 1886; see Nakano (1936: 410).

11 Or so the Army and its supporters claimed. Art. 11 gave the Emperor control over the military command, and Art. 12 gave him control over administrative matters, but neither gave any crucial detail about what any of this might mean. At least from the text of the Constitution, one might have inferred a variety of different organizational structures – but one would not normally have inferred that the command was independent and the administration was not (Momose, 1990: 256). Nonetheless, the pre-Constitution practice of placing the command directly under the Emperor and the administration under the Ministry of Army continued under the Constitution. Most commentators deferred (Momose, 1990: 256), though some continued to criticize the constitutional interpretation involved (for example, Nakano, 1936).

12 See *Sanbō honbu jōrei*, supra note 5, §5; Koyama (1944: 230–31); Momose (1990: 256–57); Nakano (1936: 368–73, 440–46).

13 *Rikugun shō kansei*, Chokurei No. 193 of May 19, 1900, App.; *Kaigun shō kansei*, Chokurei No. 194 of May 19, 1900, App. This requirement was deleted by Chokurei No. 165 of June 13, 1913 (army requirement) and Chokurei No. 168 of June 13, 1913 (navy requirement). This lasted until the active duty requirement was reinstated in 1936. Momose (1990: 258). On the procedures for the selection of the Ministers within the military branches, see Momose (1990: 259).

14 As noted later, it was not a clear veto, since the key to the veto lay in the personnel office. The personnel office was in the Ministry rather than the General Staff, and Yamagata did not always control the Ministry.

15 The veto sometimes failed. For example, when Yamagata's protege Katsura tried to form a cabinet in 1912, the Navy (over budgetary quarrels) refused to name a Navy Minister. Because Yamagata had access to the Emperor, however, Katsura could trump the Navy. He obtained an imperial memorial ordering the Navy to appoint a Minister, and formed his Cabinet. See Crowley (1966: 12–13). When naval officer Yamamoto Gonnohyōe became Prime Minister the next year, he removed the active-duty requirement. In turn, the services responded by shifting more personnel authority to the General Staff (Inoue, 1975). Similarly, when Yamagata wanted Katsura to boycott Itō Hirobumi's cabinet in 1900, Itō appealed to the Emperor to induce Katsura to accept the position. See Matsushita (1967: I-333–34).

16 *Koshiki rei*, Chokurei No. 6 of Jan. 31, 1907; *Kobun shiki*, Chokurei No. 1 of Feb. 24, 1886.

17 Gunrei No. 1 of Sept. 11, 1907, §2. The logical inappropriateness of using a military order to establish the procedures for military orders was noted at the time (Momose, 1990: 69).

18 See the factional affiliations in, for example, Kyōto (1958: 726). As of 1879, of

the 3,005 Army officers, 14 percent were from Yamagata's home province and 8 percent from Saigō's home province; of the 887 Naval officers, 29 percent were from Saigō's home province and 5 percent were from Yamagata's home province. See Matsushita (1967: I-216–17). The Yamamoto-Saigō faction lost some influence in the Navy after a munitions bribery scandal involving Siemens and Vickers came to light in 1914 (Murakami, 1973: 186). This seems to have been temporary. By 1923, Yamamoto's son-in-law Takarabe Takashi was Navy Minister (Nihon kindai, 1971: 103, 230).

19 See, for example, *Sangun kansei*, Chokurei No. 24 of May 12, 1888; *Rikugun sanbō honbu jōrei*, Chokurei No. 25 of May 12, 1888; *Kaigun sanbō honbu jōrei*, Chokurei No. 26 of May 12, 1888.

20 *Sanbō honbu jōrei*, Chokurei No. 25 of Mar. 7, 1889; *Kaigun sanbōbu jōrei*, Chokurei No. 30 of Mar. 7, 1889; *Kaigun gunreibu jōrei*, Chokurei No. 27 of May 19, 1893, §2.

21 Maverick Tokyo University professor Minobe Tatsukichi, for example, warned that if the military "is given an unduly extended latitude, . . . the government of the state will be controlled by military power and the evils of militarism will arise." *Quoted in* Miller (1965: 10). Similarly, Diet member Oka Ikuzō, argued for the complete abolition of military autonomy, and the *Tokyo asahi shimbun* provided editorial support.

22 Koku v. Miyada, 21 Daihan keishū 178, 184–85 (Sup. Ct. April 6, 1942). Although some scholars (for example, Hozumi, 1910: 688–89) argued that a statute could not void or suspend an order, basic rules of constitutional interpretation (the Constitution did provide that an order could not suspend a statute, but did not provide the converse), Itō's commentaries (1889: 23), and the scholarly consensus all indicated otherwise. See Fukushima (1926: 253); Ichiki (1892: 33); Minobe (1926: 458); Nomura (1935: 378); Uesugi (1935: 53–54).

23 As explained in note 2, Chapter 1, we address primarily the process by which power devolved to the politicians, and from them to the military. We do not, except cursorily, deal with the period of military rule after 1932.

24 See Crowley (1966: 12–13); Kimura (1985: 138); Toyoda (1983: 304–07).

25 See generally Aoki (1958: 76–92); Crowley (1966: chap. 1).

26 See Colegrove (1936: 919); Nobuo (1952: 1058–1061); Aoki (1958: 92–93); Coox (1989: 405).

27 See Matsushita (1963b: 258–59). Teranuma (1986: 300) claims that the military considered having Minami resign his cabinet post – and in doing so force the entire Minseitō cabinet to resign – as a way of getting support for the war in China. In the end, the military did not have to go to those extremes: the mere threat was enough.

28 After World War II, Ugaki's plans to run for a seat in the House of Representatives were foiled by the Occupation's "purge" of military-related figures from the political scene. Again he bided his time, and in 1953 he finally won a Diet seat – as the top vote-getter in the House of Councillors. He was never penitent, however, of the Army's role in the war. To the day he died a year later, he maintained that "The Pacific War was not Japan's fault. Japan was just protecting itself" (Inoue, 1975: 280).

29 The April 1937 election was the last before the 1942 non-party election. In 1940, political parties were disbanded in favor of a "unified political movement" called the Imperial Rule Assistance Association.

30 Though the February 26, 1936, coup failed, the young perpetrators managed

to assassinate Finance Minister Takahashi Korekiyo to protest his efforts to cut defense spending. For an illuminating discussion of the clashes between Takahashi and the military, see Ōkurashō ed. (1977: 130–136). The rebels also killed the Keeper of the Privy Seal, a general, and the Prime Minister's brother. This was the last of a long line of random assassinations and several foiled coup attempts, including one on October 21, 1931. See Aoki (1958: 97–99).

31 *Tokyo asahi shimbun,* Mar. 6,7, and 8, 1936.

32 See Snyder (1991) on the territorial log roll.

33 On the failure of the oligarchs to groom heirs, see Chapter 1.

34 Moreover, Yamagata was no altruist – and we do not claim that in making his decisions he necessarily considered consequences to Japanese citizens with whom he had no connections.

8. FINANCIAL POLITICS

1 As with the industries discussed in Chapters 9 and 10, the government manipulation of the banking industry becomes most prominent under the party politicians of the 1920s – after the oligarchs had largely lost power.

2 See Sakairi (1988: 191). Until 1928, the banking industry was under the Banking Regulations (*Ginkō jōrei,* Law No. 72 of 1890). The regulations set no capital requirements.

3 Shibusawa (1956: 263–264).

4 See *Ginkō tsūshin roku,* 79: 6 (June 28, 1892).

5 *Ginkō gappei hō [Bank Merger Act],* Law. No. 85 of April 1896. See Kin'yū kenkyūkai (1932: 13).

6 During the pre-war period, deposit interest rates were not regulated in Japan (Teranishi, 1982: 98–101, 422–424, 476), though some groups of banks tried locally to impose maximum rates (Hashimoto, 1984: 130). After the war, rates have been regulated pursuant to Ōkurashō kokushi [MOF Orders] issued under the *Rinji kinri chōsei hō [Temporary Financial Interest Adjustment Act],* Law. No. 181 of 1947.

7 It was not until 1931 that banks got the Minseitō cabinet to limit corporate access to the bond market by imposing stiff capital requirements on issuers.

8 Yabushita and Inoue (1994: 393) note that many regional banks were owned by local landowners, a traditional Seiyūkai constituency.

9 This does not mean that the big money-center banks acquired the smallest banks; rather, we hypothesize that the Minseitō-affiliated regional banks disproportionately acquired them. According to one regional study, for example, most of the smallest banks were acquired by the larger regional banks (Abe, 1989: 102). Similarly, Sugiyama (1990: 230) writes that "the acquisition of local banks by the great metropolitan banks was rare in our country's banking history." Nonetheless, the lending and borrowing businesses became increasingly concentrated in the hands of the money-center banks.

10 The government's version of the bill actually stipulated a seven-year transition period, but rank and file Diet members agreed to a five-year transition in exchange for imposing a lower standard on banks in the smallest towns. See Ogawa (1930: 377–378), who was himself a lawyer and a Seiyūhontō member of the Finance Committee.

11 A ¥500,000 capital requirement had been imposed on savings banks, a separate category of financial institutions from regular banks, in legislation passed

in 1921. See Shūgiin jimukyoku, (1927); "Seiri gōdōhō," *Tokyo asahi shimbun* (February 11, 1927), p. 4.; Kyōto shi (1932: 161).

12 "Ginkō hōan no ichibu shūsei tōru," *Tokyo asahi shimbun*, (March 5, 1927, evening) p. 1; "Dai gojūni gikai, ginkō hōan," *Hōritsu shimbun* (Feb. 23, 1927), pp. 19–20; Teranishi (1984: 332).

13 Shūgiin (1927); Ogawa (1930: 90–101, 151–155, 377–378).

14 The Lower House's Finance Committee, which deliberated on the bill before submitting it to the floor for discussion, included ten Seiyūkai members, seven Kenseikai members, four Seiyūhontō members, and one member of the Shinsei Club. See Shūgiin (1925, 1927).

15 "Ginkō hōan [Banking Bill]," *Hōritsu shimbun* (Feb. 20, 1927), p. 19; Sakairi (1988: 1193–5); Okano (1927: 99–100). Upper and Lower House debates are recorded in Ogawa (1930: 102–112, 155–161).

16 "Seiyū mōsen shinteian ni hantaishi [The Seiyūkai Now Opposes the New Banking Act," *Tokyo asahi shimbun*, (Mar. 4, 1927), p. 2.

17 The Kenseikai cabinet had just a few months earlier achieved Diet passage of the 1927 fiscal year budget by cutting the other two main parties into the allocative decisions.

18 Formally, The Bill for Bank of Japan Special Loans and Loss Compensation, or *Nihon ginkō tokubetsu yūtsū hōan oyobi sonshitsu hōshū an.*

19 Chokurei No. 424 of Sept. 27, 1928; Law No. 35 of Mar. 30, 1925.

20 By 1927, the BOJ was already saddled with ¥270 million in defaulted bonds that it had purchased from banks at a discount. A large percentage – one report said as much as half – was purchased from the Bank of Taiwan. See Hazama (1981: 322–324).

21 By 1927 the Bank of Taiwan's loans accounted for 35 percent of Suzuki's external funding and much of this was collateralized only with stocks of Suzuki-owned companies. Since 1923, the Bank of Taiwan had received ¥9.97 million from the BOJ in rediscounted earthquake bills, of which ¥6.5 million it passed along to Suzuki. Hazama (1981: 339–341).

22 Suzuki shōten's manager, Kaneko Naokichi, had catapulted the Kōbe company into the ranks of the top trading firms with the help of political friends. Kaneko hailed from the same part of Shikoku as Kenseikai politicians Hamaguchi Osachi and Kataoka Naoharu, and nurtured those ties. See Hazama (1981: 334–335).

23 Sakairi (1988: 197–199); Hazama (1981: 321–324).

24 See Ōe (1968: 86–87). Earlier in March the Tokyo District Court had begun investigating allegations that the Watanabe Bank had sold some of its land to the MOF Reconstruction Bureau (*fukkō kyoku*), and contributed over ¥1 million of the proceeds to the Kiyoura cabinet. Soon thereafter, one of the Bureau officials committed suicide. "Ginkō no hatan to kinkyū chokurei," *Hōritsu shimbun*, (May 3, 1927), p. 3.

25 Aoki Tokuzō, a bureaucrat in the Ministry of Finance's secretariat, recounts this episode in the Diet Budget Committee in sharp detail in Ōkurashō (1977: 212–219).

26 The Fifteenth Bank was established by the Matsukata family during the Meiji period before non-peers were permitted to own bank shares. Hazama argues that one reason the Fifteenth Bank had become so weak was that its management had used its ties to the Peers and the Privy Council to resist any kind of oversight by the MOF or the BOJ. Nearly half of the bank's loans were uncollateralized loans to the Matsukata family and their various business concerns. Hazama (1981: 343–344).

27 Ginkō mondai kenkyūkai, ed. (1927: 113–124); "Ginkō no hatan to kinkyū chokurei [Bank Collapse and the Emergency Ordinance]," *Hōritsu shimbun* (May 3, 1927), p. 4; "Ginkōgyō ni taisuru kantoku no shobun [Sanctions for Bank Oversight]," *Hōritsu shimbun* (July 15, 1927), p.3; Bank of Taiwan shares fell by the largest margin, from 85.2 to 28.5. Other firms' stock also fell, including Kanebō from 248.6 to 228, and Meiji Sugar from 107.3 to 92.1. Most zaibatsu banks were little affected. Yasuda bank shares went from 75.6 to 75, for example. See Ōkurashō (1963, Vol. 10: 65–67).

28 It is not clear if the Peers were genuinely horrified at the thought of political corruption – unlikely, given their own involvement from time to time – or if a substantial number of Peers were more sympathetic to the Seiyūkai than to the Kenseikai.

29 There is further textual basis for Itō's position. While the emperor could issue Article 8 emergency orders if the Diet were in session, he could raise funds under his Article 70 emergency powers only if he could not call the Diet into session. Hence, the classic legal interpretive principle applies: If the drafters used one clause in one place (Art. 8) and a different one elsewhere (Art. 70), they must have intended a difference.

30 See Colegrove (1931: 887–888); Takahashi (1981: 124–125).

31 Takahashi (1955: 674–675). But many of Suzuki shōten's interests passed into Mitsui's hands – a shift in assets from Kenseikai/Minseitō to Seiyūkai supporters.

32 Ginkō (1932: 107–109); Teranishi (1984: 311).

33 In February 1931, sixty-five regional banks lobbied the Diet to extend the deadline for compliance with the new capitalization requirements to 1938 or 1939. Although there was some support for the extension among Minseitō backbenchers, the Minseitō leadership and the House of Peers opposed the bill (Gotō 1973: 276).

34 Matsuzaki (1933: 280–286). For a discussion of the legal procedures by which deposits of closed banks were handled, see Ginkō kenkyūsha, ed. (1932: 107–172).

35 Sakairi (1988: 218). J.P. Morgan's Norman Lamont visited Japan in October 1927, urging Japan to return to the gold standard. Although he found a receptive audience in certain business circles, his recommendations fell on deaf ears in Prime Minister Tanaka's Seiyūkai government (Itō, 1987: 248).

36 Bankers advanced these arguments in "Kin no kaikin ga kyūmu [Restoring the Gold Standard is Urgently Needed]," *Tōkyō asahi shimbun* (Feb. 5, 1928), p. 4.

37 See Ōkurashō (1977: 166); Endō (1964: 168).

38 At the time, Minister of Home Affairs Adachi Kenzō remarked on the popularity of the Kenseikai's platform of fiscal responsibility (Adachi, 1960: 235).

39 Hamaguchi was shot by a right-wing fanatic in November 1930.

40 The public criticized the zaibatsu bitterly for making large profits in anticipation of the yen's depreciation, though the zaibatsu broke no laws in guessing right. For a fuller discussion of these events, see Sasahiro (1932: 91–102).

41 In the ensuing elections, former Finance Minister Inoue Junnosuke was shot and killed while campaigning on behalf of a Tokyo candidate. The assassin, a Nichiren shōshō priest, expressed outrage at the political parties' corrupt financial dealings. Other politicians on this ambitious young man's hit list included Prime Minister Inukai Tsuyoshi, Seiyūhontō leader Tokonami Takejirō, former Home Minister Suzuki Kisaburō, Minseitō President Wakatsuki

Reijirō, former Foriegn Minister Shidehara Kijurō, Mitsui magnates Ikeda Seihin and Dan Takuma, and more (Aoki, 1958: 101).

9. RAILROAD POLITICS

1 Ito (1992: 20, 29). Other assertions about the importance of railroads and the government's role in their development appear in, for example, Minami (1986: 22–24); Fairbank, Reischauer and Craig (1965: 247).

2 Estimates of the total social savings attributable to railroads vary by scholar and by country studied, but are generally less than 5 percent of GNP (O'Brien, 1977: 26). For reviews of the voluminous debate over the cliometric studies of the railroad industry, see Fogel (1979); O'Brien (1977).

3 Because the principal competitors to the trains were the ships, the usual academic comparisons with palanquins (for example, Minami, 1986: 23) are entirely beside the point. One of the few observers to note the competitive character of railroads and coastal shipping firms was Watarai (1915: 20–23, 119–22). Note that in the U.S., too, railroad firms tended to lay tracks near water routes (Fogel, 1979: 6).

4 Trucks would not, of course, have substituted well for railroads in moving coal and other minerals to the sea. Yet these railroads were specific to mineral deposits, and thus were railroads with a minimum of externalities. Here, the owners of the railroads would have been able to capture virtually all the benefits the railroads provided.

Railroads also facilitated the growth of the silk fabric industries in some areas (cotton spinning mills, by contrast, tended to be located near the coast) (Harada, 1980). Even here, however, it is not clear that the railroads would not have internalized any positive effect that they had on those silk firms.

5 Tetsudō shō, *Kokuyū* (1920: 2–3); Tetsudō shō, *Nippon tetsudō shi* (1921: I: 92); Harada (1984: chap. 1); Kawakami (1967: I: chap. 1); Nakanishi (1963: I-chap. 1); Wakuda (1981: chap. 1).

6 For comparison, note that in 1907 when Japan had 5,013 miles of track (or 1.1 miles/10,000 inhabitants), the following track was in place in other countries (Morris, 1911: 822–24):

Country	miles of track	per 10,000 inhabitants
Australia	19,855	35.9
Argentina	13,673	28.0
USA	236,949	26.8
Mexico	13,612	9.4
Germany	36,066	7.6
UK	23,108	5.6
Egypt	3,445	3.5
India	29,893	1.0
China (excluding Manchuria)	4,162	0.12

7 Much like the benefits the U.S. government gave private railroad developers (Fogel, 1960).

8 Tetsudō shō, *Nippon tetsudō shi* (1921: I-403, 695, 698–99).

9 Tetsudō shō, *Kokuyū* (1920: 3); Tetsudō shō, *Nippon tetsudō shi* (1921: I-695, 699).

10 Tetsudō shō, *Kokuyū* (1920: 3–4); Tetsudō shō, *Nippon tetsudō shi,* (1921: I-839, 865, 890–91); Wakuda (1981: 25).

11 Tetsudo sho (1920: 3–4); Nakanishi (1963: I: 51). The figures are for paid-in capital as of 1904.

12 The *Tetsudō kokuyū hō [Railroad Nationalization Act]*, Law No. 17 of Mar. 30, 1906.
13 Harada (1984: 48–51); Tetsudō shō, *Kokuyū* (1920: 5–10); Wakuda (1981: 38–49).
14 In order to account for companies that had only recently put new lines into service, the formula provided the following price: 20 times the product of (a) the total construction costs incurred as of the date of purchase and (b) the applicable multiplier. The applicable multiplier was two times the mean of (1) the firm's semi-annual profits, divided by (2) the total construction costs as of the end of that half year (for each of the half years from the middle of 1902 through the middle of 1905). *Tetsudō kokuyū hō*, supra note 12, at §5.
   The price was payable in government bonds bearing 5 percent interest. In 1906, the official discount on loans secured by government securities was 6.57 percent; 6-month deposits at banks earned 5 percent interest. Nihon tōkei (1988: III-160).
15 We have not compared the stock prices for the firms subject to nationalization, since the price would have incorporated the possibility of nationalization itself. Because (as seems likely) the railroads nationalized were not a random sample of railroads, this comparison should be seen as suggestive only.
16 To be sure, the Mitsui group had at one point taken a lead in railroad development, helping to promote, for example, Kansai tetsudō (Tetsudō shō, *Nippon tetsudō shi*, 1921: I-116–17). It also had some ties to both the San'yō and Kyūshū railroads. By the turn of the century, however, the Mitsui had begun withdrawing from the railroad industry, and even Kansai had developed Mitsubishi ties.
17 Of course, one cannot determine what the multiple would otherwise have been by looking at pre-nationalization railroad stock prices. The prospect of nationalization itself would have affected price.
18 For an argument impliedly to the contrary, see Banno (1983) (the Seiyūkai had little power at the time).
19 Table 9.6 does not prove that the popularly elected politicians subsidized fares, for after nationalization the difference in mean ride and traffic density between public and private railroads increased. Even if a profit-maximizing firm were running the national railroads, it would probably have charged less than the other private firms. For a careful discussion of the level of services provided by the various railroads, see Ericson (1989b).
20 This is consistent with the literature on regulation from other countries – government actors may underprice the goods and services they provide in order to maximize their electoral gains
21 *Kaikei hō [Accounting Act]*, Law No. 4 of Feb. 1889.
22 Even if the zaibatsu manipulated matters elsewhere, the government did not buy their rails. Instead, it bought almost all of its rails from its own steel yard (Yahata seitetsu). Private firms seem not even to have tried to sell it rails (Nihon kokuyū, 1971: 637)).
23 On Mitsubishi production and sales, see Kawakami (1967: I-144); Mitsubishi (1981: 434–36); Mitsubishi (1982: XXXV-64–65, 176–77, 309–10). On total government locomotive purchases, see Tetsudō shō, *Tetsudō shō nempō* (various years).
24 Chapter 4. The shareholding patterns are based on the shareholder lists published in the semi-annual reports of the firms at issue.
25 From 1924 to 1927, the government's steam locomotive purchases increased

14.3 percent. Nihon Kokuyū (1971: 633). Profit figures represent profits before depreciation, based on semi-annual company reports. The figures cover the period after the Kenseikai lost power because we suspect contracts for railroad equipment are long–term projects that affect profits for several subsequent accounting periods.

26 One could restate the lesson of Table 9.7 more precisely as follows: Although both parties had strong rural support, the Seiyūkai relied more heavily on the rural vote than the Kenseikai, since the Kenseikai was more successful in the cities than the Seiyūkai was.

27 The railroad plans for Hara and his predecessors appear in Tetsudō shō, "Tetsudō kensetsu" (various years). For a detailed discussion of Hara's strategy, see Najita (1967: 69–79).

28 Tokyo shisei (1932: 11, 16). Of these amounts, the 262 "local railroad" (*chihō tetsudō*) firms operated 7,018 km of track, and the 148 "tramway" (*kidō*) firms operated 2,707 km.

29 Tokyo shisei (1932: 11). In 1920, the national railroad ran 10,913 km of track the carried 406 million passengers. The 276 private railroads and tram firms ran 5,278 km. of track and carried 1,387 million passengers. Nakanishi (1963: II-195–56).

30 The subsidy was initially limited to five years. *Keiben tetsudō hojo hō [Light Railroad Subsidy Act]*, Law No. 17, of Mar. 21, 1911, renamed the *Chihō tetsudō hojo hō [Local Railroad Subsidy Act]* by Law No. 53 of Apr. 9, 1919.

31 The subsidy was limited to ten years. The government paid a maximum of 5 percent, however, since the private railroads were now expcted to earn the first 2 percent of their profits themselves. Amendment to *Chihō tetsudō hojo hō*, Law No. 14 of Mar. 29, 1921.

32 The national railroad relied relatively heavily on freight (¥22 million revenue from passengers, ¥182 million from freight, in 1930), and the private railroads relied relatively heavily on passengers (¥59 million from passengers, ¥20 million from freight). Tokyo shisei (1932: 11).

33 Nakanishi (1963: II-200 to II-205). For example, from 1928 to 1930, annual operating expenses averaged 31.2 percent of annual revenues at the Tokyo subway company of Tokyo chikatetsu, 58.9 percent at the Tokyo commuter line of Tōbu tetsudō, and 57.3 percent at the Osaka commuter line of Hanshin tetsudō. By contrast, annual operating expenses averaged 85.7 percent of annual revenues at the Okinawan prefectural lines and 94.3 percent of revenues at the Miyazaki prefectural lines. Tokyo shisei (1932: 150–56).

34 On the political independence of pre-war prosecutors, see Chapter 6; on the independence of bureaucrats, see Chapter 5.

35 Ōshima (1970); Koku v. Ogawa, 4045 Hōritsu shimbun 3 (Sup. Ct. Sept. 19, 1936).

10. COTTON POLITICS

1 This introduction borrows heavily from Ramseyer (1993).

2 Abe (1990: 170); Seki (1954: 13, 164, 436).

3 Mutō (1927: 5) (cotton consumption in 1927); Seki (1954: 60) (yarn production in 1935); id. at 435 (of all manufacturing workers, 42.5 percent was in one of the textile industries in 1934–36).

4 Abe (1990: 165); Hashimoto (1935: 12–17); Saxonhouse (1974: 151–52); Seki (1954: 23–27).

5 Ōyama (1935: 167–73). More specifically, the returns on total paid-in and accumulated equity spinning firm capital.
6 See Shōkō (1938: 2, 5); Tsūshō (1961: 30, 40).
7 Law No. 28 of Mar. 28, 1925. The Act was amended by Law No. 62 of 1931, and renamed the "Industrial Associations Act" (§1).
8 Act, §8. Curiously, not until 1933 could member firms be punished by the government. See Law No. 20 of 1933. Note that membership in these associations was voluntary. Id. at §24. At least according to the text of the statute, renegade firms could (prior to 1933) have evaded cartel rules by joining the cartel.
9 Shōkō shō kokushi No. 6 of Aug. 28, 1925 (designating woven cotton products).
10 See Isobe (1936: 431–48); Kōgyō shō (1936: 13); Zaisei (1936: 14–16). Double counting is possible: The data do not disclose whether (and how many) firms were members of more than one association.
11 According to Isobe (1936: 634). By contrast, Kōgyō (1936: 43) lists forty-one price-fixing agreements, but without giving details; the discussion in Isobe suggests these may have been local labor market wage agreements. Even Isobe notes that some associations tried to coordinate production cuts – which of course can accomplish the same thing as a price-fixing agreement. Isobe (1936: 634, 653–72). By tradition, firms in the striped cotton twill sector were said to have successfully set monopoly prices. See Shōkō shō rinji (1931).
12 One would of course expect smaller cartels where price-fixing is illegal (for example, the modern U.S.) than where it is legal (for example, pre-war Japan).
13 Zaisei (1936: 18–19); Kōgyō (1936: 22–25). The government made additional loans to the associations under various programs totalling ¥969,100. Id. at 24. On interest rates generally, see Nihon tōkei (1988: III-160–61). Note that the Seiyūkai continued to patronize the firms after taking control in 1928.
14 Electoral data from Seisen (1930: app.). The "weaving districts" are those so designated by Abe (1990: 190).
15 In the giant metropolitan centers of Tokyo, Osaka, Kyōto, Nagoya, Kobe and Yokohama, the Minseitō won 757,990 out of 2,207,713 votes. This gave it 39 out of the 76 seats available. Seisen (1930: app.).
16 Note that the fact that some factories closed did not necessarily cause a decrease in the total number of spindles in use. The factories closing down could sell their spindles to their competitors, and expanding firms could continue to purchase new spindles even while other firms closed their factories.
17 Saxonhouse (1976: 122; 1991). For a discussion of what purposes this spinning cartel did serve, see Ramseyer (1993).
18 The Mitsubishi zaibatsu also would have suffered losses, though smaller ones. It too sold some spinning machines, and through the NYK handled the delivery of raw cotton.
19 Katō (1967: 94, 96–97); Tatsuki (1990a); Sugiyama (1990).
20 Wada (1937: 257–58). The firm was remarkably successful. From ¥1.0 million in spinning machine sales in 1931, it grew to ¥38.8 million in spinning machine sales in 1937. See Tsūshō (1960: 274–75).
21 The Mitsui figures are from a secret unpublished company memorandum cited as Mitsui (1928) and from published accounts that appear in Matsumoto (1979, tabs. 56–59, 82–86). Note that the large pre-war Japanese firms generally paid out as dividends 60–70 percent of their profits (Okazaki, 1991: 371).
22 Figures are for 1910. Unfortunately (for the scholar), by 1928 the cotton trade

had been moved to a separate Mitsui company (known as Tōyō menka). Some suggestive later figures: During the first half of 1928, Tōyō menka handled raw cotton trades of ¥83.6 million, cotton yarn trades of ¥18.3 million, and cotton fabric trades of ¥15.1 million (Mitsui, 1928). In the first half of 1928, the Mitsui earned Kanebō dividends (see Table 10.5) of only ¥280,000.

23 Note that the elected politicians themselves did not have an interest in organizing the spinning firms comparable to their interest in organizing the weaving firms. The politicians had organized the weaving firms because the firms had been so fragmented. Fragmented, they had not been helpful either to extract rents or or to divide votes. By contrast, the spinners were a smaller group, and had already organized themselves into the Bōren.

24 *Jūyō sangyō no tōsei ni kansuru hōritsu [An Act Regarding the Control of Major Industries]*, Law No. 40 of March 31, 1931.

25 Act, §2. The cartel had to include at least half of the members of the industry. Act, §1.

26 Chokurei No. 209 of August 8, 1931.

27 Shōkō shō kokushi No. 64 of December 5, 1931.

28 For arguments to the contrary – that "the zaibatsu profited most from 'control' and 'industrial order,' and that the 1931 Act "helped curtail competition and profitability in cotton spinning" – see Johnson (1982: 110).

29 Law No. 25 of May 27, 1936.

30 Shōkō shō, Nōrin shō, Teishin shō, joint shō rei No. 1 of Aug. 10, 1931.

31 For example, [No names given], 4494 Hōritsu shimbun 4 (Sup. Ct. Nov. 17, 1939); Koku v. Nakamura, 4547 Hōritsu shimbun 13 (Sup. Ct. Mar. 19, 1940).

32 *Kōjō hō [Factory Act]*, Law No. 46 of Mar. 28, 1911.

33 Chokurei No. 8 of Jan. 21, 1916. On the constitutional requirement that the Emperor implement statutes, see Chapter 2.

34 Law No. 33 of Mar. 29, 1923.

35 Chokurei No. 152 of June 5, 1926.

36 See also Lewchuk (1993) (male-only policy at Ford reduced worker alienation by building fraternal esprit de corps).

37 For the argument that the ban primarily concerned issues of sex roles, see Hunter (1989).

38 A point some historians suggest. See Nishikawa (1987: 178).

39 Nardinelli (1980) argues that the British Factory Act was largely without effect, as the shift away from child labor was already occurring for technical reasons. Anderson and Tollison (1984) argue that the adult male operators promoted the British law to restrict the use of competing laborers (women and children). As Japanese mill operators used adolescent girls and young women almost exclusively both before and after the factory legislation, neither argument applies to Japan.

40 In 1905, only three of the forty-nine Bōren firms relied exclusively on water power. They were all in the smallest quintile. Two firms relied partially on water power: one in the first quintile, one in fourth. By 1925, only one firm (the second largest in the country) had any water-powered machines. See Dai-Nippon (various years).

41 Some scholars have tried to explain the statute by arguing that the larger firms had by this time moved to higher count yarn (thinner yarn) (Okazaki, 1987). The evidence is ambiguous: as of mid-1925, the largest quintile of firms produced yarn with an average count of 25.4, followed by 22.8, 27.4, 20.8

and 19.7. Moreover, we find little difference among firms in the length of work shifts by average yarn count. Firms with an average count of 30 or above worked 20.7 hours/day (7 firms), those with a count of $20 \leq x < 30$ worked 20.7 hours/day (22 firms), and those with a count of less than 20 worked 20.1 hours/day (17 firms). See Dai-Nippon (1925) (excluding 2 firms working only 1 shift).

42 Saxonhouse (1977: 297) cites arguments to the effect that the move to the eight-hour shift benefited both workers and employers, because it sufficiently improved the morale and attentiveness of the employees. Were that the case, it is not clear why anyone would need a law to reduce hours.

43 The assumption here is that many workers were willing to leave home or to defer marriage for a stated period only if they thereby could earn enough in total income during that period. If the Act effectively prevented them from making that income, they would either remain part of their parents' household (and workforce) or marry.

44 This follows from our highly elastic S_{10}. Given this elastic supply curve, workers differ from each other primarily only in their preference for leisure.

45 Over time, one would expect workers to dissipate the gains as those with a stronger preference for leisure disproportionately compete for work in the regulated eight-hour factories, and those who value leisure less switch to the unregulated ten-hour factories.

46 Males over age twenty-five could vote.

To make the point explicit, we note that we are here assuming that the male head of the household acts altruistically toward his children and seeks to raise their utility. Thus, if the female worker's utility were increased, her household head's utility increased as well. The point is commonplace in the rational-choice tradition. See Becker (1991: chap. 8). Because most female spinning workers lived in company dormitories, shorter hours would not have increased the hours they worked at home.

11. CONCLUSION

1 By efficiency, we (and they) mean it in the Paretian sense: Institutions are efficient if there is no adjustment that would improve the utility of one actor without making someone else worse off.

2 "Strong state" refers, in most political science literature, to governments in which the bureaucracy is well-insulated from, if not autonomous of, societal pressures. See, for example, Katzenstein (1978); Zysman (1983).

3 Stinchcombe (1990: 307). Although Stinchcombe's emphasis on "rational faculties" stands out among sociologists, the gist of his argument follows in a venerable tradition of sociological thinking on institutions. Polanyi (1947), for example, attributes the post-war rise of the welfare state to the desire of societies to protect themselves from "the ravages of unfettered capitalism."

4 See also Levi (1988); North (1981, 1988). North and Weingast (1989) argue that Britain gained the needed revenue base to defeat France in the Hundred Years' War only when the king gave the legislature a genuine veto on his actions.

5 This view is at least as old as Marx, but for more recent explications, see, for example, Bates (1981, 1988), Roemer (1986), Levi (1990), Knight (1992), and Calvert (1992). These authors contend that political entrepreneurs cannot always, for whatever reason, sufficiently subsidize the collective action costs of

the masses. Collective action costs thus persist as an entry barrier to the political market. Note the underlying assumption: that the rules limiting competition, and thereby dampening the urge to represent the unrepresented, are hard to change. We will return to this subject later.

6 The third feature of unstable cartels – high demand – seems to us less useful for cross-national or inter-temporaral comparisons. We are not sure how or why national populations should differ in their desire for political accountability. Perhaps, as Susanne Lohmann (1994) has suggested, populations differ substantially in the quality of information they have about the likelihood of violent government repression in the event of a mass revolt. If that is the case, populations that can discount the probability of incurring personal injury in a mass rebellion may express a stronger demand for political change.

7 Some scholars invoke "path dependence" without distinguishing between situations of political equilibrium (when the relevant actors support the status quo) and of structure-induced equilibrium (when existing institutions operate independently and sometimes at cross-purposes with the interests of the actors). Instances of political equilibrium should not be termed "path dependence" at all, since the situation gives us no clue as to how the "path" would change when underlying interests change. We therefore concern ourselves exclusively with the concept of structure-induced equilibrium (for example, Shepsle and Weingast, 1981).

8 Recall that Navy Minister Takarabe was forced into early retirement after he defied the Navy General Staff's position on the London Naval Treaties.

9 For notable exceptions, see Rosovsky (1961: 55–104) and Smith (1988: 42–46).

References

Abe, Takeshi. 1990. "Men kōgyō [The Cotton Industry]." In Abe and Nishikawa (1990).

—— and Nishikawa, Shunsaku (eds.). 1990. *Sangyōka no jidai [The Age of Industrialization]*. Tokyo: Iwanami shoten.

Adams, T.F.M., and Iwao Hoshii. 1964. *A Financial History of Modern Japan*. Tokyo: Dai Nippon Press.

Akamatsu, Paul. 1967. *Meiji 1868: Revolution and Counter-Revolution in Japan*. New York: Harper & Row.

Akamatsu, Ryōko (ed.). 1977. *Nippon fujin mondai shiryō shūsei [Collection of Materials Relating to Women's Issues in Japan]*. Tokyo: Domesu shuppan.

Akita, George. 1967. *Foundations of Constitutional Government in Modern Japan: 1868-1900*. Cambridge: Harvard University Press.

Alchian, Armen A. and Harold Demsetz. 1972. "Production, Information Costs, and Economic Organization." *American Economic Review*, 62: 777.

Allen, George C. 1981. *A Short Economic History of Modern Japan (4th Ed.)*. New York: St. Martin's Press.

Anderson, Gary M., and Robert D. Tollison. 1984. "A Rent-Seeking Explanation of the British Factory Acts." In Colander (1984: 187–201).

Andō, Yoshio. 1968. "Kisei zaibatsu ka, narikin zaibatsu ka [An Established Zaibatsu or a Parvenue Zaibatsu?]." *Ekonomisuto*, Jan. 23: 84–89.

Aoki, Tokuzō. 1958. *Wakatsuki Reijirō, Hamaguchi Osachi*. Tokyo: Jiji tsūshinsha.

Asahi shimbun seiji keizai bu (ed.). 1930. *Sūmitsuin mondai [The Issue of the Privy Council]*. Tokyo: Asahi shimbunsha.

Atack, Jeremy, and Fred Bateman. 1992. "How Long Was the Workday in 1880?" *Journal of Economic History*, 52: 129–60.

Baba, Tsunegō. 1930. "Itō Miyoji ron [An Essay on Itō Miyoji]." *Chūō kōron*, Vol. 45: 202–212.

—— 1946. *Konoe naikakushi ron [A Study of the Konoe Cabinet]*. Tokyo: Takayama shoin.

Bank of Japan. 1935. *Honpō keizai tōkei [Economic Statistics of Japan]*. Tokyo: Bank of Japan.

Banno, Junji. 1983. "External and Internal Problems After the War." In Wray and Conroy (1983: 163–69).

Barzel, Yoram. 1991. "Property Rights and the Evolution of the State." Unpublished manuscript.

201

References

—— 1992. "Confiscation by the Ruler: The Rise and Fall of Jewish Lending in the Middle Ages." *Journal of Law & Economics*, 35: 1–13.

Bates, Robert. 1981. *Markets and States in Tropical Africa: The Political Basis of Agricultural Policies*. Berkeley: University of California Press.

—— 1989. *Beyond the Miracle of the Market: The Political Economy of Agrarian Development in Kenya*. Cambridge: Cambridge University Press.

Bawn, Kathy. 1993. "The Logic of Institutional Choice: German Electoral Law as a Social Choice Outcome." *American Journal of Political Science*, 37: 965–989.

Beasley, W.G. 1989. "Meiji Political Institutions." In Jansen, ed. (1989: 618–73).

Becker, Gary S. 1991. *A Treatise on the Family (Enlarged Edition)*. Cambridge: Harvard University Press.

Bendor, Jonathan. 1985. *Parallel Systems: Redundancy in Government*. Berkeley: University of California Press.

Berle, Adolf, and Gardiner Means. 1932. *The Modern Corporation and Private Property*. New York: Macmillan.

Cain, Bruce, John Ferejohn, and Morris Fiorina. 1987. *The Personal Vote: Constituency Service and Electoral Independence*. Cambridge: Harvard University Press.

Calvert, Randall L. 1992. "The Rational Choice Theory of Social Institutions: Cooperation, Coordination, and Communication." Unpublished University of Rochester manuscript.

Clement, Ernest W., and Etsujiro Uyehara. 1925. "Fifty Sessions of the Japanese Imperial Diet," *The Transactions of the Asiatic Society of Japan, Vol. II*. Tokyo: The Asiatic Society of Japan.

Coase, R.N. 1937. "The Nature of the Firm." *Economica (n.s.)*, 4: 386.

—— 1960. "The Problem of Social Cost." *Journal of Law & Economics*, 3: 1.

Colander, David C. (ed.). 1984. *Neoclassical Political Economy: The Analysis of Rent-Seeking and DUP Activities*. Cambridge: Ballinger Publishing Co.

Colegrove, Kenneth. 1929. "Labor Parties in Japan." *American Political Science Review*, 23: 329–63.

—— 1931. "The Japanese Privy Council." *American Political Science Review*, 25: 589–614, 881–905.

—— 1933. "Powers and Functions of the Japanese Diet." *American Political Science Review*, 27: 885–898.

—— 1934. "Powers and Functions of the Japanese Diet, II." *American Political Science Review*, 28: 23–29.

—— 1936. "The Japanese Cabinet." *American Political Science Review*, 30: 903–23.

Coleman, James S. 1990. *Foundations of Social Theory*. Cambridge: Harvard University Press.

Connors, Lesley. 1987. *The Emperor's Advisor: Saionji Kinmochi and Pre-War Japanese Politics*. London: Croom Helm.

Coox, Alvin. 1989. "The Kwantung Army Dimension." In Peter Duus, Ramon Myers, and Mark Peattie (eds.), *The Japanese Informal Empire in China, 1895–1937*. Princeton: Princeton University Press.

Cox, Gary W. 1990. "Centripetal and Centrifugal Incentives in Electoral Systems." *American Journal of Political Science*, 34: 903–935.

—— 1991. "SNTV and d'Hondt are 'Equivalent.'" *Electoral Studies*, 10: 118–132.

Crawcour, E. Sydney. 1988. "Industrialization and Technological Change, 1885–1920." In Duus (1988: 385–450).

References

Crowley, James B. 1966. *Japan's Quest for Autonomy: National Security and Foreign Policy, 1930–1938.* Princeton: Princeton University Press.

Dai-Nippon bōseki rengō kai (ed.). Various years. *Dai-Nippon bōseki rengō kai geppō [Great Japanese Spinning Federation Monthly Newsletter].* Osaka: Dai-Nippon bōseki rengō kai.

Daiwa ginkō (ed.). 1958. *Daiwa ginkō yonjūnen shi [A Forty-Year History of Daiwa Bank].* Tokyo: Kabushiki gaisha Daiwa ginkō.

De Long, J. Bradford, and Andrei Shleifer. 1992. "Princes and Merchants: European City Growth Before the Industrial Revolution." NBER Working Paper, No. 4274.

Dore, Ronald. 1973. *British Factory-Japanese Factory: The Origins of National Diversity in Industrial Relations.* Berkeley: University of California Press.

Duus, Peter. 1968. *Party Rivalry and Political Change in Taisho Japan.* Cambridge: Harvard University Press.

—— (ed.). 1988. *The Cambridge History of Japan, Volume VI: The Twentieth Century.* Cambridge: Cambridge University Press.

—— 1989. "Japan's Informal Empire in China, 1895–1937: An Overview." In Peter Duus, Ramon Myers, and Mark Peattie (eds.), *The Japanese Informal Empire in China, 1895–1937.* Princeton: Princeton University Press.

Duverger, Maurice. 1955. *Political Parties: Their Origin and Activity in the Modern State.* Translated by Barbara and Robert North. London: Methuen.

Endō, Shōkichi, Toshihiko Katō and Makoto Takahashi. 1964. *Nihon Ōkura daijin [Japan's Finance Ministers].* Tokyo: Nihon hyōron sha.

Ericson, Steven J. 1989a. "Railroads in Crisis: The Financing and Management of Japanese Railway Companies During the Panic of 1890." In Wray (1989: 121).

—— 1989b. "Private Railroads in the Meiji Era: Forerunners of Modern Japanese Management?" In Yui and Nakagawa (1989: 51–77).

Fairbank, John K., Edwin O. Reischauer, and Albert M. Craig. 1965. *East Asia: The Modern Transformation.* Cambridge: Harvard University Press.

Fogel, Robert William. 1960. *The Union Pacific Railroad: A Case of Premature Enterprise.* Baltimore: Johns Hopkins University Press.

—— 1964. *Railroads and American Economic Growth: Essays in Econometric History.* Baltimore: Johns Hopkins University Press.

—— 1979. "Notes on the Social Saving Controversy." *Journal of Economic History,* 39: 1–54 (1979).

Friedman, James W. 1986. *Game Theory with Applications to Economics.* New York: Oxford University Press.

Fujii, Shinichi. 1940. *The Essentials of Japanese Constitutional Law.* Tokyo: Yūhikaku.

—— 1965. *The Constitution of Japan: A Historical Survey.* Tokyo: Kokushikan University, Hokuseido Press.

Fujimura, Michio. 1961. *Yamagata Aritomo.* Tokyo: Yoshikawa kōbunkan.

Fujino, Shōzaburō, Shino Fujino, and Akira Ōno. 1979. *Chōki keizai tōkei: Sen'i kōgyō [Long-Term Economic Statistics: The Textile Industry].* Tokyo: Tōyō keizai shimpō sha.

Fujisawa, Rikitarō. 1928. *Sōsenkyo dokuhon [Reader on the General Election].* Tokyo: Iwanami shoten.

Fukai, Eigō. 1953. *Sūmitsuin jūyō giji oboegaki [Notes on Important Privy Council Discussions].* Tokyo: Iwanami shoten.

Fukuchi, Shigetaka. 1954. "Kensei shoki no daigishi no seikaku [The Character

References

of Diet Members in the Early Constitutional Period]." *Nihon rekishi*, 79: 778–783.

Fukushima, Giichi. 1926. *Nippon teikoku kempō ron [Japanese Imperial Constitutional Theory]*, 4th ed. Tokyo: Kyōbundō shoten.

Fukutake, Tadashi. 1977. *Gendai Nihon shakairon [Contemporary Japanese Society]*. Tokyo: Tokyo daigaku shuppan kai.

Furushima, Kazuo. 1951. "Rimpō kakumei o ki ni: ichi rōseijika no kaisō [On the Occasion of Nearby Revolutions: The Reflections of One Old Politician]." *Chūō kōron*, Vol. 46, No. 1: 159–168.

Gaimushō (ed.). 1969. *Gaimushō no hyakunen [The Foreign Ministry's One Hundred Years]*. Tokyo: Hara shobō.

Garon, Sheldon. 1987. *The State and Labor in Modern Japan*. Berkeley: University of California Press.

Gerschenkron, Alexander. 1962. *Economic Backwardness in Historical Perspective*. Cambridge: Harvard University Press.

"Ginkō hōan no ichibu shūsei tōru [The Banking Bill Passes with Amendment]." 1927.*Tokyo asahi shimbun*, Mar. 5 (evening edition): 1.

Ginkō kenkyūsha (ed.). 1932. *Kyūgyō ginkō no hōritsu mondai [Legal Issues Involving Closed Banks]*. Tokyo: Bungadō.

Ginkō mondai kenkyūkai. 1927. "Kin'yū kyōkō ni taisuru hihan [Criticizing the Financial Panic]." *Ginkō ronsō*, Vol. 9, No. 2: 113–124.

"Ginkō no hatan to kinkyū chokurei," 1927. *Hōritsu shimbun*. May 3: 3.

Gluck, Carol. 1985. *Japan's Modern Myths: Ideology in the Late Meiji Period*. Princeton: Princeton University Press.

Gotō, Shin'ichi. 1973. *Honpō ginkō gōdōshi [A History of Bank Mergers in Japan]*. Tokyo: Kin'yū zaisei jijō kenkyūkai.

Green, E., and R. Porter. 1984. "Non-cooperative Collusion Under Imperfect Price Information." *Econometrica*, 52: 87–100.

Hackett, Roger F. 1971. *Yamagata Aritomo in the Rise of Modern Japan, 1838–1922*. Cambridge: Harvard University Press.

Haley, John O. 1991. *Authority without Power: Law and the Japanese Paradox*. New York: Oxford University Press.

Hani, Gorō. 1956. "Itō Hirobumi to Yamagata Aritomo." *Chūō kōron*, Vol. 71, No. 1: 311–318.

—— 1967. *Hani Gorō rekishi roncho sakushū [A Collection of Hani Gorō's Writings on History]*. Tokyo: Aoki shoten.

Hara, Keichirō, and Shirō Yamamoto (eds.). 1982. *Hara Takashi o meguru hitobito*. Tokyo: NHK Books.

Hara, Takashi. 1965. *Hara Takashi nikki [Diary of Hara Takashi]*. Tokyo: Fukumura shuppan.

Harada, Katsumasa. 1977. *Tetsudō no kataru Nihon no kindai [Early Modern Japan Through the Railroads]*. Tokyo: Soshiete.

—— 1980. "Technological Independence and Progress of Standardization in the Japanese Railways." *Developing Economies*, 18: 313–32.

—— 1981. *Mantetsu [The Manchurian Railroad]*. Tokyo: Iwanami shoten.

—— 1984. *Nihon no Kokutetsu [The National Railway of Japan]*. Tokyo: Iwanami shoten.

Hashimoto, Jūrō. 1984. *Daikyōkōki no Nihon shihon shugi [Japanese Capitalization During the Great Depression]*. Tokyo: Tokyo daigaku shuppan kai.

Hashimoto, Takahiko. 1935. *Nippon menshiseki gyō shi nempō [A Time Line for*

References

the Japanese Cotton Yarn Spinning Industry]. Tokyo: Bunka shi nempyō seisaku kenkyū kai.

Hata, Ikuhiko. 1981. *Senzenki Nihon kanryōsei no seido, soshiki, jinji [The System, Organization, and Personnel of the Pre-war Japanese Bureaucracy]*. Tokyo: Tokyo daigaku shuppankai.

Hay, George, and Daniel Kelley. 1974. "An Empirical Survey of Price Fixing Conspiracies." *Journal of Law and Economics*, 17: 13.

Hazama, Otohiko. 1981. *Shōwa kyōkō no seiji keizaigaku: Inoue Junnoseke o hyōteisuru [The Political Economy of the Shōwa Depression: Evaluating Inoue Junnosuke]*. Vol. 1. Tokyo: Sōgō keizai kenkyū sentaa.

Hida, Takuji. 1955. *Seitō kōbō gojūnen [The Vicissitudes of Political Parties Over Fifty Years]*. Tokyo: Kokkai tsūshinsha.

Horie, Kiichi. 1927. *Kin'yū to kyōkō [Finance and Recession]*. Tokyo: Daitōkaku.

Hosojima, Yoshimi. 1964. *Ningen Yamaoka Mannosuke den [An Account of Yamaoka Mannosuke, the Man]*. Tokyo: Kōdansha.

Hozumi, Yatsuka. 1910. *Kempō teiyō [Constitutional Summary]*. Tokyo: Yūhikaku.

Hunter, Janet. 1989. "Factory Legislation and Employer Risistance: The Abolition of Night Work in the Cotton Spinning Industry." In Yui and Nakagawa (1989: 243–72).

Ichiki, Kotokurō. 1892. *Nippon hōrei yosan ron [The Theory of Japanese Statutes, Regulations, and Budgets]*. Tokyo: Tetsugaku shoin.

Ichimura, Mitsuyoshi. 1927. *Teikoku kempō ron [Imperial Constitutional Theory] (13th ed.)*. Tokyo: Yūhikaku.

Ienaga, Saburō. 1962. *Shihō ken dokuritsu no rekishi teki kōsatsu [A Historical Inquiry into Judicial Independence]*. Tokyo: Nihon hyōron sha.

Ikeda, Jun. 1984. "Seitō naikakuka no futatsu no chihō zeisei kaikaku to kanryō [Two Local Tax Reforms Under Party Cabinets, and the Bureaucrats]." In Nihon gendaishi kenkyūkai (1984: 111–152).

Inoue, Kiyoshi. 1954. *Nihon no gunkoku shugi [Japanese Militarism]*. Tokyo: Tokyo daigaku shuppan kai.

—— 1956. "Jiyū minken undō o meguru rekishiteki hyōka ni tsuite [Concerning a Historical Assessment of the Popular Rights Movement]." *Shisō*, 379: 47–63.

—— 1975. *Ugaki Kazunari*. Tokyo: Asahi shimbunsha.

Inoue, Masaru. 1906. *Nippon teikoku tetsudō sōgyō dan [Discussion of the Establishment of the Japanese Imperial Railways]*. Reprinted, Tokyo: Inoue koshaku dōzō kensetsu dōshi kai.

Iriye, Akira. 1989. "Japan's Drive to Great Power Status." In Jansen (1989: 721–82).

Isobe, Kiichi. 1936. *Kōgyō kumiai ron [Industrial Association Theory]*. Tokyo: Kōbundō shoten.

Itō, Hirobumi. 1889. *Teikoku kempō gikai [Commentaries on the Constitution] (1935 ed.)*. Tokyo: Kokka gakkai. English translation by Miyoji Ito, *Commentaries on the Constitution of the Empire of Japan* (Tokyo: Igirisu hōritsu gakkō).

Itō, Masanori. 1956. *Daikaigun wo omou [Remembering the Great Navy]*. Tokyo: Bungei shunju shinsha.

Itō, Masaya. 1984. *Nihon no seiji: Hiru no ishito yoru no ishi [Japanese Pol-*

References

itics: The Intent of the Day and the Intent of the Night]. Tokyo: Chūō kōron sha.

Itō, Shirusu. 1930. *Kakuretaru jijitsu: Meiji rimenshi [The Hidden Truth: An "Inside" History of Meiji]*. Tokyo: Narimitsu kan shuppanbu.

Itō, Takashi. 1981. *Taishō shoki Yamagata Aritomo tanwa hikki [Conversations and Writings of Yamagata Aritomo in the Early Taishō Period]*. Tokyo: Yamakawa shuppansha.

Ito, Takatoshi. 1992. *The Japanese Economy*. Cambridge: MIT Press.

Itō, Yukio. 1987. *Taishō demokurashii to seitō seiji [Taishō Democracy and Party Politics]*. Tokyo: Yamada shuppan sha.

Iwai, Tadakuma. 1976. "Gunji keisatsu kikō no kakuritsu [The Establishment of the Military and Police Structures]." In *Iwanami kōza: Nihon rekishi [Iwanami Lectures: History of Japan]*, vol. 15. Tokyo: Iwanami shoten.

Iwasaki, Uichi. 1921. *The Working Forces in Japanese Politics: A Brief Account of Political Conflicts: 1867–1920*. New York: Columbia University Press.

Iwata, Masakazu. 1964. *Ōkubo Toshimichi: The Bismarck of Japan*. Berkeley: University of California Press.

Izu, Takao, and Matsushita, Yoshio. 1938. *Nihon gunji hattatsu shi [A History of the Development of the Japanese Military]*. Tokyo: Mikasa shobō.

Jansen, Marius B. 1971. *Sakamoto Ryōma and the Meiji Restoration*. Stanford: Stanford University Press.

—— (ed.). 1989. *The Cambridge History of Japan, Volume 5: The Nineteenth Century*. Cambridge: Cambridge University Press.

Jensen, Michael C., and Willliam H. Meckling. 1976. "Theory of the Firm: Managerial Behavior, Agency Costs, and Ownership Structure." *Journal of Financial Economics*, 3: 305.

Johnson, Chalmers. 1972. *Conspiracy at Matsukawa*. Berkeley: University of California Press.

—— 1982. *MITI and the Japanese Miracle: The Growth of Industrial Policy, 1925–1975*. Stanford: Stanford University Press.

Jones, F.C. 1931. *Extraterritoriality in Japan, and the Diplomatic Relations Resulting in its Abolition, 1853–1899*. New Haven: Yale University Press.

Kaji, Yasuo. 1926. *Teikoku kempō yōkō [An Outline of the Imperial Constitution]*. Tokyo: Teikoku kōgaku kai.

Kamijō, Sueo. 1988. "Shōsenkyoku saiyō o meguru shomondai [Various Problems in Adopting the Single-member District Electoral System]." In Nakamura (1988).

Kanamori, Tokujirō. 1927. *Teikoku kempō yōkō [An Outline of the Constitution] (4th ed.)*. Tokyo: Yūhikaku.

Kaneko, Kentarō. 1937. "Naikaku seido sōshi tōji no tsuikai [Recollections of the Establishment of the Cabinet System]." *Chūō kōron*, Feb., Vol. 51: 115–122.

Katō, Saisaburō. 1967. "Kigyō gōdō ka, kyōsō ka [Firm Combination or Competition?]." *Ekonomisuto*, Mar. 1967, pp. 92–97.

Katzenstein, Peter (ed.). 1978. *Between Power and Plenty: Foreign Economic Policies of Advanced Industrial States*. Madison: University of Wisconsin Press.

Kawabe, Kisaburo. 1924. *The Press and Politics in Japan*. Chicago: University of Chicago Press.

Kawakami, Yoshiyuki. 1967–68. *Shin Nippon tetsudō shi [A New History of Japanese Railroads] (3 vols.)*. Tokyo: Tetsudō tosho kankō kai.

References

Kawato, Sadafumi. 1992. *Nihon no seitō seiji, 1890–1937 [Japan's Party Politics, 1890–1937]*. Tokyo: Tokyo daigaku shuppankai.

Kimbara, Samon. 1967. *Taishō demokurashii no shakaiteki keisei [The Social Structure of Taishō Democracy]*. Tokyo: Aoki shoten.

Kimura, Ki. 1985. *Saionji Kinmochi [Saionji Kinmochi]*. Tokyo: Jiji tsushin sha.

"Kin no kaikin ga kyūmu [Lifting the Gold Embargo is High Priority]." 1928. *Tokyo asahi shimbun*, Feb. 5: 4.

Kin'yū kenkyūkai (ed.). 1932. *Chūshō nōshōkōgyōsha ni taisuru kin'yū ni oite [Concerning Financing of Small- and Medium-sized Farmers, Retailers, and Manufacturers]*. Tokyo: Kin'yū kenkyūkai.

Kishimoto, Kōichi. 1990. *Gikai wa ikiteiru [The Legislature is a Living Thing]*. Tokyo: Jiji tsūshinsha.

Kitaoka, Hisaichi. 1929. "Bōseki gyō no shin'ya gyō kinshi to sōtan mondai [The Ban on Night Work in the Spinning Industry and the Problem of Production Cutbacks]." *Shakai seisaku jihō*, 114. Reprinted in Akamatsu (ed.) (1972, III: 337–48).

Klein, Benjamin R., and Keith B. Leffler. 1981. "The Role of Market Forces in Assuring Contractual Performance." *Journal of Political Economy*, 89: 615–41.

Knight, Jack. 1992. *Institutions and Social Conflict*. Cambridge: Cambridge University Press.

Kobayakawa, Kongō. 1944. *Meiji hōseishi ron [A Legal History of Meiji]*. Tokyo: Ganshodō shoten.

Kōgyō kumiai chūō kai (ed.). 1936. *Kōgyō kumiai gaikyō [Overview of Industrial Associations]*. Tokyo: Shōkō shō kōmu kyoku.

Konishi, Shirō. 1968. *Meiji hyakunen no rekishi [A Hundred Years of Meiji History]*. Tokyo: Kōdansha.

Koyama, Hirotake. 1944. *Kindai Nihon gunji shi gaisetsu [An Outline of Early Modern Japanese Military History]*. Tokyo: Itō shoten.

Krehbiel, Keith. 1992. *Information and Legislative Organization*. Ann Arbor: University of Michigan Press.

Kusunoki, Seiichirō. 1989. *Meiji rikken sei to shihō kan [The Meiji Constitution and Judicial Officers]*. Tokyo: Keiō tsūshin K.K.

Kyōto daigaku bungaku bu (ed.). 1958. *Nihon kindai shi jiten [Dictionary of Early Modern Japanese History]*. Tokyo: Tōyō keizai shimpō sha.

Kyōto shi kyōiku bu shakai ka (ed.). 1932. *Kyōto shi ni okeru shomin kin'yū ni kansuru chōsa [A Survey of Consumer Finance in Kyoto City]*. Kyōto: Gigyoku dō.

Kyū sanbō honbu (ed.). 1966. *Ishin, Seinan sensō [The Restoration, The Seinan War]*. Tokyo: Tokuma shoten.

Landes, Elisabeth M. 1980. "The Effect of State Maximum-Hours Laws on the Employment of Women in 1920." *Journal of Political Economy*, 88: 476–94.

Landes, William M., and Richard A. Posner. 1975. "The Independent Judiciary in an Interest-Group Perspective." *Journal of Law & Economics*, 18: 875–901.

Levi, Margaret. 1990. *Of Rule and Revenue*. Berkeley: University of California Press.

Lewchuk, Wayne A. 1993. "Men and Monotony: Fraternalism as a Managerial Strategy at the Ford Motor Company." *Journal of Economic History*, 53: 824.

Lewis, Michael. 1990. *Rioters and Citizens: Mass Protest in Imperial Japan*. Berkeley: University of California Press.

References

Lohmann, Susanne. 1994. "Dynamics of Informational Cascades: The Monday Demonstrations in Leipzig, East Germany, 1989–91." *World Affairs*, 47: 42–101.

Lowi, Theodore. 1969. *The End of Liberalism*. New York: Norton.

Luney, Percy R., Jr. 1990. "The Judiciary: Its Organization and Status in the Parliamentary System." *Law & Contemporary Problems*, 53: 135–162.

McCubbins, Mathew, and Frances Rosenbluth. 1995. "Party Provision for Personal Politics: Dividing the Vote in Japan." In Peter F. Cowhey and Mathew D. McCubbins (eds.), *Structure and Policy in Japan and the United States*. New York: Cambridge University Press.

—— and Thomas Schwartz. 1984. "Congressional Oversight Overlooked: Police Patrols versus Fire Alarms." *American Journal of Political Science*, 28: 165–79.

Maeda, Renzan. 1934. "Kempō no bannin, Itō Miyoji [Itō Miyoji, the Guardian of the Constitution]." *Chūō kōron*, Vol. 49, No. 4: 191–201.

Marlow, Michael L. 1986. "Private Sector Shrinkage and the Growth of Industrialized Economies." *Public Choice*, 49: 143–54.

Marvel, Howard P. 1977. "Factory Regulation: A Reinterpretation of Early English Experience." *Journal of Law and Economics*, 20: 379–402.

Mason, R.H.P. 1969. *Japan's First General Election, 1890*. Cambridge: Cambridge University Press.

Masuda, Kowashi. 1954. "Dainiji Itō naikaku [The Second Itō Cabinet]." *Kōbe hōgaku zasshi*, 4: 469–502.

Masugo, Masahiro. 1968. *Jinji gyōsei nijūnen no ayumi [Twenty Years of Personnel Administration]*. Tokyo: Jinji in.

Masumi, Junnosuke. 1986. *Nihon seitō shi ron [A Treatise on Japan's Political History]*. Tokyo: Tokyo daigaku shuppankai.

Matsumoto, Hiroshi. 1979. *Mitsui zaibatsu no kenkyū [A Study of the Mitsui Zaibatsu]*. Tokyo: Yoshikawa kōbunkan.

Matsuo, Takayoshi. 1989. *Futsū senkyo seido seiritsu no kenkyū [Research on Establishing the Universal Suffrage Electoral System]*. Tokyo: Iwanami shoten.

Matsushita, Yoshio. 1963a. *Meiji no guntai [The Meiji Military]*. Tokyo: Shibundō.

—— 1963b. *Nihon gunji shi sōsho [Library of Japanese Military History]*. Tokyo: Tsuchiya shoten.

—— 1966a. *Kindai no sensō, I [Early Modern Wars, I]*. Tokyo: Tsuchiya shoten.

—— 1966b. *Nihon no gunji shi jitsuwa [Accounts from Japanese Military History]*. Tokyo: Tsuchiya shoten.

—— 1967. *Nihon gunbatsu no kōbō, I-III [The Vicissitudes of Japanese Military Factions, I-III]*. Tokyo: Jimbutsu ōrai sha.

Matsuzaki, Hisashi. 1933. *Ginkō oyobi kin'yū shijō [Banks and Financial Markets]*. Tokyo: Bungadō.

Miller, Frank O. 1965. *Minobe Tatsukichi, Interpreter of Constitutionalism in Japan*. Berkeley: University of California Press.

Miller, Gary J. 1992. *Managerial Dilemmas: The Political Economy of Hierarchy*. Cambridge: Cambridge University Press.

Minami, Ryōshin. 1986. *The Economic Development of Japan: A Quantitative Study*. Houndsmills, U.K.: Macmillan Press.

Minobe, Tatsukichi. 1926. *Kempō satsuyō [An Outline of the Constitution] (4th ed.)*. Tokyo: Yūhikaku.

—— 1930. "Senkyohō hihan [A Criticism of the Electoral Law]." *Hōritsu jihō,* Mar. 1: 41–48.

Mitani, Taiichiro. 1980. *Gendai Nihon no shihōken to seitō [The Modern Japanese Judiciary and Political Parties].* Tokyo: Hanawa Shobo.

Mitchell, Richard H. 1992. *Janus-Faced Justice: Political Criminals in Imperial Japan.* Honolulu: University of Hawaii Press.

Mitsubishi Kōbe zōsenjo 75 nen shi henshū iinkai (ed.). 1981. *Mitsubishi Kōbe zōsenjo 75 nen shi [A 75-Year History of Mitsubishi's Kōbe Shipbuilding Facilities].* Kōbe: Mitsubishi jūkō.

Mitsubishi shashi kankō kai (ed.). 1982. *Mitsubishi shashi [Mitsubishi Company History].* Tokyo: University of Tokyo Press.

Mitsui bussan (ed.). 1928. *Mitsui bussan kabushiki kaisha Shōwa 3-nen jōhanki gyōnin sōshi [Report of Business Activities of the Mitsui Bussan K.K. for the First Half of 1928].* Secret internal company memorandum on file at the University of Tokyo Faculty of Economics library, catalogued at 13/1336.

Miyake, Yūjirō. 1911. "Ōkuma haku ron [An Essay on Prince Ōkuma]." *Chūō kōron,* Vol. 26, No. 1: 122–168.

Moe, Terry. 1990. "Political Institutions: The Neglected Side of the Story." *Journal of Law, Economics, and Organization,* 6: 213–266.

Momose, Takashi. 1990. *Shōwa senzenki no Nihon: seido to jittai [Pre-war Japan: Its Structure and Practice].* Tokyo: Yoshikawa Hirobumi bunkan.

Mōri, Kahei. 1982. *Muhin kin'yūshiron [On the Financial History of Mutual Banks].* Tokyo: Hōsei daigaku shuppankyoku.

Moriguchi, Shigeji. 1925. *Hirei daihyōhō no kenkyū [Research on the Proportional Representation Law].* Tokyo: Yūhikaku.

Morris, Ray. 1911. "Railways – General Statistics." In *Encyclopædia Brittanica,* 11th ed., 22: 822–24.

Morton, William F. 1980. *Tanaka Giichi and Japan's China Policy.* Kent: William Dawson.

Murakami, Ichirō. 1973. *Nihon guntai ron josetsu [An Introduction to the Theory of the Japanese Military].* Tokyo: Shin jinbutsu ōrai sha.

Murase, Shin'ichi. 1988. "Kokuritsu ginkō shobun mondai to Jiyūtō [Treatment of National Banks and the Liberal Party]." *Nihon rekishi,* 486: 71–84.

Murobushi, Tetsuo. 1988. *Jitsuroku Nihon oshoku shi [A History of Japanese Corruption].* Tokyo: Chikuma shobō.

Muroyama, Yoshimasa (ed.). 1984. *Kindai Nihon no gunji to zaisei [Military Affairs and Fiscal Policy in Modern Japan].* Tokyo: Tokyo daigaku shuppan kai.

Mutō, Sanji. 1927. "Bōsekigyō [The Spinning Industry]." In *Shakai keizai taikei [Overview of Social Economics].* No publication information; catalogued in the University of Tokyo Department of Economics library at 12/120P.

Naitō, Seichō. 1968. *Jiyū minken undō no kenkyū [Research on the People's Rights Movement].* Tokyo: Aoki shoten.

Najita, Tetsuo. 1967. *Hara Kei in the Politics of Compromise, 1905–1915.* Cambridge: Harvard University Press.

—— and J. Victor Koschman (eds.). 1982. *Conflict in Modern Japanese History: The Neglected Tradition.* Princeton: Princeton University Press.

Nakagawa, Keiichirō, Hidemasa Morikawa, and Tsunehiko Yui (eds.). 1990. *Kindai Nihon keiei shi no kiso chishiki [Basic Information Regarding Early Modern Japanese Management History].* Tokyo: Yūhikaku.

Nakamura, Katsunori (ed.). 1988. *Kindai Nihon seiji no shōsō: jidai ni yoru*

References

tenkai to kosatsu [Various Aspects of Modern Japanese Politics: Historical Development and Other Considerations]. Tokyo: Keiō tsūshin.

Nakanishi, Ken'ichi. 1963. *Nippon shiyū tetsudō shi kenkyū [A Study of the History of Private Japanese Railroads]* (2 vols.). Tokyo: Nippon hyōron sha.

Nakano, Tomio. 1936. *Tōsuiken no dokuritsu [The Independence of Military Command]*. Reprinted, 1973, Tokyo: Hara shobō.

Nardinelli, Clark. 1980. "Child Labor and the Factory Acts." *Journal of Economic History*, 40: 739–55.

Neustadt, Richard E. 1964. *Presidential Power*. New York: New American Library.

Nihon gendai shi kenkyūkai, ed. 1984. *1920 nendai no Nihon no seiji [Japanese Politics in the 1920s]*. Tokyo: Ōtsuki shobō.

Nihon kindai shiryō kenkyūkai (ed.). 1971. *Nihon rikukaigun no seido, soshiki, jinji [The System, Organization, and Personnel of Japan's Army and Navy]*. Tokyo: Tokyo daigaku shuppankai.

Nihon kingendai shi [Modern and Contemporary Japanese History]. 1978. Tokyo: Tōyō keizai shimpōsha.

Nihon kokusei chōsakai (ed.). 1978. *Sangiin meikan [A Directory of the House of Councillors]*. Tokyo: Kokusei shuppan shitsu.

Nihon kokuyū tetsudō (ed.). 1971. *Nihon kokuyū tetsudō hyakunen shi [The Hundred-Year History of the Japanese National Railroads]*. Tokyo: Nihon kokuyū tetsudō.

Nihon shinshi roku [A Record of Japan's Aristocracy]. 1934. Tokyo: Kōjunsha.

Nihon tōkei kyōkai (ed.). 1988. *Nihon chōki tōkei sōran [Historical Statistics of Japan]*. Tokyo: Nihon tōkei kyōkai.

Nishikawa, Hiroshi. 1987. *Nippon teikoku shugi to mengyō [Japanese Imperialism and the Cotton Industry]*. Kyoto: Minerubwa shobō.

Nisshin bōseki K.K. (ed.). 1969. *Nisshin bōseki hyakunen shi [A One-Hundred-Year History of Nisshin Bōseki]*. Tokyo: Nisshin bōseki K.K.

Niwa, Kunio. 1962. *Meiji ishin no tochi henkaku [The Meiji Restoration's Land Tenure Changes]*. Tokyo: Ochanomizu shobō.

Nobuo, Kiyosaburō. 1952. *Taishō seiji shi [A Political History of Taishō]*. Vols. 1–4. Tokyo: Kawade shobō.

Nomura, Masao. 1966. *Hōsō fūsō roku [Window into a Record of the Vicissitudes of the Law]*. Tokyo: Asahi shimbun sha.

Nomura, Nobutake. 1935. *Kempō taikō [Fundamental Principles of the Constitution]*. Tokyo: Ganshōdō shoten.

North, Douglass C. 1981. *Structure and Change in Economic History*. New York: W.W. Norton.

—— 1990. *Institutions, Institutional Change and Economic Performance*. Cambridge: Cambridge University Press.

—— and Barry R. Weingast. 1989. "Constitutions and Commitment: The Evolution of Institutions Governing Public Choice in Seventeenth-Century England." *Journal of Economic History*, 49: 803–32.

Ō, Y.K. 1930. "Hompō bōseki saikin jūnen shi [A History of Our Nation's Spinning Industry in the Last Ten Years]." *Dai-Nippon bōseki rengō kai geppō*, 454: 7–16.

Odera, Tetsunosuke. 1967. *Sainan no yakusatsugun kūsyōsho [A Record of the Satsuma Army During the Satsuma Rebellion]*. Tokyo: Yoshikawa Hirobumi kan.

O'Brien, Patrick. 1977. *The New Economic History of the Railways*. New York: St Martin's Press.

References

Oda, Hiroshi. 1993. *Japanese Law*. London: Butterworths.

Odanaka, Toshiki. "Osarizawa dōzan jiken [The Osarizawa Copper Mine Case]." In Wagatsuma (1968: 313).

Ōe, Sada. 1907. "Seikai kaikodan [Reflections on the Political World]." *Taiyō*, Feb.: 173–177.

Ōe, Shinobu. 1968. "Kyūsai ka, seiri ka [Bail-out or Consolidation?]." *Ekonomisuto*, Jul. 16: 86–91.

Ogawa, Kōtarō. 1930. *Shin ginkōhō riyū [The Reason for the New Banking Act]*. Tokyo: Nihon hyōronsha.

Ohkawa, Kazushi, Tsutomu Noda, Nobuyuki Takamatsu, Saburō Yamada, Minoru Kumazaki, Yūichi Shinoya, and Ryōshin Minami. 1967. *Chōki keizai tōkei: Bukka [Long-Term Economic Statistics: Prices]*. Tokyo: Tōyō keizai shimpō sha.

Ōishi, Kaichirō. 1989. *Jiyūminken to Ōkuma, Matsukata zaisei [The People's Rights Movement and Ōkuma's and Matsukata's Fiscal Policies]*. Tokyo: Tokyo daigaku shuppan kai.

Ōishi, Kiichirō (ed.). 1992. *Senkanki Nihon no taigai keizai kankei [Japan's International Economic Relations during the Inter-war Years]*. Tokyo: Nihon keizai hyōron sha.

Ōishi, Makoto. 1990. *Giinhō seiteishi no kenkyū [Research on Establishing the Diet Laws]*. Tokyo: Seibundō.

Okano, Bunnosuke. 1927. "Ginkō hōan o hyōsu [Critiquing the Banking Bill]." *Ginkō ronsō*, Vol. 8, No. 5: 90–102.

Okazaki, Tetsuji. 1987. "Senji keikaku keizai to kakaku tōsei [The Wartime Planned Economy and Price Controls]." *Kindai Nihon kenkyū*, 9: 175.

——— 1991. "Seiji keikaku keizai to kigyō [The Wartime Planned Economy and Firms." *Gendai Nihon shakai*, 4: 363.

Ōkubo, Toshiaki. 1986. *Bakumatsu, Ishin no yogaku [A Look Back at the End of the Tokugawa Period and the Meiji Restoration.]* Tokyo: Yoshikawa kōbunkan.

Ōkuboke zōban (ed.) 1928. *Ōkubo Toshimichi bunsho [The Writings of Ōkubo Toshimichi]*. Tokyo: Nihon shiseki kyōkai.

Ōkuma, Shigenobu. 1909. *Fifty Years of New Japan*. Translation by Marcus Huish. London: Smith, Elder.

Ōkura shō (ed.). 1906. *The Sixth Financial and Economic Annual of Japan*. Tokyo: Ōkura shō.

——— (ed.). 1921. *Ōkurashō dai yonjūrokkai nenpō [The Finance Ministry's 46th Annual Report]*. Tokyo: Takashima insatsu sho.

——— (ed.). 1928. *Ōkurashō dai gojūsankai nenpō [The Finance Ministry's 53rd Annual Report]*. Tokyo: Tōa insatsu kabushiki gaisha.

——— (ed.). 1936. *Ōkurashō dai rokujūikkai nenpō [The Finance Ministry's 61st Annual Report]*. Tokyo: Naikaku insatsu kyoku.

——— (ed.). 1977. *Ōkura daijin kaikiroku [The Reflections of Finance Ministers]*. Tokyo: Ōkura zaimu kyōkai.

Ōkurashō Shōwa zaiseishi henshū shitsu (ed.). 1963. *Shōwa zaiseishi [A History of Showa Finance]* Vols. 10, 13. Tokyo: Tōyō keizai shimpōsha.

Olson, Mancur. 1982. *The Rise and Decline of Nations: Economic Growth, Stagflation, and Social Rigidities*. New Haven: Yale University Press.

Osadake, Takeki. 1930. *Nippon kenseishi [A Constitutional History of Japan]*. Tokyo: Nippon hyōronsha.

——— 1937. "Gunjin seiji ni kanshō sebekarazu [Military Men Should Not Interfere in Politics]." *Hōritsu jihō*, Sept.: 3–4.

References

——— 1938. "Kempō seiji no ichi katei [A Procedure of Constitutional Politics."
Kokka gakkai zasshi, 58: 1–39.

Ōshima, Kiyoshi. 1972. Nihon kyōkōshiron [History of Japan's Recessions]. Tokyo: Tokyo daigaku shuppan kai.

Ōtani, Yoshitaka. 1939. Dainihon kempō ron [A Theory of the Great Japanese
Constitution]. Tokyo: Ganshōdō shoten.

Ōyama, Hisashi. 1935. Hompō bōsekigyō ni kansuru chōsa [An Investigation
into Our Nation's Spinning Industry]. No publication Information; catalogued in the University of Tokyo Department of Economics library at
12/482.

Ozaki, Yukio. 1918. "On the Obstacles to Democracy in Japan." In George O.
Totten (ed.) Democracy in Prewar Japan (1965), pp. 50–58.

Pearse, Arno S. 1929. "Nippon bōseki hatten no gen'in [The Reasons for the
Development of the Japanese Spinning Industry.]" Dainihon bōseki rengō kai
geppō, 443: 12–15.

Peltzman, Sam. 1971. "Pricing in Public and Private Enterprises: Electric Utilities
in the United States." Journal of Law & Economics, 14: 109–47.

Polanyi, Karl. 1947. "Our Obsolete Market Mentality: Civilization Must Find a
New Thought Pattern." Commentary, Feb.: 109.

Przeworski, Adam. 1991. Democracy and the Market: Political and Economic
Reforms in Eastern Europe and Latin America. Cambridge: Cambridge University Press.

Ramseyer, J. Mark. 1991. "Indentured Prostitution in Imperial Japan: Credible
Commitments in the Commercial Sex Industry." Journal of Law, Economics
and Organization, 7: 89–116.

——— 1993. "Credibly Committing to Efficiency Wages: Cotton Spinning Cartels in
Imperial Japan." University of Chicago Law School Roundtable, 1993: 153.

——— 1994. "The Puzzling (In)dependence of Courts: A Comparative Approach."
Journal of Legal Studies, 23: 721.

——— and Frances McCall Rosenbluth. 1993. Japan's Political Marketplace. Cambridge: Harvard University Press.

Ritsumeikan daigaku (ed.). 1993. Saionji kinmochi den, III [Account of Saionji
Kinmochi]. Tokyo: Iwanami shoten.

Roberts, John G. 1989. Mitsui: Three Centuries of Japanese Business. New York:
Weatherhill, 2nd ed.

Roemer, John. 1981. Analytical Foundations of Marxian Economic Theory. Cambridge: Cambridge University Press.

Rosovsky, Henry. 1961. Capital Formation in Japan, 1868–1940. Glencoe: The
Free Press.

Rōyama, Masamichi. 1930. "Senkyo seido no seijiteki igi o ronjite, kusei mondai
no jūyōsei ni oyobu [A Consideration of the Political Significance of the
Electoral System, Including the Importance of District Magnitude]." Hōritsu
jihō, Mar.: 59–63.

Saitō, Hideo. 1971. "Saikōsai no shihō gyōsei no arikata [The Proper Method of
Judicial Administration by the Supreme Court]." Jurisuto, 480: 66–71.

Sakai, Tetsuya. 1992. Taishō demokurashii no hōkai [The Collapse of Taishō
Democracy]. Tokyo: Tokyo daigaku shuppan kai.

Sakairi, Nagatarō. 1988. Taishō Shōwa shoki zaiseishi [A Financial History of the
Taishō and Early Shōwa Periods] Tokyo: Sakai shoten.

Sasahiro, Yū. 1931. Seiji no hinkon [The Poverty of Politics]. Tokyo: Chigura shobō.

——— 1932. Taishū seiji dokuhon [A Reader on Mass Politics]. Tokyo: Chūō kōron sha.

References

Sasaki, Sōichi. 1932. *Nippon kempō yōran [General Theory of the Japanese Constitution]*. Tokyo: Kinshi hōryūdō.

Satō, Seirō. 1954. "Meiji jūshichinen gogatsu no Jiyūtō meibō ni tsuite [Concerning the Liberal Party Roster in May, 1884]." *Rekishigaku kenkyū*, Vol. 12, No. 178: 31–38.

Satō, Tatsuo. 1975. *Kokka kōmuin seido [The Civil Service System]*. Tokyo: Gakuyō shobō.

Satō, Ushijirō. 1936. *Teikoku kempō kōgi [Lectures on the Imperial Constitution] (10th ed.)*. Tokyo: Yūhikaku.

Satow, Ernest. 1983. *A Diplomat in Japan: An Inner History of the Japanese Reformation*. Tokyo: Charles E. Tuttle Co.

Sawai, Minoru. 1992. "Tetsudō sharyō kōgyō to 'Manshū' shijō [The Rolling Stock Industry and the Manchurian Market]." In Ōishi (1992: 131).

Saxonhouse, Gary. 1974. "A Tale of Japanese Technological Diffusion in the Meiji Period." *Journal of Economic History*, 34: 149–65.

—— 1976. "Country Girls and Communication among Competitors in the Japanese Cotton-Spinning Industry." In Hugh Patrick and Larry Meisner (eds.), *Japanese Industrialization and its Social Consequences*. Berkeley: University of California Press, pp. 97–125.

—— 1977. "Productivity Change and Labor Absorption in Japanese Cotton Spinning 1891–1935. *Quarterly Journal of Economics*, 91: 195–219.

—— 1991. "Mechanisms for Technology Transfer in Japanese Economic History." *Managerial and Decision Economics*, 12.

—— and Gavin Wright. 1984a. "Two Forms of Cheap Labor in Textile History." *Research in Economic History*, supp. 3: 3–31.

—— and Gavin Wright. 1984b. "Rings and Mules around the World: A Comparative Study in Technological Choice." *Research in Economic History*, supp. 3: 271–300.

Scalapino, Robert. 1953. *Democracy and the Party Movement in Prewar Japan*. Berkeley: University of California Press.

Schmitter, Philippe. 1979. "Still the Century of Corporatism?" In Philippe Schmitter and Gerhard Lehmbruch (eds.), *Trends Toward Corporatist Intermediation*. Beverly Hills: Sage.

Scully, Gerald W. *Constitutional Environments and Economic Growth*. Princeton: Princeton University Press.

"Seiri gōdō hōhō [The Method of Consolidating and Merging]." 1927. *Tokyo asahi shimbun*, Feb. 11: 4.

Seisen kiroku shi kankō kai (ed.). 1930. *Dainihon seisen kiroku shi [A Historical Record of the Political Battles in Great Japan]*. Tokyo: Seisen kiroku shi kankō kai.

Seki, Keizō. 1954. *Nihon mengyō ron [A Theory of the Japanese Cotton Industry]*. Tokyo: Tokyo daigaku shuppan kai.

Shakai kyoku rōdō bu (ed.). 1931. *Shin'ya gyō kinshi no eikyō chōsa [Investigation into the Effects of the Ban on Night Labor]*. Tokyo: Shakai kyoku rōdō bu.

Shepard, Walter. 1927. "Foreign Governments and Politics: Parliamentary Government in Japan." *American Political Science Review*, 21: 835–52.

Shepsle, Kenneth A., and Barry R. Weingast. 1981. "Structure-Induced Equilibrium and Legislative Choice." *Public Choice*, 37: 503–19.

Shibusawa Seijun kinen zaidan ryūmon sha (ed.). 1956. *Shibusawa Eiichi denki shiryō [Materials from Shibusawa's Writings]*. Tokyo: Shibusawa Seijun kinen zaidan ryūmon sha.

References

Shihō shō (ed.). 1939. *Shihō enkaku shi [A Documentary History of the Judiciary]*. Tokyo: Hōsō kai. Reprinted, Tokyo: Hōsō kai, 1960.

Shima, Yasuhiko. 1950. *Nippon shihon shugi to kokuyū tetsudō [Japanese Capitalism and National Railroads]*. Tokyo: Nippon hyōron sha.

Shindō, Takejirō. 1958. *Mengyō rōdō sankō tōkei [Reference Statistics Regarding Labor in the Cotton Industry]*. Tokyo: Tokyo daigaku shuppan kai.

Shinmyō, Takeo. 1961. *Shōwa seiji hishi [A Secret History of Shōwa]*. Tokyo: Sanichi shobō.

Shinohara, Miyohei. 1972. *Chōki keizai tōkei: kōkōgyō [Long-term Economic Statistics: The Mining and Manufacturing Industries]*. Tokyo: Tōyō keizai shimpō sha.

Shōkō daijin kanbō tōkei ka (ed.). Various years. *Kōjō tōkei hyō [Census of Manufactures]*. Tokyo: Tokyo tōkei kyōkai.

—— Various years. *Shōkō shō tōkei hyō [Statistical Tables for the Ministry of Commerce and Industry]*. Tokyo: Tokyo tōkei kyōkai.

Shōkō shō rinji sangyō gōri kyoku (ed.). 1931. *Kōsanryo oyobi menchijimi tōsei no hanashi [The Story of the Regulation of Triple Striped Twill and Cotton Crepe]*. Tokyo: Shōkōshō.

Shūgiin jimukyoku (ed.). 1925. *Shūgiin yōran*. Tokyo: Shūgiin.

—— 1927. *Shūgiin iinkai giroku*. Tokyo: Shūgiin.

Shūgiin and Sangiin (eds.). 1990. *Gikaiseido hyakunenshi [A Hundred Year's History of the Parliament]*. Tokyo: Ōkurashō insatsu kyoku.

Silberman, Bernard. 1982. "The Bureaucratic State in Japan: The Problem of Authority and Legitimacy." In Najita and Koschman (1982: 226–57).

—— 1993. *Cages of Reason: The Rise of the Rational State in France, Japan, the United States, and Great Britain*. Chicago: University of Chicago Press.

Skocpol, Theda. 1979. *States and Social Revolutions: A Comparative Analysis of France, Russia and China*. Cambridge: Cambridge University Press.

Smith, Thomas C. 1988. *Native Sources of Japanese Industrialization, 1750–1920*. Berkeley: University of California Press.

Snyder, Jack. 1991. *Myths of Empire: Domestic Politics and International Ambition*. Ithaca: Cornell University Press.

Soma, Masao. 1986. *Nihon senkyo seidoshi [A History of Japan's Electoral System]*. Tokyo: Kyūshū daigaku shuppankai.

Spaulding, Robert M. 1967. *Imperial Japan's Higher Civil Service Examinations*. Princeton: Princeton University Press.

Stigler, George S. 1964. "A Theory of Oligopoly." *Journal of Political Economy*, 72: 44.

—— 1961. "The Theory of Economic Regulation." *Bell Journal of Economics & Management Science*, 2: 3.

Stinchcombe, Arthur L. 1990. *Information and Organizations*. Berkeley: University of California Press.

Sugiyama, Kazuo. 1990a. *Ginkō gōdō [Bank Unions]*. In Nakagawa et al. (1990: 229–230).

—— 1990b. "Sangyō kakumei to kin'yū [Finances and the Industrial Revolution]." In Nakagawa et al. (1990: 75–76).

Sumitomo ginkō, ed. 1979. *Sumitomo ginkō hachijūnen shi [An Eighty-Year's History of Sumitomo Bank]*. Tokyo: Kabushiki gaisha Sumitomo ginkō.

Sundquist, James. 1969. *Politics and Policy*. Washington, D.C.: Brookings Institution.

"Tagaku nōzeisha meibō [Roster of High-end Tax Payers]." 1933. In *Nihon shinshi roku furoku [A Record of Japan's Gentlemen]*. Tokyo: Kōjun sha.

References

Tagawa, Daikichirō. 1910. "Yamagata kō ni taishite omou tokoro [Reflecting on Prince Yamagata]." *Chūō kōron,* Vol. 25, No. 10: 64–67.

Taishō Shōwa Nihon zenkoku shisanka jinushi shiryō shūsei [Collected Data on Capitalists and Landlords in the Taishō and Shōwa Periods]. Tokyo: Fukkoku.

Takahashi, Kamekichi. 1925. *Nihon no kin'yū [Japan's Finance].* Tokyo: Tōyō keizai shimpōsha.

—— 1930. *Nippon zaibatsu no kaibō [An Analysis of the Japanese Zaibatsu].* Tokyo: Chūō kōron sha.

—— 1932. *Henkakuki no zaikai to sono taisaku [The Business World and Business Policies in Period of Flux].* Tokyo: Chigura shobō.

—— 1955. *Zaikai hendō shi [A History of Changes in the Business World],* Vol. 2. Tokyo: Tōyō keizai shimpōsha.

Takahashi, Masanori. 1981. *Seitō seiji no kenkyū [Research on Party Politics].* Tokyo: Kōbundō.

Takahashi, Yōsai. 1976. *Meiji nendai no keisatsu buchō [Police Chiefs During the Meiji Period].* Tokyo: Ryōsho fukyōkai.

Takamura, Naosuke. 1971. *Nihon bōseki gyō shi josetsu [An Introduction to the History of the Japanese Spinning Industry].* Tokyo: Hanawa shobō.

—— 1989. "Comment [on Hunter]." In Yui and Nakagawa (1989: 273–76).

Takayanagi, Kenzo. 1963. "A Century of Innovation: The Development of Japanese Law, 1868–1961." In von Mehren (1963: 5–40).

Tamai, Kiyoshi. 1989. "Seiyūkai no Terauchi naikaku ni taisuru kensei to kyōryoku [The Seiyūkai's Restraint Towards and Cooperation With the Terauchi Cabinet]." *Hōgaku kenkyū,* Vol. 62, No. 9: 56–86.

Tatsuki, Mariko. 1990a. "Mitsui Bussan no setsuritsu to hatten [The Establishment and Development of Mitsui Bussan]." In Nakagawa et al. (1990: 36–37).

Teikoku gikai, ed. 1927. *Kizokuin giji sokkiroku [Minutes of the House of Peers].* Tokyo: Teikoku gikai.

Teishin shō tetsudō kyoku (ed.). Various years. *Tetsudō kyoku nempō [Annual Report for the Railroad Bureau].* Tōkyō: Teishin shō tetsudō kyoku. Reprinted, Tokyo: Nihon keizai hyōron sha, 1991.

Teranishi, Jūzō. 1982. *Nihon no keizai hatten to kin'yū [Finance and Economic Development in Japan].* Tokyo: Iwanami shoten.

Terao, Gorō. 1975. *Satchō rengō no butai ura [Behind the Satsuma-Chōshū Alliance].* Tokyo: Shin jinbutsu ōraisha.

Tetsudō shō (ed.). 1920. *Kokuyū jūnen: Hompō tetsudō kokuyūgo no shisetsu narabi seiseki [Ten Years of Nationalization: The Facilities and Performance of the Railroads of our Country After Nationalization].* Tokyo: Tetsudō shō. Reprinted, Nihon keizai hyōron sha, 1983.

—— 1921. *Nippon tetsudō shi [A History of Japanese Railroads] (3 vols.).* Tokyo: Tetsudō shō.

—— Various years. "Tetsudō kensetsu oyobi kairyō hi yosan nendo wari hyō [Chart Showing Railroad Construction and Repair Costs, by Year]." *Tetsudō kaigi giji sokki roku [Records of the Proceedings of the Railroad Meetings].* Tokyo: Tetsudō shō. Reprinted, Nihon keizai hyōron sha, 1988.

—— Various years. *Tetsudō shō nempō [Annual Report for the Railroad Ministry].* Tokyo: Tetsudō shō. Reprinted, Tokyo: Nihon keizai hyōron sha, 1990.

—— Various years. *Tetsudō tōkei shiryō [Railroad Statistical Materials].* Tokyo: Tetsudō shō. Reprinted, Tokyo: Nihon keizai hyōron sha, 1991.

References

Tiedemann, Arthur E. 1971. "Big Business and Politics in Prewar Japan." In James W. Morley (ed.), *Dilemmas of Growth in Prewar Japan.* Princeton: Princeton University Press.

Tirole, Jean. 1988. *The Theory of Industrial Organization.* Cambridge: MIT Press.

Titus, David Anson. 1974. *Palace and Politics in Prewar Japan.* New York: Columbia University Press.

Tokufuku, Inoichirō. 1937. "Itō, Ōkuma, Yamagata." *Chūō kōron,* Vol. 52, No. 5: 273–287.

Tokyo kabushiki torihiki sho (ed.). 1928. *Tokyo kabushiki torihiki sho 50 nen shi [A 50-Year History of the Tokyo Stock Exchange].* Tokyo: Tokyo kabushiki torihiki sho.

Tokyo shisei chōsa kai (ed.). 1932. *Hompō chihō tetsudō jigyō ni kansuru chōsa [A Survey of the Local Railroad Business in Our Country].* Tokyo: Tokyo shisei chōsa kai. Reprinted, Tokyo: Hōbunkaku shuppan, 1988.

Tomita, Nobuo. 1986. "Shūgiin giin sōsenkyo no shiteki bunseki [A Historical Analysis of Lower House Elections]." *Senkyo kenkyū,* 1: 65–93

—— 1987. "Shūgiin giin sōsenkyo no shiteki bunseki (II) [A Historical Analysis of Lower House Elections, Part II]." *Senkyo kenkyū,* 2: 64–88.

Toriumi, Yasushi. 1967. "Minryoku kyōyō ka, gunbi zōkyō ka [Resting the Private Sector or Strengthening the Military]." *Ekonomisuto,* Apr. 11: 86–91.

Totten, George O.(ed.). 1965. *Democracy in Prewar Japan: Groundwork or Facade?* Boston: D.C. Heath.

Tōyama, Shigeki (ed.). 1988. *Tennō to kazoku [The Emperor and the Aristocracy].* Tokyo: Iwanami shoten.

Tōyama, Shigeki and Yoshiko Adachi. 1961. *Kindai Nihon seijishi hikkei [A Primer on Modern Japanese Political History.]* Tokyo: Iwanami shoten.

Toyodai, Jō. 1983. *Saionji Kinmochi Meiji taitei hōgyo [Saionji Kinmochi and the Death of the Great Meiji Emperor].* Tokyo: Kōdansha.

Tsuji, Kiyoaki. 1944. "Naikaku seido no juritsu [The Establishment of the Cabinet System]," *Kōbe hōgaku zasshi,* 58: 78–126.

—— 1952. *Nihon kanryōsei no kenkyū [Research on Japan's Bureaucracy].* Tokyo: Kōbundō.

Tsurumi, Yōsuke. 1924. "Universal Suffrage Seen as the Antidote to Big Money Elections." In Totten (1965: 59–62).

Tsūshō sangyō daijin kanbō chōsa tōkei kyoku (ed.). 1961. *Kōgyō tōkei 50 nenshi [A Fifty Year History of the Manufactures Census].* Tokyo: Ōkura shō insatsu kyoku.

Tsūshō sangyō shō (ed.). 1960. *Nihon no kikai kōgyō [The Japanese Machine Tool Industry].* Tokyo: Nihon jūkōgyō kenkyū kai.

Tsutsui, Masao. 1988 "'Seitō seiji' kakuritsuki ni okeru chiiki shihai kōzō [The Structure of Local Control under the Early Period of Party Politics]." *Hikone ronsō,* 248: 53–90.

Uchida, Kenzō, Samon Kanehara, and Tetsuo Furuya (eds.). 1991. *Nihon gikai shiroku [A Record of Japan's Legislature], vols. I-III.* Tokyo: Daiichi hōki shuppan.

Uesugi, Jūjirō. 1956. "Katsura Tarō." *Chūō kōron,* Vol. 71, No. 1: 326–331.

Uesugi, Shinkichi. 1918. *Teikoku kempō kōryo [Thoughts on the Imperial Constitution.].* Tokyo: Yoshikawa.

—— 1935. *Teikoku kempō chikujō kōgi [Imperial Constitutional Annotated Lectures].* Tokyo: Nippon hyōron sha.

216

References

Umetani, Noboru. 1984. *Nihon kindaika no shosō [Aspects of Japan's Modernization]*. Kyoto: Shibunkaku shuppan.

Uyehara, George Etsujiro. 1910. *The Political Development of Japan: 1867–1909*. London: Constable.

Vlastos, Stephen. 1989. "Opposition Movements in Early Meiji, 1868–1885." In Jansen (1989: 367–431).

von Mehren, Arthur Taylor (ed.). 1963. *Law in Japan: The Legal Order in a Changing Society*. Cambridge: Harvard University Press.

Wada, Hidekichi. 1937. *Mitsui kontsuerun dokuhon [Reader on the Mitsui Conglomerate]*. Tokyo: Shunjō sha.

Wagatsuma, Sakae (ed.). 1968. *Nihon seiji saiban shi roku [A Historical Record of Political Trials in Japan]*. Tokyo: Daiichi hōki shuppan.

Wakatsuki, Reijirō. 1983. *Meiji Taishō Shōwa seikei hishi [A Secret Political History of Meiji Taishō and Shōwa]*. Tokyo: Kōdansha.

Wakuda, Yasuo. 1981. *Nihon no shitetsu [The Private Railways of Japan]*. Tokyo: Iwanami shoten.

Watanabe, Ikujirō. 1958. *Ōkuma Shigenobu*. Tokyo: Jiji tsūshin sha.

Watarai, Toshiharu. 1915. *Nationalization of Railways in Japan*. New York: Columbia University Political Science Dissertation.

Weingast, Barry. 1984. "The Congressional Bureaucratic System: A Principal-Agent Perspective (with Applications to the SEC)." *Public Choice*, 44: 147–91.

Whaples, Robert. 1990. "Winning the Eight-Hour Day, 1909–1919." *Journal of Economic History*, 50: 393–406.

White, James W. 1988. "State Growth and Popular Protest in Tokugawa Japan." *Journal of Japanese Studies*, 14: 1–25.

Williamson, Oliver E. 1985. "Credible Commitments: Using Hostages to Support Exchange." *American Economic Review*, 73: 519.

Wray, William D. (ed.). 1989. *Managing Industrial Enterprise: Cases from Japan's Prewar Experience*. Cambridge: Harvard Council on East Asian Studies.

Yabushita, Shiro, and Atsushi Inoue. 1993. "The Stability of the Japanese Banking System: A Historical Perspective." *Journal of the Japanese and International Economies*, 7: 387–407.

Yamamoto, Shirō. 1985. *Terauchi Masatake naikaku kankei shiryō [Materials Related to the Terauchi Cabinet]*. Tokyo: Kyōto joshi daigaku.

Yano, Fumio. 1907. "Yo ga seitō jidai [Political Parties in My Era]." *Taiyō*, Vol. 13, No. 3: 165–170.

Yoshino, Sakuzo. 1928. *Meiji bunka zenshū, II [The Complete Meiji Culture, II]*. Tokyo: Nihon hyōron sha.

Yui, Tsunehiko and Keiichiro Nakagawa. 1989. *Japanese Management in Historical Perspective*. Tokyo: Tokyo daigaku shuppan kai.

Zaisei keizai jihō sha (ed.). 1936. *Nippon sen'i kōgyō sōran okutsuki [An Overview of the Japanese Textile Industry, with Appendix]*. Tokyo: Zaisei keizai jihō sha.

Zenkoku chihō ginkō kyōkai, ed. 1988. *Zenkoku chihō ginkō kyōkai gojūnen shi [A Fifty-Year's History of the National Local Bank Association]*. Tokyo: Zenkoku chihō ginkō kyōkai.

Zysman, John. 1983. *Governments, Markets, and Growth*. Ithaca: Cornell University Press.

Index

219

Index

Index

Index

223

Index